VICTORIAN LITERARY CRITICS

VICTORIAN LITERARY CRITICS

George Henry Lewes, Walter Bagehot,
Richard Holt Hutton, Leslie Stephen,
Andrew Lang, George Saintsbury
and Edmund Gosse

by

HAROLD OREL

MACMILLAN

First published 1984 by
THE MACMILLAN PRESS LTD
London and Basingstoke
Companies and representatives
throughout the world

ISBN 0 333 36162 8

Printed in Hong Kong

To Frank and Marjorie Pinion

Contents

List of Plates

Acknowledgement

This investigation was supported by University of Kansas General Research allocation no. 3675–Xo–0038.

Introduction

We know so much about Matthew Arnold's contribution to literary criticism, and so little about his contemporaries who wrote as professional men of letters, that a book of this sort, reviewing the careers of seven major bookmen, has become a needed contribution to our understanding of the Victorian landscape. It is much too easy to assume that Arnold's most striking formulations – his definition of culture, his handy dichotomy of Hebraist versus Hellenist, his attack on Philistines and a large assortment of barbarians, his notion that poetry is a criticism of life, his firm conviction that we must acquaint ourselves with the best that has been thought and said in the world, his touchstones of literary perfection – were wholly original; that, indeed, Arnold was as contemptuous of his fellow critics as he was of members of the middle class who read and understood superficially the finest productions of Western culture. In fact, Arnold learned from his contemporaries, and read their writings with great care. The more we know about those critics who actively pursued their literary pleasures through the pages of widely read periodicals (including the newspapers that printed their reviews of dramatic productions and equally ephemeral writings in a wide variety of fields), collections of essays, full-length studies, and textbook surveys of several national literatures, the better able are we to see Arnold plain.

For this kind of survey of Victorian letters, it has not been deemed necessary to summarise, still one more time, the major tenets of Arnold's critical essays, or to express reservations about various inconsistencies and elements of an unpleasant (and occasionally unearned) snobbism. Arnold's influence on Victorian thought was, on the whole, salutary, and the shock that he administered to set modes of viewing both the past and the present highly necessary. Moreover, Arnold's receptivity to new developments in Continental literature, although more rigidly selective and narrowly based than perhaps even he perceived, was of enormous benefit to those who wanted to make available to the reading public works that might otherwise have remained untranslated and unpublished. The notion that Arnold was 'a coxcomb of letters' was destroyed long before his death. One test of a critic's greatness is the readiness with which we employ his catchphrases, not always remembering to attribute them properly, and Arnold's popularity attests to his continuing influence.

The critics whose writings I examine in this study of nineteenth-century culture are George Henry Lewes, Walter Bagehot, Richard Holt Hutton, Leslie Stephen, Andrew Lang, George Saintsbury and Edmund Gosse. They wrote voluminously, but only the most dedicated student of Victorian literature is familiar with their major works, or even the major lines of thought that they represented. In part this decline in the attention we pay to critical studies now a century or more old is inevitable, an understandable by-product of the pressures created by new creative works, new literary controversies, new critical theories and stratagems for reading. In part, too, we are considering the decline in attention given to all kinds of serious literature. Because it is difficult to get a quick overview of any one of these seven figures, or to identify rapidly the precise nature of the contribution made by these men to the literary scene, I have attempted to review the following elements of each career: sufficient biographical data to enable a reader to see how and in what respects a life experience leads to a literary concern; the most important publications, not necessarily restricted to those which earned the critic the greatest popularity in his own time; an evaluation of the major features of his opinions on books and the literary life; and a consideration of the continuing viability of some of his writings for the late twentieth century. (My concern is the *readability* of critical texts, and not whether they are currently being read by large numbers of readers.) A bibliographical note · for each chapter identifies standard editions (if such exist), important critical books and articles, and the in-print availability of individual texts.

Altogether these seven individuals were responsible for almost one thousand books coming into print, though not all of these volumes dealt with literary subjects. A surprising number are so lively and witty in their treatment of important subjects that the total achievement is bound to communicate a sense of boundless good spirits dedicated to a worthy cause: the elucidation of literary merit. The audience for which these seven men wrote was assumed to be literate, intelligent and curious, but relatively uninterested in technical nomenclature and the specialised concerns of research scholars. That awareness of the existence of a homogeneous audience – which has largely gone from both English and American criticism – was seldom patronising, and would surely have been resented if it had been. (Bagehot's remarks about an intellectually undernourished reading public were, more often than not, graceless, and consequently all the more noticeable.) The relationship of a critic to his audience, even more than his ties to previous generations of writers or to a contemporary school of criticism, was a crucial matter in the thinking of each of these men of letters.

Victorian critics at their best wrote with sensibility, intelligence and style. Although this work is not a history of literary criticism in the second half of the nineteenth century, I seek to provide enough information to demonstrate that these seven bookmen, no less than Matthew Arnold, were seriously dedicated to meeting the challenges of an honourable profession. They behaved responsibly in their role as mediators between serious literature and an intelligent, educable public. By means of review articles, books, lectures and reference works, they exhibited the openmindedness of their intelligence; a sensitivity to man's past; and a capacity to appreciate the best works of art, literature, history, and philosophy that have come down to us from previous generations. They believed that true culture is humanistic, and that good literary criticism can be, and often is, a potent force in producing a civilised society.

Some critical texts, as the modern reader will soon see, aimed at the defining and clarifying of a literary problem. On occasion a work reinforced prejudices held in common by a critic and his audience; or sought to impress others with a sense of the rightness and grandeur of the critic's insights. Such critical studies were, fortunately, atypical of their total production. Most often these British men of letters wanted to inspire a reader to seek out the literary work in order to see whether the judgement of a given critical essay was well grounded, and, surprisingly often, they succeeded in that objective.

Closer inspection of their writings will do a great deal to refute the casually disseminated notion that British literary criticism before the Great War was undisciplined, slack in its definition of key terms, irresponsibly impressionistic, and unworthy of serious attention in our time. We may legitimately wonder whether the techniques for analysing and evaluating literary texts used in our century are all that superior to those used by Victorian critics, or whether indeed the ability to read a text intelligently has been improving in recent decades. Newer modes of discussing literature may not necessarily be better, or more effective in helping a reader to understand and appreciate the author's achievement. The change, as I. A. Richards once noted, with some unhappiness, is related to an ever-increasing professionalism in the study of literature, and to the coming-in of another professional study, linguistics; but the literary and critical works produced by Lewes, Bagehot, Hutton, Stephen, Lang, Saintsbury and Gosse, taken one by one and collectively, are among the most impressive and regrettably underestimated achievements of Victorian culture. They remain relevant to the concerns of all who regard literature as a serious art.

1 George Henry Lewes

The Life of Goethe, first printed in 1855, illustrates the importance in Lewes's mind of the biographical component of literary art. It was not only his most substantial effort in the field, exceeding in length and ambitiousness the sketches contained in *A Biographical History of Philosophy* (2 vols, 1845) and *The Life of Maximilien Robespierre with Extracts from his Unpublished Correspondence* (1849), but it was to remain the finest biography of Goethe in English published during the century.

The study gave a full treatment to Goethe's scientific writings. Lewes was extraordinarily well qualified to discuss these from a position of authority; as he explained in his Preface to the second edition, partly rewritten in 1864, 'Science filled a large portion of Goethe's Life', and 'even in Germany' there had been 'nothing like a full exposition of his aims and achievements in this direction'.

Moreover, for those English readers baffled by contradictory opinions on the value of Goethe's poetry (Coleridge, for example, had sharply censured *Faust* as a series of 'mere magic-lantern pictures'), Lewes supplied numerous examples of the difficulties created by the translations of English-born poetasters, and reasons why an important element of Goethe's genius would forever remain ineffable. Lewes, not a poet himself, originally read *Faust* with the aid of a dictionary, and confessed that his first acquaintance with Goethe's poem had not overwhelmed him with its greatness. But rereadings, and an improving mastery of the German language, led him to see why more was needed than a shudder of disgust at inadequate versions prepared for an English public. At any rate, there was something charming – and attractive – about the manner in which Lewes promised to 'translate every word cited' (though, in point of fact, he did not live up to the promise). These were 'approximative' translations, which Lewes declared were better than nothing: 'to leave German untranslated is unfair to those whose

5

want of leisure or inclination has prevented their acquiring the language'.[1]

Lewes's use of sources, although wide-ranging and intelligent, would frustrate any graduate student in a modern language department. The notes are casually generalised; all too often the provocative fact appears from nowhere, and cannot easily be checked. For example, Lewes distrusted *Dichtung und Wahrheit* because of its 'abiding inaccuracy of tone', though how or in what respects it was inaccurate remains unclear. 'The picture of youthful follies and youthful passions comes softened through the distant avenues of years. The turbulence of a youth of genius is not indeed quite forgotten, but it is hinted with stately reserve. Jupiter serenely throned upon Olympus forgets that he was once a rebel with the Titans.' For the later period Lewes did considerable interviewing, and used manuscript materials (their nature and authorship unidentified for the most part). But he did not anticipate that his second edition would be superseded: 'As there is little probability of any subsequent publication bringing to light fresh material of importance, I hope that this reconstruction of my book will be final.'

In format, the book is unadventurous, subdividing Goethe's life into the seven ages of man and proceeding in a straightforward line from birth to death. In two respects, however, Lewes believed that his function as biographer of a great man might prove of special interest to a reading audience who could remember the living man. Since he had not known Goethe himself, no 'personal connexion' had affected his desire to get at the truth – that is, he was not a partisan in his praise or blame of a controversial world figure. Moreover, the essays of varying length that Lewes inserted at appropriate moments in the chronology for the specific purpose of analysing and criticising Goethe's works took little for granted. Plots were reviewed, crisply and helpfully (save in the case of *Wilhelm Meister*, a novel which intrigued Lewes, rather atypically, because of some considerations of form and structure rather than of characterisation or moral message); and Lewes consistently interpreted his position to be that of *lector* in the best sense, a guide. 'By these analyses,' Lewes wrote in his Preface, 'I have tried to be of service to the student of German literature, as well as to those who do not read German; and throughout it will be seen that pains have not been spared to make the reader feel at home in this foreign land.'

The Life of Goethe illustrates dramatically the sympathy held by a Victorian critic toward the evolving tastes of a large and not always self-confident middle class. Lewes, who thought of his calling as distinguished, and who fulfilled his educative obligations entirely outside the charmed circle of university lectureships, appreciated the fact that criticism could not, and indeed should not, deny a reader his honest enjoyment. *Egmont* is a classic case of a drama that 'is far, very far, from a masterpiece', but there is no hint of scolding in Lewes's recognition of the fact that 'it is a universal favourite. As a tragedy, criticism makes sad work with it; but when all is said, the reader thinks of Egmont and Clärchen, and flings criticism to the dogs.'

Lewes held the most fundamental kind of reservations against *Egmont*. Goethe had not devised 'a collision of elemental passions from whence the tragic interests should spring' (a fault of conception), nor constructed dramatic situations to embody them. 'It is in certain passages dramatic, but the whole is undramatic. It approximates to the novel in dialogue.' Lewes did not accept as full compensation the local colouring of history that Schiller had praised, though when it subserved a larger interest, as in Scott's romances, he fully appreciated its usefulness. 'The merit, such as it is, belongs to erudition, not to poetry . . . .'[2] He was more interested in Schiller's factual correction of Egmont's marital status, Goethe having eliminated from the drama any mention of Egmont's wife and children. Lewes rendered a balanced judgement: some loss ('he deprived himself of some powerful dramatic situations'), but ultimately more gain, for Clärchen is 'the gem of the piece', and, since Goethe read much of himself into Egmont's character, 'a healthy, noble, heroic man' comes before us as all the more human because he is in love.

In an age when the techniques of evaluating masterpieces written in different languages were still being worked out, Lewes's perceptions of the relationships between Shakespeare's example and Goethe's practice had behind them no full-scale aesthetic; yet the occasional *aperçu* still retains the capacity to stimulate a line of thought. Goethe manipulated puppets to get through his necessary exposition and prehistory: 'We see the author's *intention* in all they say; in Shakespeare the men betray themselves, each with some peculiar trick of character.' Unimpressed by the sacredness of a text, Lewes approved of Schiller's stage adaptation that had lopped away the character of the Duchess altogether, and made other drastic alterations. Yet, in his quotations of dialogue that presented complexities of nuance, Lewes italicised lines that seemed to him to be 'taken from the life', 'exquisitely touched'. In part this eagerness to discover and identify the gems of a somewhat rocky landscape is related to Lewes's awareness that many of his comments on the dramatic viability of *Egmont* are broad-sweeping in their implications: for instance, the irrelevance of the entire third act. To an impatient 'poetic reader' who might object to his insistence on 'technical demands' that the action be advanced, that something new be said, Lewes responded with gentle firmness, 'If the poet has attempted a drama, he must be tried by dramatic standards.' Shakespeare was more than a poet, 'he was also a dramatic poet', and his technique was superior to that of Goethe.

The problem is compounded because *Egmont* was conceived at a time when Goethe was under the influence of Shakespeare, and might have learned more about how to tighten his dramatic construction if – during that same period – he had completed the play. But the length of time needed for the writing of *Egmont* extended over three different periods of Goethe's career. Lewes saw the advantages to be derived from careful revision after the work had been completed, but remained largely negative about fragmentary composition. 'A work of Art should be completed before the paint has had time to dry . . . .' Completion, delayed until the stormy period had subsided into the classical phase of Goethe's creativity, proved deadly to the drama if not to the poetry. Lewes conceded that criticism was powerless to diminish public approval of *Egmont*, and, with a mildly amused shrug, moved on to the next non-dramatic work, *Tasso*. If, then, no *drama* in the acted story, what remains? The poetry. And that, as Lewes has gone to great lengths to demonstrate, 'cannot be reproduced in a translation'.

Certain strands of continuity weave through the critical summations of the merits and flaws of Goethe's works. First, Lewes brings a fresh feeling to his valuations; not for him are the awestruck and hero-worshipping dithyrambs of those who, following Carlyle's lead, saw Goethe as a great man whose very errors of judgement in the execution of a poem or drama were superhuman, beyond criticism. He has a sceptical, and at times a bitingly mordant, attitude toward 'all learned apparatus', 'the industry and ingenuity of commentators', and the efforts of his predecessors to translate art into philosophy. In particular, he regarded as wrong-headed the efforts of generations of critics to provide an exposition of 'the Idea of Faust'. Such an artist as Goethe was not primarily interested in developing an Idea. His public, too, was not primarily anxious to learn about the Idea, but left it entirely to the critics, who, as Lewes noted, could not agree among themselves. 'In studying a work of Art,' as Lewes wrote in his admiring review of the first part of *Faust*,

> we should proceed as in studying a work of nature: after delighting in the effect, we should try to ascertain what are the *means* by which the effect is produced, and not at all what is the Idea lying behind the means. If in dissecting an animal we get clear conceptions of the mechanism by which certain functions are performed, we do not derive any increase of real knowledge from being told that the functions are the final causes of the mechanism, while, on the other hand, if an *a priori* conception of purpose is made to do the work of actual inspection of the mechanism, we find ourselves in a swamp of conjectural metaphysics where no dry land is to be found.[3]

In brief, one must look at the work itself, and hope for the best: story, art, human interest. Whatsoever interferes with these diminishes our pleasure – and all for the sake of other and lesser joys, which come from pursuing abstract and dehumanised axioms. In brief, the first principle of Lewes's *The Life of Goethe* is to enjoy the literary work as a literary experience.

Second would seem to be the primacy, in Lewes's mind, of the binding ties between life and art. *The Life of Goethe* has no particularly sophisticated or complicated vision of the differences between epochs in Goethe's imaginative works, only the most obvious kind of differentiation between a turbulent, romantic spirit who visualises life as things and (in later life) an over-reflective, mysticising mind that became 'as fond of symbols as a priest of Isis'. This accounts for Lewes's general devaluation of the poems written in Goethe's final years, particularly the second part of *Faust*. Though Lewes well understood the attractiveness of the art that so conveniently created symbols of philosophy, he himself found that Goethe's hieroglyphs – 'the encroachment of Reflection' – signified the weakening of an artist's vital powers. 'It is quite true that Modern Art, as representative of the complexity of Modern Life, demands a large admixture of Reflection; but the predominance of the reflective tendency is a sign of decay.'[4] Or, as Lewes phrases it elsewhere, 'Art is picture-painting, not picture-writing. . . . . The poet who has only profound meanings, and not the witchery which is to carry his expression of those meanings home to our hearts, has failed. The primary requisite of poetry is that it shall move us; not that it shall instruct us.' Thus, one may have the key to a work without being able to respond emotionally to its imaginative dimension; the work may not have been conceived intensely enough; and its failure to engage the reader's emotions may, in turn, be related to an artist's shifting allegiances to what he considers significant. And there is no doubt that Goethe changed both his subject-matter and his sense of what might be appropriate to his old age: 'If we remember that all Goethe's works are biographical, are parts of his life, and expressions of the various experiences he underwent, and the various stages of culture he passed through, there will be a peculiar interest in examining this product of his old age . . . .'[5]

A corollary of this belief – namely, that Goethe, writing about himself concerning German myths or the German national character, became less rather than more interesting as he aged – was that the first fine frenzy of inspiration counted for more, artistically, than any sober second thought about form or meaning. Thus, Lewes preferred the *Geschichte Gott-friedens von Berlichingen mit der eisernen Hand, dramatisiert* of 1771 ('the one I most admire, and the one which, biographically, has most interest') to *Götz von Berlichingen, Schauspiel,* of 1773, and the subsequent adaptation prepared by both Goethe and Schiller as part of their efforts to establish a national stage at Weimar. Lewes quotes with approval the process whereby Goethe, exhilarated by his readings in Shakespeare, his admiration of the autobiography of Götz von Berlichingen, and his conversations with his sister Cornelia, began one morning to write, 'without having made any previous sketch or plan'. Goethe continued to write: 'Hope increased with the daily communications, and step by step everything gained more life as I mastered the conception. Thus I kept on, without interruption, looking neither backwards nor forwards, neither to the right nor to the left . . . .'

In similar fashion, Goethe's uncanny accuracy in depicting the Wertherism of his age (the detestation of all control, the boundless enthusiasm for the 'rhetorical trash' of Ossian, the disregard of 'the grave remonstrances of reason and good sense') derived from the fact that one part of Goethe lived in Werther, even though, as Lewes hastened to add, Werther was not Goethe in any simple sense. 'Goethe was one of those who are wavering because impressionable, but whose wavering is not weakness; they oscillate, but they return into the direct path which their wills have prescribed.' At any rate, no man completely 'confesses' when he delineates himself. 'Our moral nature has its modesty. Strong as the impulse may be to drag into light that which lies hidden in the recesses of the soul, pleased as we may be to create images of ourselves, we involuntarily keep back something, and refuse to identify ourselves with the creation.' Despite this codicil, Lewes admired the *candour* of the revelation, and wrote with sympathy about the 'wondrous popularity' of *Werther*. It was 'a people's book' in Germany, 'hawked about the streets, printed on miserable paper, like an ancient ballad', and Napoleon carried it in his pocket during his expedition to Egypt. It came from somewhere deep within Goethe; it spoke to something deep within a generation of Europeans, Americans and even Chinese; it became a secular bible for Romanticism.[6]

It is not surprising, therefore, that a fourth constant in Lewes's criticism should be an impatience with rules that are too narrowly conceived and too inflexibly applied. The pettifogging fussiness that yearns backward in time frequently misunderstands the models that it praises. As one illustration we may cite Lewes's treatment of *Iphigenia*, a play that frequently was singled out as quintessentially Greek in its spirit (Lewes quotes Schlegel: 'an echo of Greek song'). As Lewes pointed out, with some exasperation, critics had continually failed to look at the Greek plays that disregarded Unity of Time, and on occasion violated the 'rule' of Unity of Place; they could not appreciate comedy and tragedy mingled in more than one Greek play; and they overstressed the importance of Destiny in a majority of Greek dramas. *Iphigenia* had little or nothing to do with 'repose', and even the term proved singularly inappropriate to the subject-matter of a tragedy; it was borrowed from a term appropriate to another art altogether (sculpture); and it generalised from a few facts, largely related to scenic necessities, such as raised footwear and masks with fixed expressions, to misrepresent the dark passions that were the true subject-matter of the Greek playwrights, passions that represented the very opposite of calmness and repose. As a consequence, Goethe's play was German in both its ideas and its sentiments. (Lewes had some severe things to say about its failing to meet the standard of a *drama*; rather, it was a dramatic poem, though a marvellous one.) How could one call it Greek, without simultaneously confessing a misapprehension as to what constituted the essence of Greek drama? Lewes argued that Goethe's *Iphigenia*, as a character, was 'in every way superior to the Greek priestess' – if only because she had 'the high, noble, tender, delicate soul of a Christian maiden'. Her very rebellion against 'the barbarous practice of human sacrifices' marked her as un-Greek; after all, she was allowing personal feelings 'to rise up in rebellion against a religious rite'. An elaborate analysis of Teutonic and Greek characteristics concludes with allusions to two additional points of difference. The Furies – in Euripides –

> are terrible Apparitions, real beings personated by actors; in Goethe they are Phantasms moving across the stage of an unhappy soul, but visible only to the inward eye; in like manner the Greek *dénouement* is the work of the actual interference of the Goddess in person, whereas the German dénouement is a loosening of the knot by a deeper insight into the meaning of the oracle.[7]

What did it matter, in any crucial sense, if *Hermann und Dorothea* invited discussion of its genre? Goethe had written it in Homeric hexameters, 'with Homeric simplicity'. The critics, 'copious in distinctions and classifications', had exercised great ingenuity in differentiating the Epos proper from a Romantic Epos and from a Bourgeois Epos. But Lewes was impatient with such questions. The debate over whether Goethe intended to write an epic or an idyll or – if compromises seemed desirable – an idyllic epic, bored him. 'Well! if these discussions gratify the mind, and further any of the purposes of Literature, let those whose bent lies that way, occupy themselves therewith.' Lewes would have none of it. The poem was filled with 'life, character, and beauty', and the rest was, and remains, busy-work. 'If it be unlike all other poems, there is no harm in that; if it resemble some other poems, the resemblance does not enhance its charm.'[8] This distaste for fences (that wall out more than they enclose) is directly related to a wariness against rhetorical tropes that obscure one's sense of what the thing is in itself. Time and again Lewes praised Goethe's avoidance of metaphor. Instead of seeing similarities, Goethe sees the *thing*. This simplicity may be mistaken for baldness, but it is far superior to tropes created for the pleasure of rhetorical showiness, and it arises from a concept of art fundamentally different from that practised by Shakespeare in such plays as *Romeo and Juliet*, where the playwright's delight in language obscures our understanding of how credible or incredible the behaviour of the *dramatis personae* may be.

Clarity, simple diction, tight structure: these are the qualities that

Lewes finds praiseworthy. One would expect a full exploration of this critical position in any consideration of the two parts of *Faust*, and Lewes, proudly adopting the stance of the common reader, does not disappoint us. One may argue over the First Part; it may seem to be constituted of fragments, the elements may appear 'discordant', the tone may be irreverent, some readers will desire a heavier stress on metaphysics. But even a single reading 'is enough to impress us with a sense of its interest, its pathos, its poetry, its strongly-marked character'. The substance fascinates; the execution of details is more controversial. Reading it again will increase our familiarity, our respect for Goethe's achievement.

The Second Part raises objections not only to execution but also to the whole conception, 'both in respect to the story itself, and to the mode of working out that story'. Uneasy during a first reading, Lewes discovered that familiarity gained through rereadings only confirmed his objections. The scenes, incidents, and characters borrowed their interest from the meanings they were supposed to symbolise.

> Only in proportion to your ingenuity in guessing the riddle is your interest excited by the means. Mephisto, formerly so marvellous a creation, has become a mere mouthpiece; Faust has lost all traces of individuality, every pulse of emotion. The philosophic critics will point out how this change is necessary, because in the *Second Part* all that was individual has become universal. But this is only a description, not a justification; it is dignifying failure with a philosophic purpose.

Hence, the objection lies not in the degree of occult meaning lying behind the poetic picture, but in the weakness of the poetic invention.

> A lion may be the symbol of wakefulness, of strength, of kindness, of solitariness, and of many other things, according to the arbitrary fancy of the artist, and it matters comparatively little whether we rightly or wrongly interpret the artist's meaning; but his lion must be finely executed, must excite our admiration *as* a lion, if we are to consider it a work of Art.[9]

Lewes opposed formal academic criticism as diverting a reader's attention from the literary text to questions of form and historical analogy. 'Critics are judges who rely on precedents with the rigour of judges on the bench', he writes (in relation to *Götz*, but much the same elsewhere).

They pronounce according to precedent. That indeed is their office. No sooner has an original work made its appearance, than one of these two courses is invariably pursued: it is rejected by the critics because it does not range itself under any acknowledged class, and thus is branded because it is not an imitation; or it is quietly classified under some acknowledged head.[10]

All of which suggests that Lewes regarded the true challenge of a critic to be to rise to the meeting of an original work in terms of its own premises; to understand the objective of the artist who does not conform, and to evaluate his achievement at least partially in terms of what he or she set out to do. That challenge, Lewes implied, had proved too much for most of his fellow critics.

The issue has to do with a critic's sympathy for modernness, and his capacity for recognising the value of a creative originality. For the Victorians a number of writers seemed baffling because of their unconventionality. Lewes adopted some significant, and very characteristic, attitudes toward their creations. Charles Dickens, for one, had alarmed a number of critics who identified (without difficulty) defects of exaggeration, fantasy and melodrama in his fiction. Lewes did not defend Dickens against these charges, and indeed documented them. But the very popularity of Dickens's writings suggested that 'Dickens had powers which enabled him to triumph in spite of the weaknesses which clogged them': 'an imagination of marvellous vividness', so vivid that it àpproached closely to hallucination. No other perfectly sane mind came so close to the brink. Lewes added, parenthetically, that Blake may not have been perfectly sane. Admitting that Dickens enjoyed great health of mind and spirit, Lewes maintained that 'there is considerable light shed upon his works by the action of the imagination in hallucination'. Dickens could see – in all its sharpness – and believe in his own creations, 'no matter how fantastic and unreal'. It was possible to analyse these figures and to find them merely masks, 'not characters, but personified characteristics, caricatures and distortions of human nature', and yet, even so, admit that 'Against such power criticism was almost idle.' Dickens 'spoke in the mother-tongue of the heart'; he emphasised the emotions that we all feel, and as a consequence can understand. 'Even critical spectators who complained that these broadly painted pictures were artistic daubs, could not wholly resist their effective suggestiveness.' Dickens was not a thinker; 'the world of thought and passion lay beyond his horizon'; he lacked the reflective tendency, and could not spend time on 'the general relations of things' because his was merely 'an *animal* intelligence, i.e., restricted to perceptions'. Lewes confessed astonishment at how thoroughly Dickens, 'an almost unique example of a mind of singular force in which, so to speak, sensations never passed into ideas', had committed himself to the logic of feelings at the expense of all thought. Dickens, in brief, would never have had the patience or the necessary talent to become a student.

But Lewes did not count himself among those critics who wrote of Dickens with 'mingled irritation and contempt'. He instead thought it desirable to identify two biases that had led to their censoriousness. The first, called the bias of opposition, derived from Dickens's extraordinary failure to create genuine human beings in his fictions, though 'touches of verisimilitude' are everywhere. 'It is indeed surprising that Dickens should have observed man, and not been impressed with the fact that man is, in the words of Montaigne, *un être ondoyant et diverse*.' Dickens knew that his characters were grotesque; what he failed to recognise was his own occasional grotesqueness of attitude. Dickens confided to Lewes, on one occasion, that he had distinctly heard every word uttered by his characters. Lewes, puzzled, could explain the failure of a great writer to perceive the unreality of his own dialogue only by relating it to the phenomena of hallucination. The bias of opposition, then, is the tendency of Victorian critics to treat only the weaknesses of Dickens's art, while ignoring the potency of Dickens's imagination for so many thousands of his ordinary readers. (One recalls how often Lewes noted – before raising objections to a poem or play by Goethe – how popular the work was with Goethe's countrymen; it was never enough to attack the deficiencies of an art without simultaneously recognising the wellsprings of its appeal.)

The second, the bias of technical estimate, threw Lewes into conflict with many of his contemporaries. Believing that the primary purpose of art is to delight, and that delight may be divided into two kinds – emotional pleasure at what the artist does, and technical pleasure at how the artist does it – Lewes declared that it was all too easy for reviewers to overvalue technical skill; to misjudge Dickens by applying to him technical 'rules' derived from the works of others, to accuse him of working 'in delf, not in porcelain'. Lewes called them back to the fact that Dickens's 'prodigal imagination created in delf' forms which delighted a vast reading public. 'He only touched common life, but he touched it to "fine issues". . . .' The 'universal heart' was stirred by the murder of Nancy, the deaths of little Nell and little Paul, and the seduction in Peggoty's boathouse. 'Captain Cuttle and Richard Swiveller, the Marchioness and Tilly Slowboy, Pecksniff and Micawber, Tiny Tim and Mrs Gamp, may be imperfect representations of human character, but they are types which no one will forget.'[11]

Criticism, in Lewes's view, is an imperfect art, all too often anxious to elevate its understanding of literature (a word usually capitalised by Lewes) to a doctrine. 'My first objection . . . is, that it must necessarily be so incomplete as to be tyrannically oppressive; because at the best it could only exhibit the laws which great artists had followed, it could not embrace the laws which great artists to come would follow.'[12]

Lewes, functioning as a responsible and accountable man of letters, exerted a strong influence on Matthew Arnold; but on one point, the value of the classics, Lewes held views that Arnold disagreed with sharply, and that must have disconcerted many of those trained in the classics. He admired Homer as the owner of a 'vivid, graphic, direct' style, one 'adapted to the thoughts'. But a balanced reckoning demanded the comment, ' It is at the same time rude, careless, naive, tautologous – all which, though charming to us as indications of the antiquity of the poem, are not to be regarded as poetical excellencies. . . .' Homer shared the merits of his style with 'all early poets', and no less so his faults. 'In fact, the style is not an elaborate – not a cultivated – not an artistic style.'[13]

The point is related not so much to the greatness of the *Iliad* and the *Odyssey*, which Lewes did not contest; these works ranked with the *Aeneid*, *The Divine Comedy*, *Paradise Lost* and *Faust*. Looking for the man behind the Homeric poems, Lewes found himself baffled. There was only one Goethe, Milton or Virgil. But identifying the one Homer cannot be satisfactorily accomplished 'We find no difficulty in conceiving twenty Homers . . . .' Moreover, we go to Homer expecting 'traits of simplicity, indications of early barbarism, pictures of a bygone creed and a bygone civilization', and these satisfied expectations, though they yield delight, have nothing to do with Homer's *merits*. They deal, rather, with critical and historical judgements:

We always read the poem with a secret understanding that we are to find in it the expression of an antique period, and do not, therefore, demand from it the refinements of modern poetry, the qualities of modern art; nor are we shocked at *any* faults, *any* rudenesses, *any* tautologies. The very faults for which we should pitilessly condemn a Virgil or a Milton, become positive sources of delight when we meet with them in Homer. In Homer, artlessness has the effect of exquisite art. But *is* it art?

On closer examination, this turns out to be Lewes's usual distinction between a poet's delight in things rather than words, as well as an argument that insists that, the closer a poet is to the origins of his own language, the more apt will he be to see all objects round about him with an imagination-vivified intensity. Later poets have grown away from the things that *are* to a more meditative appreciation (perhaps sadder as a consequence) of things that *were*. For Lewes, all chatter about the exactitude or complexity of Homer's characterisations misses the point. 'The characters are *true*; but they are merely outlined. They are to the characters of Shakespeare – to which rash admiration has sometimes compared them – as the rude outline of a figure on the wall is to the perfect sculpture of a Phidias.'

These are more than the philistine judgements Arnold would later deplore in less knowledgeable critics. Indeed, there should have been self-evident in the elements of Lewes's attack (the ability of a poet to succeed in portraying passion is commonplace and not specially to be praised in Homer; the Homeric verse is 'a mere jingle . . . stuffed out with idle epithets and particles, or with tautologies, merely thrust in to keep up the jingle') an intense desire to differentiate his own views from those of the conventional wisdom, and to provide something of a philosophical base for the higher valuation of nineteenth-century writers. Lewes praised in more than one context the meaning of Solon's self-satisfaction at having provided his countrymen with the best laws that they were capable of receiving. Understood more widely, the saying could have minimised much grief, anger and mutual persecution. 'It means this: that all truths are *truths of periods*, and not truths for eternity.' In part related to an enlightened Christian consciousness of the nineteenth century – Protestantism replaced Catholicism because the latter had become obsolete, just as the revelations of the Jewish religion had been superseded by the New Testament as more *fitting* –

and in part related to a sense that the best writing of the Victorian
Age could not be seen plain until the literary idols of the past were
more objectively measured, Lewes underscored the need for encouraging the literature of own's own time. It has more to teach about
modern problems (many of them social in nature, and without
parallel or analogue in the cultures of ages past). It was a fire built
within one's hearth. Thus, Shelley speaks of futurity, and gives his
life to it. Shelley's dreams are of 'humanity, perfectability, civilization, democracy', 'the goal, admitted or not, of every human
energy!' There was no question in Lewes's mind that Shelley had
more to say to his century than most writers of previous ages, and for
that matter more than most of his fellow Romantics. 'Scott resorted
to the past, called up the dead spirit of chivalry before our eyes, and
passed in panoramic manner the whole bygone days, with their
border forays. . . . But it was the dead past, and bore in its womb no
living future.' Wordsworth, Southey and Coleridge may have begun
with 'wild youthful theories of Pantisocracy', but they were unable
to sustain their momentum or their direction for very long; while
Byron mirrored the disease of the age ('unbelief and self-anatomy'),
Moore sought the remote past and knew 'no Gospel', and Keats,
'remote and unsettled', saw much that was wrong, but did not
clearly see 'where and how it could be righted'. Shelley, the only
poet 'standing completely on his truth', saw man's life and
endeavour as 'a stammering and confused utterance of eternal
truth', and refused to accept the view that man restlessly whirled
'round in a circle, like a blind horse in a mill'. (Even so, Lewes did
not exaggerate Shelley's achievement as an artist. Though Shelley
'had a most marvellous command of language, music, and imagery',
in most of his larger poems there was 'too much glare and brilliancy',
and his mind had to be characterised as 'sensitive and reflective,
rather than plastic and creative.'[14])

Lewes rejected the principle of imitation of the classics, particularly as promulgated by Matthew Arnold in his Preface to a new
edition of his own poems (1853). Though he conceded the value of
studying Homer, Aeschylus and Virgil, he saw nothing automati-
cally right in their productions that eliminated the need for
selectivity in models. 'Study the Classics and the Moderns too', he
wrote. He contradicted Arnold's thesis that the Moderns had
become enervated as a consequence of heeding 'syren-charms', and
hence were no longer able to sustain the admiration of younger
writers. Lewes went on,

But beware of the rudeness and baldness of the one, no less than of the rhetoric and glitter of the other! That is our text. For we believe the Ancients to have had every virtue and every vice conspicuous in the Moderns, over and above the remoteness of their ideas and feelings, which to us moderns becomes a vice. When the classics are good, they are so by virtue of qualities essential in all excellent works of Art; when they are bad, which is mostly the case, they are so by vice of qualities noticeable in every age – rudeness, incongruity, untruth, greater regard for manner than for matter, and for the mere fopperies of manner.

Homer, despite virtues, 'is as rude as hemp', and Aeschylus and Virgil have limitations in their style that rival the worst excesses of 'the very worst specimens which can be selected from eminent poets of Modern times'.[15]

Emulation rather than imitation – such was the advice Lewes gave his contemporaries. 'Instead of following the mere fashions of Greek Art, follow no fashions but those which bear the general verdict of your age . . . .' All great artists have lessons to teach, and there is no reason to suppose that the Greeks did not have their share of great men. But the past is precisely that, something with historical, not absolute significance; 'it is our Ancestry, and not our Life'. Lewes took issue with Arnold's conviction that 'the highest problem of an art is to imitate actions'. If the practical application of such an exhortation is to deny the status of art to such a work as *Faust* – a work which does not conceive of the imitation of actions as its highest goal – then *The Divine Comedy* must be similarly slated, and what are we to do with a drama about Philoctetes, 'of which no one will say that the interest or beauty lies in the action'? 'Actions are not ends in Art, but means to an end; they are not for their own sake, but for the sake of the thoughts and emotions they excite in us.'

Lewes was remarkably consistent in preaching that 'the purpose of Literature' is 'the sincere expression of the individual's own ideas and feelings'. He believed in the right of a distinctive personality to modify the rules governing literature to suit himself. 'Unless a man thinks and feels precisely after the manner of Cicero and Titian it is manifestly wrong for him to express himself in their way. . . . They ought to be illustrations not authorities, studies not models.' To some extent, of course, this controverts Arnold's admiration of the 'chastity and elegance' of French models of the seventeenth century. The notion that the Ancients had 'discovered all wisdom', Lewes believed, explained – at least in part – why French literature was not richer. As a student of science, Lewes was more familiar than most with the irrelevance of practically all Greek scientific treatises to the 'secrets of the universe'. The universe itself has to be studied before one can surprise its secrets. Science, advancing, has exposed the limitations of the science of an earlier age. But criticism remains bound to the past, 'overawèd by tradition'. (Lewes entertained no undue reverence for the five-act structure of a drama, though he recognised the utility of a general rule based upon observation of a great many plays successfully produced over a period of time.) 'Great writers should be our companions if we would learn to write greatly; but no familiarity with their manner will supply the place of native endowment.'[16]

The denigrating tendency of nineteenth-century criticism – the argument that the tendency of the epoch 'is to destroy poetry, by placing everywhere material instead of moral agency', and by introducing an iron machine 'without a soul, without beauty', to take the place of the spinning-wheel – was formulated by Ernest Renan; but Lewes's attack on Renan's polemics has not dated a great deal. 'We lose much in passing from our old and consecrated conditions. But is there not compensation for the loss? No one remembers the old days of coach-travelling without a sigh; but does he not, on the whole, prefer the railway? ' To some extent, the terms of the dialogue were being set by the new forces abroad in the land. 'The creation of art is not industrialism', Lewes wrote in his review.

> The disposal of a work of art is. All the gold of California would be insufficient to buy a single poem, or a single picture, unless the poet and the painter had seen and suffered what their art expressed. All that industrialism can do to favour art, is by stimulating the artist to labour more; and all that it can do to deteriorate art, is by seducing the artist to become a rapid manufacturer.

Lewes rejected the pessimism of Renan, which had developed as a consequence of artists becoming more conscious than ever before of the rewards ('in hard cash and present renown') attending upon their work. An artist, Lewes maintained, would continue to produce his work 'because he is an artist', and because 'the noble impulse lives within him'. But to say such things, no matter how deeply believed, may be depressing, because the very fact of having to say such things seems like a new development. Perhaps, too, the optimism that Europe would be unlikely to forgo its birthright for a mess of pottage betrayed insufficient awareness of the symbiotic relationships between an artist anxious to reach as wide a public as possible, and a public complacently willing to be titillated and 'entertained'.[17]

The virtues of Lewes's mode of critical inquiry lie in an eagerness to turn from the past as stultifying and inhibiting; a carefully worked-out distinction between Imitation and Emulation; a faith in national character (the Englishness of an artist's work provides an early score – though not necessarily the decisive one – in its favour); an admiration of sincerity as a writer's irrefutable strength ('It is belief which gives momentum'); and a faith in the long-run certifying value of popular success. It is in some ways more interesting to watch these principles put to direct use in the review of a particular play or novel than to read Lewes's earnestly titled collection of highly generalised essays, *The Principles of Success in Literature*. These pieces were first printed in the *Fortnightly Review*, and ran in six instalments between May and November 1865. George Saintsbury was only one of many readers who found the dogged humourlessness of the title repellent, and Lewes did not avoid the danger inherent in serial publication: such views might seem overstated or inconsistent when printed as a book. Or – to an extent not often admitted by summarisers of Lewes's career – platitudinous, and a weariness to the spirit.

In one respect *The Principles of Success in Literature* served a worthwhile purpose. Lewes, like Wordsworth in an earlier age, revealed a testiness about the sorry state of much (if not most) modern literature which must have proved salutary to most readers of the *Fortnightly*. Lewes had no use for 'fine writing', which he called 'the plague-spot of Literature', and which raged like an epidemic during the middle years of the century. 'The "fine writer" will always prefer the opinion which is striking to the opinion which is true', Lewes wrote, with some exasperation. A sentence which is 'determined by some verbal suggestion' rather than by the thought that it should be seeking to convey vulgarises the language, which should be reserved for grand thoughts. Lewes was fighting against imprecise communication, against 'slapdash insincerity'. First the real emotion; then the expression, which will inevitably become 'moving'. Images, antithese, witty epigrams and rolling periods do not strike deeply into the imagination, 'whereas some simpler style, altogether wanting in such "brilliant passage"', may gain the attention and respect of a large public.[18]

Lewes, in reviewing the laws of style, stressed simplicity. But he also made room for the law of variety, which occasionally would complicate a text to the benefit of both text and the pleasure of the reader, and he had some particularly kind things to say about the drama: 'The limitations of time compel the dramatist to attend closely to what is and what is not needful for his purpose. A drama must compress into two or three hours material which may be diffused through three volumes of a novel, because spectators are more impatient than readers . . . .' A scene may be 'charmingly written', and may even excite applause, but it must serve a purpose by forwarding the progress of the action or intensifying the interest in the characters. Speeches and sentences have to be relevant; they cannot be used simply to show off the author's wit and wisdom.

This kind of analysis implies a greater looseness in the novel form. 'The novelist is not under the same limitations of time, nor has he to contend against the same mental impatience on the part of his public.' If a novelist chooses to linger, to digress, to introduce (and dismiss) characters who bear no important relationship to the plot, he has greater privileges in these regards than a dramatist. Though Lewes reminded his reader that 'the parts of a novel should have organic relations', his implicit assumption, that a novel is coarser in its structure and less demanding in its sense of what is needed at a given moment in the narrative, comes through unmistakably.[19]

Lewes lavished considerable time and talent on the theatre. Partly of course, the middle-class habit of attending the theatre on a regular basis had been sanctified by the Queen. Partly, too, the movement toward greater realism and naturalness in stage presentations (for example, Tom Robertson's *Society*, first produced in 1865) illustrated exactly the kind of reform in literature and literary values that Lewes had been fighting for. The rant and violence of over-written plays seemed less and less attractive to the audiences who read Lewes's columns with attention. Lewes's strictures were part of a reform movement that demanded greater realism, that responded warmly to recognisable locales in plays, and that cheered on the development of a quieter acting-style. By mid century prostitutes were banned from the lobbies and special 'walks' of theatres. Greater care was being taken on costumes. Only one play was being offered for an evening's entertainment, rather than two, three and even four productions that might last until 1 a.m.

Substantial increases in ticket-prices inevitably cut down on rowdiness and eating during (as well as between) acts. More detailed stage directions, a better-articulated control over stage business, and the improvement of dramatic roles for subsidiary members of the cast undercut the star system. Indeed, Lewes's theatrical reviews, which may have been read with greater care than his literary essays, proved influential in the invention of stage management as we know it today.

When Lewes wrote his dramatic reviews for the *Leader* (1850–4) under the pen-name 'Vivian', and on an even more frequent basis for the *Pall Mall Gazette* (1865–6), he was concentrating for the moment on well-developed interests in drama that had already been recorded, over a longer period of time and in a large number of periodicals, on such subjects as Alfieri's relationship to the Italian drama, Shakespeare in France, dramatic reform, the criticism of *Antigone*, *Faust* as a drama, '*Strafford* and the Historical Drama', and contemporary examples of tragedy. Still recommended to students of the age is his book *The Spanish Drama: Lope de Vega and Calderon* (1846). For a full three decades Lewes enjoyed plays on the stage and in the study; wrote some seventeen original plays and adaptations; and was called – by Archer – 'probably the most highly-trained thinker who ever applied himself to the study of theatrical art in England', a comment that prefixed a selection of Lewes's dramatic essays reprinted from the *Leader*.[20]

Lewes, as early as 1841, entertained some ambitions to act. As one of the Dickens amateurs, he tried his hand in minor roles in Shakespeare and Jonson before essaying Shylock in a Manchester production of 1849. The evidence left behind by contemporary reviewers suggests that Lewes's interpretation was gentle, thoughtful and restrained (perhaps a little subdued by a throat ailment). Lewes also played the principal role of Don Gomez de la Vega in his own play, *The Noble Heart* (1850); but the play was undistinguished fustian, even if Lewes's acting won some commendations for its restraint. Apparently the dialogue won no friends for its high level of abstraction, or what the *Morning Herald* called 'the nervous force of the Elizabethan rhapsodies, . . . the morality of the admonitions, . . . and the felicitousness of the metaphors'. Whether the arrest of the manager of the Olympic Theatre, London, where Lewes's play was being produced, and the manager's subsequent suicide in Newgate Prison (the crime being embezzlement from the ledgers of the Globe Insurance Company), terminated Lewes's

acting ambitions is unclear; but he continued to write directly for
the theatre for several years after the production of *The Noble Heart*.

Lewes's examination of Macready's interpretation of Shylock has
for us a special poignance, not only because it appeared a year after
Lewes's own enacting of the role, but also because Macready, in his
work as Shylock, Lear and Macbeth, was winding down his career
on the stage, and this performance (9 November 1850) was among
his last. Charles Kean – the only actor whose interpretation Lewes
thought worthy of offering as a comparison – 'took what one may
call the obvious view of Shylock, representing all that the plain *text*
has given, and not troubling himself about anything lying *involved* in
the text; hence, as Shakespeare gives no language of tenderness
toward Jessica, Kean represents none'. Lewes saw Shylock as a
father, who had a measure of paternal tenderness that Macready
denied the character, Macready represented Shylock as 'self-
occupied, gloomy, irritable' in a 'strange misconception' of the trial
scene, when Shylock should have been personally outraged, and his
'whole being centred in the one fierce passion of hatred about to be
satisfied'. Lewes in some ways anticipated Irving (as Archer noted
in his Preface) when he stressed all the provocation which led to
Shylock's intense hatred of Antonio, and to his deliberate risking of
community status and personal fortune for the sake of exacting a
bitter revenge. 'Shylock, to hereditary hatred of the Christians, adds
his own personal wrongs, and his malignity is the accumulation of
years of outrage silently brooding in his soul. . . . I want to keep
Shylock's human nature steadily in view.' But Lewes acknowledged
that Shakespeare had written the play in such a way that an actor
might – for understandable reasons – misinterpret the playwright's
intention and degrade the human relationships to 'a brutal
melodrama, not a great tragedy'. His characterisation of Jessica ('a
heartless, frivolous girl, who robs her father, throws away her
mother's turquoise for a monkey, speaks of her father in a tone as
shocking as it is gratuitous') is an 'outrage' against 'nature and art'.
And Shylock's worst and most ferocious outbursts must be carefully
balanced against speeches scattered through the text.[21]

Lewes insists on the actor's paying attention to the artist's
intention. The actor must become a scholar of the whole text rather
than fasten on a few convenient speeches as the rationale of a
character. He must know something of the historical context, too.
Lewes insisted that an effort mightier than usual would have to be
made to appreciate the double dilemma of Antigone, for what

impressed the Athenians as fundamental to their understanding of her rebellion – 'the holiness of the rites of sepulture and the sanctity of the laws' – cannot and does not have the same immediacy of impact on nineteenth-century Englishmen. The actress (Miss Vandenhoff) who 'throws herself into some picturesque attitudes' and who 'at times . . . reminded us of the figures on the ancient vases' does not feel deeply enough; does not go back in time far enough to appreciate the instinctive and necessary responses of Antigone to her situation.[22]

Indeed, what disturbed Lewes was the scandalous lack of interest in history shown by producers, managers and actors who exploited whatever struck their fancy. One of his more eloquent tirades broke out on the occasion of the production of Jules Lacroix and A. Maquet's *Valeria* (1851). The play, presumably based on the writings of Tacitus and Juvenal dealing with the age of Claudius, outraged Lewes particularly for its effort to rehabilitate Messalina. The playwrights had chosen to deny the evidence of how Messalina undertook orgies while bearing the name of Lysisca, and their stratagem – to pretend that Lysisca was a real person, thus washing away all the debaucheries of Messalina – struck him as frivolous. Not only were the rules of evidence ignored (the preciseness of the *Annals* of Tacitus had simply been put to one side), but no effort was made by the authors to argue the case for Messalina's innocence; it was simply assumed as a fact. 'All through the piece,' Lewes wrote,

> I felt that the attempt to make this imperial courtesan a chaste and noble woman was an insult to the audience. But it is in keeping with the rest! These men look upon history as an old warehouse, wherein theatrical masks and costumes are kept for the caprices of theatrical amateurs: enter and choose what you like!

Admitting that Lacroix and Maquet would laugh at him for being serious with them – 'They who have not been serious with themselves!' – still Lewes was depressed by this sinister development in pandering to the insatiable craving for amusement at the expense of art.

> What do they care about Art, about History, about Taste? All they think of is 'effect'. Don't talk to me about Taste, tell me if such a surprise will bring down the bravos! Poetry, character,

passion, consistency – all very respectable things in their way, – but the drama can so well dispense with them![23]

There is moral indignation here, of exactly the sort that reacted with passion against the popularity of *La Dame aux Camélias*, by Alexandre Dumas, *fils*, during the decade of the 1850s:

> I declare I know of few things in the way of fiction more utterly wrong, unwholesome, and immortal. . . . How men who have within them the capacity for high and deep feelings, who think of Love as something more than a 'heat and fervour of the blood', can be delighted at this hideous parody of passion, and tolerate this idealisation of corruption, would be a mystery, if one did not know the strange contradictions even honest minds will allow to live side by side. . . . The *banale* excuse that 'such things are', is no justification; every hospital has its horrible realities, which it must keep from the public eye, and which Art refuses to acknowledge as materials. I am not prudish, nor easily alarmed by what are called 'dangerous' subjects, but *this* subject I protest against with all my might; – a subject not only unfit to be brought before our sisters and our wives, but unfit to be brought before *ourselves*.

Something deep has been offended, for it is not Lewes's wish to make very often or very loudly a plea for censorship, based on the argument that some subjects are not amenable to artistic treatment.[24]

More important, Lewes was condemning the shallowness of taste that misunderstood the nature of dramatic greatness. He did not oppose a new interpretation of historical fact if it respected the intelligence of the playgoer, avoided the appeals of lubricity, and dramatised human emotion by means of 'the power and the music of the human voice'. Charles Kean – who regarded Lewes's criticisms of his various roles as so intolerable a burden that he took him off his Free List of tickets – should have anticipated the objection to his emphasis on 'architecture and costume' in the revival of Byron's *Sardanapalus* (1853).

> Is the Drama nothing more than a Magic Lantern on a large scale? Was Byron only a pretext for a panorama? It is a strange state of Art when the mere *accessories* become the aim and purpose of representation – when truth of archaeology supplants truth

and human passion – when "winged bulls" dwarf heroic natures! Charles Kean is so bad an actor, and his troupe is so incompetent, that the policy of subordinating drama to spectacle is undeniable from *his* point of view; but how about the public?

Historical literalness is much less important than genuine dramatic instinct, shaped over time by acquaintance with the classics of the theatre. But Lewes was not able to rest on the platitudes of received opinion, and much of what passed for the masterpieces of English drama could not survive his intense reconsideration, once he had passed beyond his 'reverential regard' for Lamb, Hazlitt and other 'fine critics' who quoted 'unmistakable beauties' in the scenes and passages they admired. 'Enthusiasm, however, was tamed by the irresistible mediocrity of these plays', he wrote on the occasion of a revival of *The Duchess of Malfi* (1850); 'no belief in their excellence could long stand up against the evidence of their dreariness and foolishness'. He distinguished between the 'noble lines of manly verse' that charmed the reader, and the impressions of the wearisome and the ludicrous that overwhelmed the spectator. Yet, rather than take an easy line of discourse and declaim against an accumulation of horrors, he protested against the childishness of the horrors ('They are not the culmination of tragic motives'), the despising of probabilities, the disregarding of all conditions of art, and the falsifying of human nature.[25] He burst into a similar tirade on the occasion of a revival of Marston's *The Malcontent*:

> Whoever has more than a second-hand acquaintance with Kyd, Peele, Marlowe, Webster, Dekker, Ford, Marston, Chapman, Heywood, Middleton, Shirley, Cyril Tourneur, and the rest, will probably agree with us that their plays are as poor in construction (artistic as well as theatric) as they are resplendent in imagery and weighty lines – that their characters are sketched rather than developed – that their situations for the most part are violent, horrible, and clumsily prepared, and that, besides being wearisome in reading, they are essentially unfit for the modern stage.

An admiration of verse drama had little to do with an understanding of genuine drama; 'imitators' of the Elizabethan form could not succeed in the nineteenth century; even James Sheridan Knowles, often cited as a true inheritor of the Elizabethan tradition, earned the respect of his audiences by his strong understanding of the domestic relationships of his characters. 'To appeal to the public taste, to move the general heart of men, you must quit the study . . . .' Again, this is an advocacy of a drama that will appeal to an audience wider 'than that of a few critics and black-letter students', a *modern* drama rather than an archeologically correct form that seeks to be 'worthy of a place beside productions of the Elizabethan age'.[26]

Shakespeare was largely exempt from this carping, though the feebleness of several of the comedies and a conviction that the minor history plays were deservedly minor may be traced in Lewes's reviews. Lewes was a great admirer of the Greeks, and of Racine; the ability of Spanish players to give room to each other in ensemble acting impressed him more than the plays they actually produced; and German theatre, on the whole, was in a far healthier condition than the English stage. Yet, for all his sharp critiques of sleaziness in the Victorian playhouse, Lewes always looked out for the possibility of hope: the perfect success of *The Day of Reckoning*, a French melodrama adapted by James Robinson Planché, and the effectiveness of the comedies of Scribe; the occasional improvement of a comic text by inspired direction and acting (Lewes in general thought poorly of English comedies); the alternation of laughter and the tears of sympathy in *Masks and Faces*, by Tom Taylor and Charles Reade, about which Lewes wrote – almost delirious with pleasure – 'bright ingenious dialogue, playing like lambent flame, stimulates the intellect; and homely pathos, homely mirth, kind hearts and loving voices, gently touch the various chords of emotion'; the 'enchantment and artistic beauty' of Planché's *Good Woman in the Wood* (1853), a play to which Lewes would gladly have applied the Greek word '*flabbergastuality*' if at all possible; 'the ingeniously-wrought drama of the modern French school' that came to London in the guise of *Plot and Passion*, by Tom Taylor and John Lang; and a number of popular plays that, despite their failings as literature, held the attention of a generous cross-section of London audiences.

Always there is the sense, in reading Lewes, that, despite a keen understanding of the staleness of particular productions, the grating mannerisms of actors and actresses, and the inevitable grimness that overtakes a playgoer who visits the theatre several nights a week because he is *obliged* to do so, Lewes found many – if not most – of his happiest moments in the gas-lit playhouses of a prosperous, intensely alive metropolis. 'I sometimes complain of the bad atmospheres of theatres,' Lewes wrote after a five-week absence from London,

> but, believe me, it is better to breathe that atmosphere, contemplating mediocre acting, and 'powerful', uninteresting pieces, than to breathe, as I have been breathing, the sea breezes of the southern coast, or the gay, intoxicating air of Paris. Yes, it is a miserable fact! I would rather sit in the upper boxes of a crowded theatre, listening to the melodious voice of Charles Kean, and watching the varied expression of his passionate countenance, than drive through the avenues of the Bois de Boulogne, or 'Hear the mighty waters rolling evermore'.[27]

This is engaging stuff, rendered even more attractive by the persona of Vivian, a personable, enthusiastic, well-informed gossip, on occasions intrigued by entertainment when 'art' proves in short supply; willing to go along with popular approval of a piece that has structural or literary defects, yet insistent, in a quiet way, on the need for not deceiving one's self about its aesthetic qualities; and it is all very modern, as William Archer noted, 'with a free-and-easiness unsurpassed even by "Spectator" or "Corno di Bassetto" in the starry youth of the New Journalism'.[28] Like many critics anxious to be liked, Lewes admitted that 'half our conversation' is 'Criticism of our friends', and committing such conversation to print is to run the risk of becoming the target of rotten eggs. There may even be some doubt as to whether criticism as practised by young men such as Vivian is 'a lawful occupation'. Yet, 'the Critic has a higher office. He is the severe guardian of public taste. . . . He is the aesthetic Policeman.' And his task is complicated by the fact that, working to meet a daily or weekly schedule, he cannot concentrate wholly on the classics and the masterpieces of many lands; he must judge as good or bad all kinds of productions before the world has had an opportunity to judge. The critic of ephemera 'has no guide but his own taste, he cannot wait, he must pronounce at once, pronounce at his peril'. The literary or artistic creation may turn out not to be ephemera at all. The only way to separate the good from the bad, to commend one work and condemn another, is to stake one's judgement on 'long experience and tact'. Ultimately, criticism, from Lewes's point of view, is lawful, perilous – and worth doing.

Lewes may be most lively, trustworthy, and useful as a theatre

guide in his criticism of particular productions, in which case the
key work is *On Actors and the Art of Acting*, printed first in 1875. The
kind of journalism that can evoke, with swift and workmanlike
language, the appearance of a Rachel or a Charles Mathews or a
Frederic Lemaître, and that can convincingly suggest for us the very
timbre of a voice, is rare in any age. In the writing of this kind of
deadline sketch, Lewes was very good indeed, and remains readable
to this day. I personally prefer Lewes's *Dramatic Essays*, not only
those reprinted by William Archer but also the dozens of additional
reviews, sketches and amiable 'impressions' dashed off for various
periodicals. *The Principles of Success in Literature* has little or no appeal
to our age; its taxonomic sensibility beclouds the pleasures of the
study; and it is, in some important respects, a didactic strain that
Lewes keeps under wise control elsewhere. The literary essays,
taken as a whole, are too scrappy, and sometimes too much at a
distance from the texts being considered, to reveal much personality, or to ingratiate their author with the reader of a full century
and a half after the event.

Behind all these works, however, with the possible exception of
Principles, is the personality of a critic of sensibility and enthusiasm,
who persuades us that rules narrowly conceived can only be the
death of genuine invention and achievement. In Lewes's world,
room exists for innovation: 'A great talent will discover new
methods', he writes in an essay entitled 'On Style and the Imitation
of Models', and he adds, with conviction, 'The strong individuality
of the artist will create special modifications of the laws to suit
himself, making that excellent or endurable which in other hands
would be intolerable.'[29] This rejection of unimaginative imitation –
even of the best elements of tradition, even of the most undeniably
great of artists past–proved delightful to Lewes's readers. And, in
The Life of Goethe, Lewes demonstrated on a large scale the value of a
clear-eyed, honest and balanced judgement, one that made a
Jovian figure more human and more accessible to intelligent
readers. It became a truism in the nineteenth century that one could
trust Lewes as a guide to drama, poetry and the novel; it is all the
more remarkable that Lewes cultivated this garden of culture while
learning as much about philosophy, the hard sciences and psychology as any layman of his time.

2 Walter Bagehot

Walter Bagehot's literary criticism fits within a fairly limited time frame: from November 1847 and an anonymous review of Philip James Bailey's *Festus*, to the period of greatest activity, a decade extending from the mid 1850s to the mid 1860s, and the final two reviews of George Grote's *History of Greece* (June 1871) and Nassau William Senior's *Journals* (August 1871). His career as editor of the *Economist*, co-editor of the *Spectator*, and author of *The English Constitution* (1867, in book form), *Physics and Politics* (1872), and a large number of essays on political figures such as Disraeli, Lord Palmerston, Bright and Gladstone, obviously distracted him from analyses of the relationship between a writer and his work. He died relatively young, at the age of fifty-one. For all his limitations in temperament and insight (no essay of his twenty-eight critiques – several impressively extended, none easily dismissible – may be rated as definitive), Bagehot may be the most modern and likable of all Victorian literary critics, and his essays the most pleasurable reading of any discussed in this volume. I do not underestimate his wit or his ability to stimulate a reader to return to the original writings under consideration; but it seems to me that, at this late date, one need not subscribe uncritically to Woodrow Wilson's idolatry (contained in two articles published in the *Atlantic Monthly* – November 1895 and October 1898 – and in a large number of other allusions) or to C. H. Sisson's searing indictment, in *The Case of Walter Bagehot* (London: Faber & Faber, 1972), that Bagehot's understanding of the greatest artists' enthusiasm for reality 'combines a silly notion of enthusiasm with an ordinary busy-body's notion of reality' (p. 42). A more restrained assessment of Bagehot's achievement and lasting legacy seems in order.

Let us begin with the paradigmatic treatment of Shakespeare that Bagehot wrote at the age of twenty-seven. Long considered it to be one of his best essays and a key document in the evolution of literary taste during the Victorian age, this review of François Guizot's

Shakespeare et son Temps: Étude Litteraire (Paris, 1852) illustrates, in several remarkable ways, what Bagehot thought important, and what he wanted to call to the attention of an educated public. The essay appeared first in *The Prospective Review* in July 1853, and was entitled 'Shakespeare – the Individual', a clear signal that Bagehot was looking for the *personality* responsible for the plays and poems.

Bagehot rejected immediately the notion that the lack of documentary evidence about Shakespeare's life inhibited the confidence of the public that they knew Shakespeare personally: 'You seem to have known Shakespeare – to have seen Shakespeare – to have been friends with Shakespeare.'[1] That confidence derived from 'the sure testimony of his certain works'.[2] For Bagehot, Shakespeare had not only a first-rate imagination but also 'a full conversancy with the world',[3] or a first-rate experience. How unlike M Guizot (Louis Philippe's first minister, 1840–8), or for that matter the English Pitt, men who – Bagehot said – were not taught by experience, who did not grow but were cast! The classic illustration provided by Bagehot came from *Venus and Adonis*. Of this 'celebrated description of the hunt'[4] Bagehot wrote, 'It is absurd . . . to say we know *nothing* about the man who wrote that; we know that he had been after a hare.'[5] Shakespeare, in an important respect, was like Sir Walter Scott, who dealt with 'the main outlines and great points of nature',[6] and unlike Wordsworth, who knew too much to hold the attention or stimulate the admiration of young people. This repeated emphasis upon youth (to whom 'beauty is more than a religion') betrays, of course, Bagehot's own age; the essay contains additional clues to Bagehot's impatience with the slow process of argumentation, the setting-forth of causes to explain and define, in some adequate way, the effect which a literary text produces on the careful reader. In a passage that Bagehot decided to omit from *Estimates of Some Englishmen and Scotchmen* (published, without notable success – perhaps because of its somewhat unappealing title – in 1858), the case is strongly made that Shakespeare knew the things themselves, and did not need general terms, abstract and recondite principles from which steps in a reasoning process might lead on to 'more practical and useful knowledge'.[7] Bagehot scoffed at the physics and metaphysics which came between an artist and his true subject-matter.

If we had eyes to see the planet Neptune, it would not have been necessary for Mr Adams to consume his valuable time in calculating where it was. The more perfect our senses, the less is the use of argument. A man who has a picture of the world in his mind will not want Natural Philosophy to inform him about it, nor will he be misled by verbose ratiocination.[8]

The confidence with which Bagehot speaks of his personal knowledge of Shakespeare – a knowledge derived not from certificates, life and death records, and the laconically worded legal depositions that pass for contemporary documentation in the Elizabethan Age, but from a careful reading of the literary texts – raises an inevitable question as to what kind of person Bagehot's Shakespeare is. A passage on dogs in *A Midsummer-Night's Dream* is quoted to show up Milton's quite different attitude toward nature:

> 'Judge when you hear.' It is evident that the man who wrote this was a judge of dogs, was an out-of-door sporting man, full of natural sensibility, not defective in 'daintiness of ear', and above all things, apt to cast on Nature random, sportive, halfboyish glances, which reveal so much, and bequeath such abiding knowledge.[9]

If we ignore Bagehot's extended digression that follows (authors who came first in time, apparently, copied from nature rather than from books, and may be considered superior to those with abstracted habits who 'read well, but write ill',[10] and lack keen exterior interests), we may conclude that we are reading more about Bagehot's taste than about Shakespeare's practice, for the subject-matter of a poetical passage proves nothing about the niceness of judgement, in real life, of the man who wrote it. The biographical heresy, which uses the text to document the assertions about the life, and then builds higher by manipulating the assertions about the life to show what must be intended in the text, is far riskier as critical strategy than Bagehot perceives. The fullness of imagination which can give life to a description of hunting demonstrates little or nothing about the degree of personal participation in the hunting of hares or foxes that an author may have experienced. And what are these 'sportive, halfboyish glances' save a rhetorical flourish?

To argue, as Bagehot does (most piquantly in this essay, but in other contexts and at length as well), that Shakespeare knew about 'the germs and tendencies of the very elements that he described' because they were within himself, that he possessed an 'amazing

sympathy with common people'[11] and appreciated stupidity as 'a
most valuable element'[12] in human life, that he enjoyed a spirited-
ness similar to that which Chaucer and Scott had enjoyed ('When
you read him you feel a sensation of motion, a conviction that there is
something "up", a notion that not only is something being talked
about, but also that something is being done'),[13] that this accounts
for the large comic element in the plays (which Bagehot claims is
peculiarly English, 'the humour of a man who laughs when he
speaks, of flowing enjoyment, of an experiencing nature'[14]), and
that, to round off the picture, Shakespeare also possessed a capacity
for solitude, 'a dark half, which is unknown to us', is simply to spread
across more than forty pages the kind of psychobiography which
Edwin Arlington Robinson created in 'Ben Jonson Entertains a
Man from Stratford'. For this Shakespeare is, ultimately, a creature
of insights, possessing an intelligence that functions in unorthodox
but strikingly effective ways; of wavering faith in the reliability of a
relationship between human virtue and divine judgement; and of
political orthodoxy, loyalty to the ancient polity of England, and a
'disbelief in the middle classes'.[15] The evidence, as always, is what
Shakespeare's characters say to heroicise or explain themselves, with
an understanding (in the reader's mind) that often they may reveal
more than they know, or wish to reveal. Bagehot argues, much more
confidently than the pattern of his chosen quotations allows, that
Shakespeare

> everywhere speaks in praise of a tempered and ordered and
> qualified polity, in which the pecuniary classes have a certain
> influence, but no more, and shows in every page a keen sensibility
> to the large views, and high-souled energies, the gentle refine-
> ments and disinterested desires in which those classes are likely to
> be especially deficient . . . .[16]

A lengthy contrast of Shakespeare's treatment of women with that of
Plato leads, unsurprisingly, to the generalisation, 'One thinks of him
(Shakespeare) as firmly set on our coarse world of common clay, but
from it he could paint the moving essence of thoughtful feeling –
which is the best refinement of the best women. Imogen or Juliet
would have thought little of the conversation of Gorgias.'[17] As for
Shakespeare's learning (or lack of it), Bagehot argues that the older
view – one that praises Shakespeare's knowledge of 'the entire range
of the Greek and Latin classics', and use of Sophocles and Aeschylus

'as guides and models' – had given way to a new school – one that stresses Shakespeare's ignorance of books[18] – without showing, in any convincing way, that either view predominated in earlier centuries or in Bagehot's own time. Bagehot evidently thought of Shakespeare as a reader very much like himself, 'a natural reader'. 'When a book was dull, he put it down; when it looked fascinating, he took it up and the consequence is, that he remembered and mastered what he read.'[19] Shakespeare liked to read, in other words, interesting books, such as the novels of his time, Plutarch, Montaigne; he would not have enjoyed reading what the critics had to say about him, had he been transported to a later age; he would 'certainly' not have read a page of Bagehot's essay on Shakespeare; and it is to Bagehot's credit that this did not seem altogether a deplorable thing in Shakespeare's temperament, for Guizot's commentary – the original point of departure for this essay – is 'a little difficult to *read*'.[20]

On two other points Bagehot convinced himself that he had caught his man, and his treatment of these illustrates some major problems in his method of analysis for literary figures. Of Shakespeare's religion much had been written, and not always to good effect. The commentary of Dr Ulrici, 'a very learned and illegible writer', sought to demonstrate 'that in every one of his plays Shakespeare had in view the inculcation of the peculiar sentiments and doctrines of the Christian religion'. Bagehot's answer to his line of investigation is somehow very characteristic: 'This is what Dr Ulrici thinks of Shakespeare; but what would Shakespeare have thought of Dr Ulrici?'[21] Bagehot disliked excess in preaching. Dr Ulrici's dullness is neither less nor more reprehensible than an Evangelical's rigidity of thought, or of a Catholic's suspicion that a poet might not be 'earnest' enough. Shakespeare had 'an objection to grim people', and 'would have liked the society of Mercutio better than that of a dreary divine'.[22] Religion is not necessarily restricted to 'pews and altar cloths', it has to do with cakes and ale also; 'there is a religion of weekdays as well as of Sundays'.[23] Shakespeare looked at England and saw 'its green fields, and its long hedgerows, and its many trees, and its great towns, and its endless hamlets, and its motley society, and its long history, and its bold exploits, and its gathering power; and he saw that they were good'. To Shakespeare these were bound together in 'a great unity', they constituted 'a great religious object'. If one could only 'descend to the inner life', and understand 'the essence of character' – Hamlet, Ophelia – 'we might, so far as we are capable of so doing, understand the nature which God has made'.[24] But Bagehot, sensitive to the unexpectedness of his new direction, and perhaps anxious lest he might offend a religiously committed reader, added hastily, 'We must pause, lest our readers reject us, as the Bishop of Durham, the poor curate, because he was "mystical and confused." '[25]

The second point – one that later readers of Bagehot have found offensive, and that is stressed here if only because Bagehot's placement of it at the very end of his essay suggests the importance which he gives it – has to do with Shakespeare's interest in making money. 'Yet it must be allowed', Bagehot writes, 'that Shakespeare was worldly, and the proof of it is, that he succeeded in the world.'[26] Shakespeare invested his money profitably. What a homecoming it must have been for the son of the wool-comber, known as poacher and vagabond, to return to Stratford 'a substantial man, a person of capital, a freeholder, a gentleman to be respected, and over whom even a burgess could not affect the least superiority'.[27] Bagehot compared the Shakespeare who had triumphed over the small, demeaning expectations of his fellow citizens at Stratford to become 'a monied man', with Disraeli, who enjoyed the duties of the Exchequer 'with so much relish' because people had said 'he was a novelist, an *ad captandum* man, and, *monstrum horrendum*! a Jew, that could not add up. No doubt it pleased his inmost soul to do the work of the red-tape people better than those who could do nothing else.'[28]

There, perhaps not unexpectedly, the essay comes to its amiable conclusion, with an admission that the author knows he has made little of a great subject. But its organisation has been disorderly, its generalisations based upon personal temperament rather than evidence, and its dogmatism, however cheery, little more than that. What can be said on its behalf has been vigorously stated by Sir William Haley in his literary appreciation, printed in volume 1 of the *Collected Works*, edited by Norman St John-Stevas. Sir William could readily imagine Bagehot 'at the club, on the hearthrug in front of the fire with Thackeray and Trollope, as much a man of the world as either of them, their equal in humour, shrewdness, and commonsense'.[29] But even this encomium must conclude, 'The essay does not at any point make us want to go back to Shakespeare – that is not its purpose – it does make us want to go on with Bagehot.'[30]

Bagehot's 'no-nonsense view of Shakespeare' leaves out a great deal (one would never suspect that 'the certain constitutional though latent melancholy '[31] in Shakespeare that Bagehot refers to was responsible for some of the most despairing and nihilistic speeches in dramatic literature), and there is a remarkable laziness about Bagehot's research that prevented him from discovering how much, in fact, was known about Shakespeare's Stratford, the quality of his schooling, the condition of the playhouses and the acting-arrangements during his lifetime, the historical circumstances leading to the composition of particular plays, and the kinds of audiences who attended productions at the Globe. Indeed, more is known about Shakespeare's life today (and was known during Bagehot's life) than about the life of any other Elizabethan playwright, including Marlowe and Jonson. It does not show up in Bagehot's essay, and only the curious anecdote about Shakespeare's unfriendly estimate of a player when he was called on by Mrs Alleyne to supply a reference ('Yes, certainly, he knew him, and he was a rascal and good-for-nothing'[32]), comes from the mass of documentation that Bagehot otherwise ignored; even here, however, Bagehot makes a characteristic point, that this is 'the proper speech of a substantial man, such as it is worth while to give a reference to'.

Yet the essay, one of Bagehot's major achievements in literary criticism, is great good fun to read. Worldly wisdom, for all its limitations in preparing us for the next world or – for that matter – a proper appreciation of this one, has its value. We all know the book-keeper Bagehot characterises with quick, slashing stroke: the man who has a ledger in his head and never can learn any more than the figures he keeps adding on the given page. If asked his opinion of Baron Rothschild, he is apt to answer, 'Yes, he keeps an account with us.'[33] And who has not met the man whose mind, like an animated dictionary, prevents him from understanding a concept: 'Unless they have got a precise word for anything they feel they know nothing about it, and where the words stop their minds stop too.'[34] It is wicked to enjoy, as much in reading as Bagehot must have enjoyed in writing, that devastating portrait of Robert Southey, who wrote poetry before breakfast ('as if anybody could'),[35] and laboured away at his epics, convinced that posterity would honour him: 'As if his epics were not already dead . . . .'[36] Bagehot's opinion of dullards did not improve from learning how industriously the dullards worked away at being dullards. One cannot but suspect that the Bagehot who had but recently recovered from a bout of depression and uncertainty about his own future (in

1851), took special delight in deriding those who devoted themselves to 'mere literature'. (The epithet is revealing.)

> They wish to produce a great work, but they find they cannot. Having relinquished everything to devote themselves to this, they conclude on trial that this is impossible. . . . A merchant must meet his bills, or he is civilly dead and uncivilly remembered. But a student may know nothing of time and be too lazy to wind up his watch.[37]

The suspicion that a writer's knowledge of things is superior to another writer's knowledge of books links Bagehot with Lewes, of course, and explains his preference for Shakespeare over Milton, for Scott over Goethe ('His works are too much in the nature of literary studies . . .'[38]). He was apt to praise Shakespeare's understanding of uneducated people, for, as he argued, in England people do not like to be committed to distinct premises.

> They like a Chancellor of the Exchequer to say, 'It has during very many years been maintained by the honourable member for Montrose that two and two make four, and I am free to say, that I think there is a great deal to be said in favour of that opinion but, without committing her Majesty's Government to that proposition as an abstract sentiment, I will go so far as to assume two and two are not sufficient to make five, which, with the permission of the House, will be a sufficient basis for all the operations which I propose to enter upon during the present year'.[39]

Bagehot's universe is all sense, and solid, and proportioned; though fancy (of a Keats, of a Shakespeare ornamenting the text) may be appreciated, and has its place.

If, in the civility of his style, Bagehot occasionally seems more accommodating to the views of others than a close reading will confirm, he also benefits from a reader's unwillingness to believe that a certain intractable crankiness runs as undercurrent through many of his literary essays, and indeed provides a major interest in his writings almost everywhere during the 1850s. For many writers Bagehot entertained a mild, if reasoned, disdain; for others, an active dislike. It may repay our time to consider some of the reasons that he found much of the literature of his century uncongenial. (Apart from a few essays on William Cowper, John Milton, Lady

Mary Wortley Montagu, Laurence Sterne and Edward Gibbon, Bagehot concentrated on the first half of his own century.)

He responded, for example, to the magisterial pronouncements of the first Edinburgh reviewers, and wrote at some length about Sydney Smith, Francis Horner and Francis Jeffrey. It was not that he considered the prejudices of a Jeffrey the essential secret to his readability or his success, and he spiritedly rejected the claim of Lord Cockburn (a biographer) that Jeffrey was 'the greatest of English critics'.[40] 'Why,' Bagehot responded, 'there is more sense, more sensibility, more keen acumen in a single paper of Christopher North, in a few pages of Coleridge, in a few lines of Hazlitt, than would be found in the whole "Selected Contributions", in the best writing of the most experienced of reviewers during a whole nine years.'[41] Partly, of course, Bagehot was expressing his dismay that Jeffrey's essays, read years after their original appearances, had lost their audience as well as their timeliness; Jeffrey would have appreciated the phrasing of Bagehot's summing-up, 'Jeffrey's essays are not read.'[42] But partly, too, it was the nature of the beast, Reviews had become characteristic of modern literature because they replaced more profound, sustained, analytical writing; because they suggested, they hurried on from topic to topic, they represented 'the talk of the manifold talker', and their life span was as limited as that of the writings they commented on. This fragmentary, allusive pseudo-literature, inevitably, was as ephemeral and casual as 'modern literature'.[43] One might observe the change in the kinds of books purveyed at a railway stall.

> People take their literature in morsels, as they take sandwiches on a journey. The volumes at least, you can see clearly, are not intended to be everlasting. It may be all very well for a pure essence like poetry to be immortal in a perishable world; it has no feeling; but paper cannot endure it, paste cannot bear it, string has no heart for it.[44]

Moreover, readers themselves have changed. The grave man 'who spends his life in study' has given way to the merchant in the railway, 'with a head full of sums, an idea that tallow is "up", a conviction that teas are "lively", and a mind reverting perpetually from the little volume that he reads to these mundane topics, to the railway, to the shares, to the buying and bargaining universe'.[45] For this kind of reader the review is suited; it lays no great claim upon his time; it frequently substitutes itself forever for the work treated; and it serves a vital pedagogical purpose. 'It is, indeed, a peculiarity of our times, that we must instruct so many persons', wrote Bagehot with some asperity. 'On politics, on religion, on all less important topics still more, every one thinks himself competent to think, – in some casual manner does think, – to the best of our means must be thought to think rightly.'[46] Democratic movements were enlarging the number of voters who could exercise the franchise. An unelected Commons, and unchosen Council, had begun to assist in the 'deliberations of the nation'. Religion now appealed to feelings and sentiments rather than to 'the technicalities of scholars, or the fictions of recluse schoolmen'. 'It is of no use addressing them [Bagehot is referring to the "many"] with the forms of science, or the rigour of accuracy, or the tedium of exhaustive discussion. The multitude are impatient of system, desirous of brevity, puzzled by formality.'[47] In all this, Bagehot is close to the distrust of 'the Citizen' that he thought he saw manifest everywhere in Shakespeare's writings. The Citizen would not read unless, in some fashion, reading had been made pleasant; and, if he were to be exhorted, educated, lifted up to a level his education or tastes had not trained him to appreciate, 'You must give him short views, and clear sentences'; you must avoid systematic completeness. Changing the subject frequently is necessary strategy for the reviewer, who has become singularly important in such a society. 'The *Edinburgh Review*, which began the system, may be said to be, in this country, the commencement on large topics of suitable views for sensible persons.'[48]

Bagehot was fully aware that the review article, for all that it filled a palpable need, represented a febrile second-best. It did not define its subject-matter. It suggested 'the lessons of a wider experience' without demonstrating in any self-confident way its possession of that experience. It encouraged dilettantism, or, in a telling and self-wounding phrase, 'It tends, as is said, to make a man fancy he knows everything.' One may have a 'cool, sharp, collected mind',[49] as Jeffrey did, and reject Wordsworth's religion; but Jeffrey's applause took place in drawing-rooms during his lifetime, and Wordsworth enjoyed the plaudits of a succeeding age, 'the fond enthusiasm of secret students, the lonely rapture of lonely minds'.[50] Bagehot, without pretending to understand 'the sublimities of the preacher', and sharing far more with Jeffrey than with the Cumberland poet, was not blind to two facts: first, that 'all cultivated men speak differently because of the existence of Wordsworth and Coleridge',[51] and second, that 'not a thoughtful English book has appeared for forty years, without some trace for good or evil of their influence'.[52] None of the essayists who wrote for the early issues of the *Edinburgh Review* 'attained to the highest rank of abstract intellect', and only one 'can be said to have a lasting place in real literature'. That one was Jeffrey, who invented the art of editorship:

> If Jeffrey was not a great critic, he had, what very great critics have wanted, the art of writing what most people would think good criticism. He might not know his subject, but he knew his readers. People like to read ideas which they can imagine to have been their own. . . . He was neither a pathetic writer nor a profound writer; but he was a quick-eyed, bustling, black-haired, sagacious, agreeable, man of the world.[53]

To which a somewhat rueful Bagehot felt compelled to add, 'He had his day, and was entitled to his day; but a gentle oblivion must now cover his already subsiding reputation.'[54]

Bagehot's attitude toward the reading public, for all its condescension, prefigures the much harsher comments of the twentieth century, and has a startling prescience about the consequences of the fact that young men, uninstructed by the aristocracy of England, in itself never 'a literary aristocracy', were turning to showy books and '*glaring* art'.[55] As Bagehot wrote in one of his characteristic essays of definition, 'Wordsworth, Tennyson, and Browning; or, Pure, Ornate, and Grotesque Art in English Poetry' (*National Review*, November 1864), 'We live in the realm of the *half* educated. The number of readers grows daily, but the quality of readers does not improve rapidly. The middle class is scattered, heedless; it is well-meaning, but aimless; wishing to be wise, but ignorant how to be wise.'[56] The times were not propitious for 'the due appreciation of pure art – of that art which must be known before it is admired', and little aid could be expected from women readers, who ever preferred 'a delicate unreality to a true or firm art'.[57]

It is not surprising, therefore, that Bagehot turned with increasing frequency from the 'dressy' and 'exaggerated' literature of mid century to the books of preceding ages which had earned their own audiences, and about which he was able to offer personal observations untainted by gloomy considerations of faddishness. Bagehot thought that the supply of readers like himself was diminishing, or at least was unable to be heard above the hubbub; he responded eagerly, and often gratefully, to any sign of 'soundness' in the writer whose works he was considering. As he wrote in his essay on Hartley Coleridge, 'Wordsworth, like Coleridge, began life as a heretic, and as the shrewd Pope unfallaciously said, "once a heretic, always a heretic". Sound men are sound from the first; safe men are safe from the beginning, and Wordsworth began wrong.'[58] The peculiar interest of the observation lies not in Bagehot's distaste for Wordsworth's concentration on the rugged aspects of nature, but in his conviction that a redeeming sanity, a due proportioning, a sense of what might be due to Caesar and what to Christ, was present in the writings of every great author from start to finish; eccentricity, or 'heresy', limited a writer's appeal both to his own age and to readers of subsequent ages. The certitude with which Bagehot apportioned praise and blame seems to have vanished with the more nervous, relativistic criticism of later decades; one remembers the wish of Lord Melbourne, that he might be as sure of any one thing as Macaulay was of everything (Bagehot wrote admiringly about Macaulay). In fairness, one must note that Bagehot occasionally cast up his hands in horror before a distorting mirror-image of himself, as when he wrote about Edward Gibbon's 'pompous cadence': 'He *cannot* mention Asia *Minor*. The petty order of sublunary matters; the common gross existence of ordinary people; the necessary littlenesses of necessary life, are little suited to his sublime narrative. . . . he scarcely gives you an idea of variety.'[59] Too much conviction of what constitutes decorum prevents an author from acknowledging the existence of vulgarity in a universe that, after all, inextricably commingles low and high elements.

Sound men are non-doctrinaire; they take the larger view. In writing of Sir Walter Scott, Bagehot recorded, with satisfaction, that 'Sir Walter had no *thesis* to maintain',[60] because his imagination was essentially conservative. 'He could understand (with a few exceptions) any considerable movement of human life and action, and could always describe with easy freshness everything which he did understand; but he was not obliged by stress of fanaticism to maintain a dogma concerning them . . . .'[61] We may talk of 'Scott's world', but Scott himself had no intention of delineating the world: 'We have vivid and fragmentary histories; it is for the slow critic of after-times to piece together their teaching.'[62]

Indeed, Scott seems to be a model that later generations should pay attention to. He had common sense. What, then, of his Jacobitism, his sentimental admiration of the Stuart cause? Bagehot admitted that this 'emotional aspect of his habitual Toryism' was '*un*sensible', but added that 'no one can have given a more sensible delineation, we might say a more statesmanlike analysis, of the various causes which led to the momentary success, and to the speedy ruin, of the enterprise of Charles Edward'.[63] Scott was never wholly unpoetical in his Toryism, but he loved administration, organisation, orderliness. 'In real life, Scott used to say that he never remembered feeling abashed in any one's presence except the Duke of Wellington's. . . . his imagination was very susceptible to the influence of great achievement and prolonged success in wide-spreading affairs.'[64]

Even if Scott's imagination 'was singularly penetrated with the strange varieties and motley composition of human life',[65] he gave to anomalous characters such as Meg Merrilies, Edie Ochiltree and Ratcliffe their due, but no more. Eccentric human character

> becomes a topic of literary art only when its identity with the ordinary principles of human nature is exhibited in the midst of, and as it were, by means of, the superficial unlikeness. Such a skill, however, requires an easy careless familiarity with usual human life and common human conduct. A writer must have a sympathy with health before he can show us how, and where, and to what extent, that which is unhealthy deviates from it . . . .[66]

Bagehot's satisfaction in Scott's healthiness is derived from the pleasure of a reader in meeting a 'manly mind', and in discovering the 'atmosphere of generosity congenial to a cheerful one'. Wrote Bagehot (much as John Stuart Mill wrote about Wordsworth's poetry),

> There are no such books as his for the sick-room, or for freshening the painful intervals of a morbid mind. Mere sense is dull, mere sentiment unsubstantial; a sensation of genial healthiness is only given by what combines the solidity of the one and the brightening charm of the other.

This admiration extends to the way in which Scott depicted his heroines, 'not with the wild ecstasy of the insane youth, yet with the tempered and mellow admiration common to genial men of this world'.[67] The phrasing has resonance: '*this world*'. Bagehot applauds Scott's 'indisposition to the abstract exercises of the intellect',[68] and suggest that Scott's unwillingness to speculate too freely even in the 'reflective portions' of his novels 'contributes to their popularity with that immense majority of the world who strongly share in that same indisposition'.[69] At a minimum his works do not disturb those who have known the passion of intellectual inquiry, 'and have had something too much of it'.

Against Bagehot's high marks for Scott one must score the failure of the style to wed words and matter. The excitement created by reading the best prose should be as great as that created by reading the best poetry. (Bagehot was adapting, and expanding, Coleridge's dicta on the untranslatability of good poetry.) Nobody rises from Scott's work 'without a most vivid idea of what is related, and no one is able to quote a single phrase in which it has been narrated'.[70] This is tantamount to declaring that there is a limitation in Scott's awareness of the fine uses to which language in a novel may be put.

> In truth, Scott's language, like his sense, was such as became a bold sagacious man of the world. He used the first sufficient words which came uppermost, and seems hardly to have been sensible, even in the works of others, of that exquisite accuracy and inexplicable appropriateness of which we have been speaking.[71]

A sound man, as we might expect, waxes less eloquent about his likes, which he tends to take for granted (doesn't everyone of equally sound constitution appreciate a sense of the variety of life?), than about his dislikes. Much of Bagehot's criticism is crotchety, and compulsively readable because of the piquancy with which those crotchets are expressed. It is impossible to forget the snort that accompanies Bagehot's review of Macaulay's praise of dead authors, and of their constancy to a reader who already knows what they have to say. 'Plato is never sullen', Macaulay had written; 'Cervantes is never petulant; Demosthenes never comes unseasonably; Dante never stays too long. No difference of political opinion can alienate Cicero; no heresy can excite the horror of Bossuet.' To which Bagehot responded,

> But Bossuet is dead; Cicero was a Roman; and Plato wrote in Greek. Years and manners separate us from the great. After dinner, Demosthenes *may* come unseasonably; Dante might stay too long. *We* are alienated from the politician, and have a horror of the theologian. Dreadful idea, having Demosthenes for an

intimate friend! He had pebbles in his mouth; he was always urging action; he spoke such good Greek; we cannot dwell on it, – it is too much. Only a mind impassive to our daily life, unalive to bores and evils, to joys and sorrows, incapable of the deepest sympathies, a prey to print, could imagine it. The mass of men have stronger ties and warmer hopes. The exclusive devotion to books tires. We require to love and hate, to act and live.[72]

(The days of Bagehot's literary reviewing were drawing to a close.)

It is debatable whether, as William Irvine maintains in his biography of Bagehot (1939), the essay on Shakespeare is 'his warmest and most enthusiastic . . . and . . . probably also his worst';[73] Irvine, after all, completed a formidable list of deficiencies in Bagehot's writings, many of them related to the truism that Bagehot had not read, studied or learned enough about the current state of knowledge concerning the literary figures he treated. In this sense, Bagehot (like Anatole France) was really writing about himself concerning Shakespeare. Measured by such a standard, of course, most Victorian literary critics would be found wanting, because their worth would be seen as intimately related to their own personalities. How interesting (for example) do we suspect Bagehot, the man, might be, as we read one of his essays? Would we want to linger in his company by checking our own impressions of an author against those recorded in one of his essays? Do the biases for 'sound' men and common sense in the literature created by such men (Bagehot has very little to say about women, and his one extended essay on Lady Mary Wortley Montagu, published in 1862, is an anomaly) excite or depress our willingness to proceed further?

The real test is a lengthy essay which provides Bagehot sufficient room to illustrate his method for interrelating an author's life and his writings, to generalise about literary intention and categories of literary form, and to elevate a personal taste to a universal preference or standard. Such an essay is the forty-page treatment of John Milton, published in the *National Review* of July 1859. Seldom, if ever, may Bagehot be seen more clearly than here. Milton did not write Bagehot's kind of poetry; Milton lacked a sense of humour (a charge, rather curiously, that Bagehot levied against Wordsworth, whose poetry he enjoyed more); he led a troubled personal life, and most of his marital difficulties, Bagehot implies, he brought upon himself; and his masterwork, *Paradise Lost*, is tendentious and well-nigh unacceptable to the Victorian Age. (Or so Bagehot says.) It is clear, at any rate, that Milton's 'deficiency in a knowledge of plain human nature'[74] unfits him for sharing the company of such writers as Scott, who did not move on a 'removed elevation',[75] who appreciated the world of cakes and ale, and who took their subject-matter from life rather than books. Milton lacked an informing, or shaping, sympathy with human relations, and his intellectual insights, Bagehot ruminated, were insufficient recompense for a failure to feel emotionally. 'The austerity of his nature was not caused by the deficiency of his senses, but by an excess of the warning instinct.'[76] Dr Johnson thought 'L'Allegro' contained melancholy; Bagehot found there solitariness.

Milton's poetry was second-hand. Although Bagehot swiftly went on to say that the process of assimilation of earlier texts was not to be confused with conscious plagiarism ('A mind like his, which has an immense store of imaginative recollections, can never know which of his own imaginations is exactly suggested by which recollection'[77]), there can be no doubt that he found Milton's works an inferior species of creation.

> A brooding, placid cultivated mind, like that of Gray, is the place where we should expect to meet with it. Great originality disturbs the adaptive process. . . . Poetry of the second degree is like the secondary rocks of modern geology, – a still, gentle, alluvial formation; the igneous glow of primary genius brings forth ideas like the primeval granite, simple, astounding, and alone. Milton's case is an exception to this rule . . . .[78]

Without denying his 'marked originality', Bagehot found it necessary to stress Milton's reliance on readings over a lifetime: his mind 'has as much of moulded recollection as any mind too'.[79]

What then shall be said of *Paradise Lost*, that epic from which (in Bagehot's unexpectedly diffident phrase) 'the imagination rather shrinks'?[80] The ambition of Milton was not merely to write a great poem, but to 'assert eternal Providence, / And justify the ways of God to men'. But so far as Bagehot was concerned (and here he was quoting a Cambridge mathematician), *Paradise Lost* had *proved* nothing.[81] To begin with, the poem was founded on a political transaction, God's conferring of the title of Lord on his only Son. The angels must henceforward obey the Son as if he were God. 'This act of patronage was not popular at court,' wrote Bagehot, 'and why should it have been? The religious sense is against it. The worship which sinful men owe to God is not transferable to lieutenants and vice-regents. The whole scene of the court jars upon a true feeling.'[82] Cognisant of the inevitable rush of sympathy toward the other side – that side to which Satan and his followers belonged, that side to which Blake and Shelley had instinctively rallied – Bagehot identified the attractiveness of Satan as a defect: 'Suppose that the source of all sin were the origin of all interest to us! We need not dwell upon this.'[83] Yet worse was to come: Milton had made God *argue*. The notion that God's 'long train of reasoning' might be understandable to men boggled Bagehot's imagination. Milton

> relates a series of family prayers in heaven, with sermons afterwards, which are very tedious. Even Pope was shocked at the notion of Providence talking like 'a school-divine'. And there is the still worse error, that if you once attribute reasoning to Him, subsequent logicians may discover that He does not reason very well.[84]

The exuberance of Bagehot's catalogue of failings in *Paradise Lost* is hard to resist. A reader would never suspect that compiling the catalogue cost Bagehot a moment of regret; that savaging England's religious epic might have been an onerous chore. Bagehot knew that Milton's interest lay in the conflict between God and Satan, but characterised as an artistic defect the manner in which the angels were portrayed as almost infinite in number, and insipid in personality.

> They appear to be excellent administrators with very little to do; a kind of grand chamberlains with wings, who fly down to earth and communicate information to Adam and Eve. They have no character; they are essentially messengers, merely conductors, so to say, of the providential will: no one fancies they they have an independent power of action; they seem scarcely to have minds of their own. No effect can be more unfortunate. If the struggle of Satan had been with Deity directly, the natural instincts of religion would have been awakened; but when an angel with mind is only contrasted to angels with wings, we sympathize with the former.[85]

Moreover, Satan's career, as recounted in *Paradise Lost*, 'scarcely acts up to his sentiments'. Satan, a superbly realised creation, an

archangel of surpassing intellect, has one grand aim, 'the conquest of
our first parents; and we are at once struck with the enormous
inequality of the conflict'.[86] Bagehot correctly points out that Adam
and Eve have just been created; are 'without guile, without
knowledge of good and evil', and yet are expected to contend with
Satan, whose powers have been delineated with 'every resource of
art and imagination, every subtle suggestion, every emphatic
simile'.[87] Bagehot, like other readers before him (though none had
expressed it so pungently), was not surprised that our first parents
should yield, but wonder-struck that Satan should not think it
beneath him to attack them. 'It is as if an army should invest a
cottage.'[88]

Dr Johnson's comment that, after all, *Paradise Lost* was one of the
books which no one wished longer, provoked Bagehot, in a later and
even more irreverent formulation, to note that some wished it
shorter: 'Hardly any reader would be sorry if some portions of the
later books had been spared him.'[89] As for Coleridge, who
discovered 'profound mysteries in the last book', Bagehot wrote,
'But in what could not Coleridge find a mystery if he wished?'[90]
Paradise Lost recounts a rebellion in heaven; but the rebellion was not
against 'known ethics, or immutable spiritual laws, but against an
arbitrary selection and an unexplained edict'.[91] What God had done
in promulgating 'a positive moral edict' is a mystery, one which can
never be explained away; its nature cannot satisfy the heart and
conscience; and it resists literary treatment. Milton has done all
readers a disservice by publishing 'so strange a problem', and giving
'only an untrue solution of it'.[92]

This essay, stimulated originally by the publication of the first
volume of David Masson's seven-volume biography (1859–94),
illustrates an impression that may be confirmed by any casual·
reader: Bagehot's criticism becomes more fun as his antipathies
toward writer, subject-matter or style increase. Masson himself did
not 'scape whipping, for his biography, though conscientious, was
overlong and stuffed with tedious detail ('We think it has been
composed upon a principle that is utterly erroneous'[93]), and it
imagined what *might* have happened ('If we are to have fancies, we
like to have our own. . . . Mr Masson has neither the humour of
imagination, nor the delicacy of style, which in other hands have
made these hypotheses pleasing'[94]). Milton's ascetic nature might be
a form of goodness; but Bagehot obviously preferred the sensuous
form of goodness. Even Milton's looks can be held against him, or,

more precisely, Milton's ability to describe his own looks with some complacency as being somehow related to virtue ('a little tinge of excessive self-respect will cling to those who can admire them-selves'[95]). The point is not unimportant, if one is to stress the human being behind the poetry as much as Bagehot does: Milton's harshness and gravity may be responsible for much that we find unattractive in his writings. Indeed, Milton's views on divorce, inseparable from 'the unusual phenomena of his first marriage',[96] are treated shrewdly, and with perhaps more compassion and patient understanding of Milton's side than is usually the case.

> We think we have shown that it is possible there may have been, in his domestic relations, a little overweening pride; a tendency to overrate the true extent of masculine rights, and to dwell on his wife's duty to be social towards him rather than on his duty to be social towards her, – to be rather sullen whenever she was not quite cheerful. Still, we are not defending a lady for leaving her husband for defects of such inferior magnitude. Few households would be kept together, if the right of transition were exercised on such trifling occasions. We are but suggesting that she may share the excuse which our great satirist has suggested for another unreliable lady: 'My mother was an angel; but angels are not always *commodes à vivre*.'[97]

Milton's art, once Bagehot turns to it, is an art of relatively simple ideas complicated by an extraordinary richness of illustration and imagery.

> His words, we may half fancifully say, are like his character. There is the same austerity in the real essence, the same exquisiteness of sense, the same delicacy of form which we know that he had, the same music which we imagine there was in his voice. In both his character and his poetry there was an ascetic nature in a sheath of beauty.[98]

Since Bagehot's temperament avoids generalising on the nature of life, art and God, it is demonstrably English in Bagehot's sense, which strikingly resembles George Henry Lewes's view of the national character. In one of his more heartfelt essays, occasioned by the publication of Robert Bell's edition of William Cowper's poems and printed in the *National Review* of July 1855, Bagehot made the

case for the determination of his contemporaries to read contemporary books by living authors; behind the humorous exaggeration one senses a deep sympathy with the point of view espoused.

> We are the English of the present day. We have cows and calves,
> corn and cotton; we hate the Russians; we know where the
> Crimea is; we believe in Manchester the great. . . . Let us be
> thankful if our researches in foreign literature enable us, as rightly
> used they will enable us, better to comprehend our own. Let us
> venerate what is old, and marvel at what is far. Let us read our
> own books.[99]

Moderation, familiarity, enjoyment of home surroundings, an
unwillingness to have the mind stretched by continual exposure to
imported ideas: 'It would be better to have no outlandish literature
in the mind than to have it the principal thing.'[100] Indeed, Cowper's
appeal for a large fraction of the English population (and, we gather,
for Bagehot himself) lies in his distrust of fancy bred at the expanse of
the imagination. Cowper draws intensely provincial pictures.
'Everything is so comfortable; the tea-urn hisses so plainly, the toast
is so warm, the breakfast so neat, the food so edible . . . .'[101] Those
who object to this kind of art, this 'torpid, in-door, tea-tabular
felicity', underestimate its appeal. Cowper's enormous popularity,
at least to the readers of the eighteenth century, arose 'from his
having held up to the English people exact delineations of what they
really prefer',[102] and to this day those who do not understand
Wordsworth (and that much greater number who cannot appreciate Shelley) can find in Cowper's dullness the proper subject-
matter of poetry, or for that matter can do so in anything that aspires
to the status of literature.

We shall not find in Bagehot's writings a set of general guidelines
to art, an explicit aesthetic. It would be easy to conclude that these
rocking-chair principles match closely a businessman's desire, at the
close of a busy day, to read escapist literature. But Bagehot's
enthusiasm for good writing, for any sign of intelligence on the
printed page, is genuine enough; it accounts for his impatience with
the second-best, or with grotesque art, or with literature that grows
out of texts rather than life, or with writers whose personal lives are
unattractive. And this accounts, in turn, for his dislike of Greek
literature, with its chill ('as of marble'); of the spirits, phantasms
and fairies who clog Shelley's poetry ('The higher air seems never to
have been favourable to the production of marked charac-

ter . . .'[103]); of the isolation and suddenness of impulse which fatally prevented Shelley from completing a long poem;[104] of fancies which ruin major talents (the word 'fancy', as used by Bagehot, denotes a lower order of talent than the word 'imagination', and is invariably used in a derogatory sense); of the disjointed novel of Dickens, which sacrifice the genius of the author to the tastes of his readers, and fail to provide 'an entire picture' of 'human life in all its spheres';[105] of the poor people in Dickens's works who 'have taken to their poverty very thoroughly', and who are 'poor talkers and poor livers, and in all ways poor people to read about'; of works which preach ('Men who purchase a novel do not wish a stone or a sermon. All lengthened reflections must be omitted, – the whole armoury of pulpit eloquence'[106]); of novels which omit *any* consideration of the soul; of the overteeming mind of Shakespeare, which creates in the reader 'a great feeling of irregularity' and 'confusion' ('men of irregular or unsymmetrical genius . . . want what the scientific men of the present day would call the *definite proportion* of faculties and qualities suited to the exact work they have in hand'[107]); of works too long delayed in composition and in the press ('extremely slow production is very rarely favourable to the perfection of works of genius',[108] as Bagehot wrote when reviewing Samuel Rogers's *Recollections*); and of Sterne's indecency, lack of form, and eccentric character.

I do not mean to superimpose a fictitious unity of feeling or logic upon Bagehot's writings, which were intended for a reading audience only slightly less impatient to be gone than Pontius Pilate, who had asked for a definition of the truth. But it is clear that Bagehot's idiom belongs to a man who has confidence in the righteousness of his classifications, and in the rankings of his hierarchy. From the perspective of more than a century later, the notion that Coleridge's 'Christabel' and 'The Rime of the Ancient Mariner' have 'no characters, no picture of life at large, no extraordinary thoughts'[109] (their only charm lies in metre and strangeness), or that they indicate 'inferior imaginative genius' to that of Tennyson,[110] is both wrong-headed and startling; many in Bagehot's generation would have willingly disputed the claim. But Bagehot's intention from the beginning was not to flatter, to be thankful, to eulogise; he felt deeply the obligation to prepare estimates; as he said in his Macaulay review, 'The business of a critic is criticism.'[111]

Although our knowledge of Bagehot's subsequent career suggests two things, the need for earning a living at better wages than book-reviewing might provide, and the voluntary (and even eager) shift in attention to precisely that English world of sums and balances that he had, with some bemusement, described on earlier occasions, there is no need to doubt Bagehot's love of the printed page, or of poetry in particular. In more than one place he spoke of the fascination that poetry exerted on young men. As he wrote about Shelley and Keats (in his essay on Tennyson's *Idylls of the King*),

> Their works had had a great influence on young men; they retain a hold on many mature men only because they are associated with their youth; they delineate

> > Such sights as youthful poets dream
> > On summer eves by haunted stream:

> and young men, who were not poets, have eagerly read them, have fondly learned them, and have long remembered them.[112]

Tennyson's poetry, like theirs, appealed at first entirely to 'young men of cultivated tastes and susceptible imaginations'.[113] Because *Maud* described (or dramatised, more precisely speaking) an unhealthy kind of hero, it exerted a pernicious effect upon the readers who were at precisely the most wavering and impressionable age. (Bagehot seems undecided whether Tennyson's choice of subject-matter had been influenced by his public of young men, in which case the audience itself had contributed to the deterioration of Tennyson's powers.) Bagehot did not believe that Tennyson had distanced himself sufficiently from the protagonist of *Maud*. The poet

> seemed to sympathise with the feverish railings, the moody nonsense, the very entangled philosophy, which he put into the mouth of his hero. . . . He sympathised with moody longings; he was not severe on melancholy vanity; he rather encouraged a general disaffection to the universe. He appeared not only to have written, but to have accepted the 'Gospel according to the Unappreciated'.[114]

It is as if in describing the kind of person who enjoys poetry most passionately, Bagehot is making an effort to understand the consequences of restless fancy and the 'diseased moodiness of feeling' that only the irreversible process of aging can alleviate. But poetry is the superior art, and worth its high esteem, if only the proper balance may be struck; poetry is – or must be – 'more intense in meaning and more concise in style than prose' ('Wordsworth, Tennyson, and Browning').[115]

Bagehot discriminated between major poets and poetasters partly on the basis of incompletely defined criteria; but his catholicity of taste was surprisingly wide. For instance, though he did not care for the rational, analytic sketch that Alexander Pope drew of the existing civilisation, he understood its place, and to some extent responded to it himself: 'Society in Pope is scarcely a society of people, but of pretty little atoms, coloured and painted with hoops or in coats – a miniature of metaphysics, a puppet-show of sylphs' ('William Cowper').[116] Bagehot preferred pure art, but recognised as legitimate the objectives and claims to attention of ornate art (after all, even Shakespeare specialised in 'indistinct illusion' and 'moving shadow'), because it did what pure art could not do:

> Illusion, half belief, unpleasant types, imperfect types, are as much the proper sphere of ornate art, as an inferior landscape is the proper sphere for the true efficacy of moonlight. A really great landscape needs sunlight and bears sunlight; but moonlight is an equaliser of beauties; it gives an unromantic unreality to what will not stand the bare truth. And just so does romantic art.[117]

He even found something positive to say about grotesque art, as exemplified by Browning's poetry, which pleased him less than either pure or ornate art. Browning had earned some successes, for example, in depicting the bourgeois nature in difficulties, 'in the utmost difficulty, in contact with magic and the supernatural. He has made of it something homely, comic, true; reminding us of what *bourgeois* nature really is.'[118] Since Browning's art was realistic, his attraction to the medieval period was appropriate, for he could treat with an understanding eye its life and legends. Bagehot readily admitted Browning's cleverness, and the challenge to the reader's 'zeal and sense of duty' which clever poems presented. 'One of his greatest admirers', Bagehot wrote, 'once owned to us that he seldom or never began a new poem without looking on in advance, and foreseeing with caution what length of intellectual adventure he was about to commence'.[119] Yet if Browning was not a type of poet that

Bagehot found congenial, there was never any doubt in his mind
that poetry was 'a serious and deep thing'.

The nineteenth century had begun with an explosion of personality and talent, and Bagehot was better on the Romantic poets
than on either the poets or novelists of his own generation. When
Lord Byron wrote, his works were as eagerly received as 'sensation
novels'.[120] *The Giaour* and *The Corsair* evoked 'wild admiration'.
Exaggeration, prettiness (as in the case of Moore), and even
greatness of soul, found their market, but that market contracted as
the taste for novelty shifted. Poetry that had once appealed to
emotion and imagination turned into an amusement 'for the lighter
hours of all classes', as the audience broadened.[121] Bagehot added,
with some gloom, that criticism of poetry consequently fell upon evil
days, inasmuch as its own fortunes depended on popular acceptance
of the art it treated. No critic in mid century could hope for the kind
of fame that Lord Jeffrey had enjoyed – or for Lord Jeffrey's kind of
authority. 'When poetry was noisy, criticism was loud; now poetry is
a still small voice, and criticism must be smaller and stiller.'[122]

Byron's sulkiness and 'dismal exaggeration' no longer entranced a
wide audience. Moreover, Bagehot entertained deep doubts about
the 'studied' spontaneity of Wordsworth's poetry. Coleridge's
achievement amounted to no more than 'two longish poems, which
have worked themselves right down to the extreme depths of the
popular memory, and stay there very firmly, in part from their
strangeness, but in part from their power'.[123] The rest is conversation, 'continuous, diffused, comprehensive', and perhaps faultily
remembered. Bagehot quoted Hazlitt: 'Great talker, certainly, *if*
you will let him start from no *data*, and come to no conclusion'
('Hartley Coleridge').[124] Blake was as invisible to Bagehot as he had
been to Shelley, who was astounded to discover that Blake was still
alive in the second decade of the century (Blake died in 1829); but,
even if Bagehot had been more familiar with his poems, Blake did
not write the kind of pure poetry that Bagehot liked. As for Keats,
Bagehot appreciated, to a limited degree, his prolonged strain of
'simple rich melody', but noted, with disdain, that Keats all too
often (like Shelley) seemed to have been hurried into song. 'He did
not carry his art high or deep; he neither enlightens our eyes much,
not expands our ears much. . . . He does not pause, or stay, or
hesitate' ('Tennyson's Idylls').[125]

Shelley, more than any of the Romantics, had appealed to
Bagehot as a young man, and, despite reservations in his years of

maturation, remained his favourite poet of the century. In a review of Mrs Shelley's edition of her husband's works, published in the *National Review* of October 1856, Bagehot confessed to feeling, at times, an unwillingness to entertain the possibility that there might be a need for a full biography of Shelley. The poet had fully delineated himself in his works; and, even without intending to, he revealed his inner character. 'Every line of his has a personal impress, an unconscious, inimitable manner.'[126] Shelley lacked inner division of the kind that had tormented St Paul and even Aristotle; he lacked self-control; but there was a sublimity about his purity of impulse that Bagehot found fascinating, perhaps even attractive. 'We fancy his mind placed in the light of thought, with pure subtle fancies playing to and fro. On a sudden an impulse arises; it is alone, and has nothing to contend with; it cramps the intellect, pushes aside the fancies, constrains the nature; it *bolts* forward into action.'[127] Easy enough to see how such intensity, how the iruption of such impulses, would puzzle bystanders and critics. Unlike a critic who is 'dark, threatening, unbelieving', Shelley is 'open, eager, buoyant'.[128] A fanatic intent upon the reform of mankind, Shelley might well have prospered, at least for a time, in the Paris of the Revolution, for he would not have scrupled over niceties in attaining his end. 'It was in him to have walked towards it over seas of blood.'[129] To such a man love might be, and was, consecrated as 'the most pure and eager of human passions', and, as Bagehot shrewdly notes, the 'Epipsychidion' could not have been written by a man 'who attached a moral value to constancy of *mind*'.[130] Shelley felt, more strongly than any other poet, 'the desire to penetrate the mysteries of existence', a 'daily insatiable craving after the highest truth'. Bagehot admitted that Shelley was never meant to be a practical reformer, or an intellectual. 'In Shelley, the habit of frequenting mountain-tops has reduced' his characters 'to evanescent mists of lyrical energy',[131] though the undiluted passion of both Beatrice and Count Cenci modifies this generalisation; their actions are 'unmodified consequences of a single principle', but as dramatic creations these two 'seem like vivid recollections from our intimate experience'.[132] They are, despite caveats, 'very high specimens' of the second class.

A natural expectation of a modern reader is to find in this characterisation of Shelley some inevitable corollaries, such as disapproval of the poet's lax religious opinions, his hastening (at Oxford) from materialism to atheism, his unwillingness to be guided, his defective conscience. And Bagehot, who wrote often enough about an Almighty God and retained throughout his life a faith in the law of divine retribution, does have some stern things to say about Shelley's brand of religious faith. It may be that his knowledge of Shelley's unattractively headstrong father and of the dreary quality of Oxford dons in the early years of the century mitigated the maximum severity of which he was capable. More probable, however, his delight in the purity of Shelley's life and in the unalloyed intensity of Shelley's poetry prevented him from making more of Shelley's 'weak' grasp of realities, or of the poet's failure ever to establish for himself a genuine religion.

This long review of Shelley's poetry, as intense an intertwining of biographical and critical perceptions as the essay on Milton, candidly admits the weaknesses of Shelley's art. If Shelley is truly delineating himself in *Julian and Maddalo*, he inevitably runs the risk of seeming insane.[133] His women characters are unchanging, and less interesting as a consequence:

> Every one of his poems almost has a lady whose arms are white, whose mind is sympathising, and whose soul is beautiful. She has many names, Cythna, Asia, Emily; but these are only external disguises. . . . She is a being to be loved in a single moment, with eager eyes and grasping breath; but you feel that in that moment you have seen the whole. There is nothing to come to afterwards . . . .[134]

Shelley could not construct whole works; his success 'is in fragments', the best of them lyrical.[135]

For Bagehot, however, he was a pure poet (a term that he preferred to 'classical'). 'We cannot know detail in tracts we have never visited; the infinite has no form; the immeasurable no outline; that which is common to all worlds is simple. There is therefore no scope for the accessory fancy.'[136] This judgement applies no less to Shelley's treatment of nature than to his 'bare treatment of the ancient mythology'.[137] Although Bagehot recognised Shelley's taste for fancies, he stressed their irrelevance to 'the concrete hearts of real men'.[138] For this kind of fancy – depending as it did upon 'slight and airy subjects' – he allowed a certain, if condescending, kind of affection. The peroration, therefore, is not unexpected:

In style, said Mr Wordsworth – in workmanship, we think his

expression was – Shelley is one of the best of us. This too, we think was the second of the peculiarities to which Mr Macaulay referred when he said that Shelley had, more than any recent poet, some of the qualities of the great old masters.[139]

Shelley's subtle mind, minute and 'acutely searching' language, even his manias, appealed to Bagehot.

As it was the instinct of Byron to give in glaring words the gross phenomena of evident objects, so it was that of Shelley to refine the most inscrutable with the curious nicety of an attenuating metaphysician. In the wildest of ecstasies his self-anatomising intellect is equal to itself.[140]

My review of Bagehot's salient characteristics as a literary critic has emphasised the wittiness which sustains one's attention even as the dogmatic generalisations, ceaseless (and almost compulsive) categorising and fitful asperities keep reminding us of the critic's fallibilities. Bagehot will always remain one of the more readable Victorian sages. Not that his self-confidence avoids complacency. More than once bathos – in the form of startling commonplaces that have little to do with the sharp insights and merciless truth-saying of the surrounding text – injures the critical thesis. For all his intelligence, Bagehot is less well-read than Lewes, less persuasive than Arnold. But his admiration of Shelley, a kind of poet whose personal life, theological convictions and artistic failings were so strongly opposed to his personal sense of decorum, suggests a broadness of sympathy that links the young reader, the passionate lover of poetry and of writing that stirs the mind to thoughts of high purpose, with the older literary critic.

3 Richard Holt Hutton

Less may be remembered of Hutton's contribution to the world of Victorian letters than of that made by any of the other critics considered in this volume. Yet a briskness and honesty of attitude, an intensity of moral integrity, a concern for the truth, instantly impress any reader who reviews Hutton's writings on important literary questions. In many respects Hutton's life provides a stunning illustration of the more attractive values of Victorian intelligence.

Born in 1826 to Joseph Hutton, a Unitarian minister at Leeds, Richard Holt Hutton grew up in a rationalistic, questioning household. His family moved to London in 1835, and he studied at University College School and University College, taking his degree, and a gold medal for philosophy, in 1845. For two semesters he studied in Heidelberg and Berlin; then, in 1847, with the intention of becoming a minister like his father, he entered Manchester New College, where his nonconformist education, pursued with the assistance of James Martineau and John James Taylor, helped to develop the strong and unconventional views that he expressed – with considerable ardour – during his two-year tenure as joint editor of the *Inquirer*. These opinions, particularly on the relationship of the laity to the formal leaders of religion, were not welcomed by the financial backers of the periodical; in 1853 he resigned, undoubtedly anticipating more severe action if he did not. His health was poor; a trip to the West Indies ended in the tragedy of his wife's death, from yellow fever, and he returned to England.

He and Walter Bagehot, a friend from University College days, became co-editors of the *National Review* (which Lady Byron may have been subsidising), and for a decade, from 1855 to 1865, Hutton's contributions were important in establishing the reputation of that journal as one of the most stimulating periodicals available to Victorian readers. During this decade Hutton's Unitarianism slowly changed into a recognition that he could, in good conscience, join the Church of England. The death of his brother-in-law, William Caldwell Roscoe, deprived the *National Review* of one of its best contributors. As an act of piety, Hutton edited a two-volume *Poems and Essays* (1860). During this same decade Hutton lectured on mathematics at Bedford College, London, and from 1858 to 1860 served as assistant editor to the *Economist*. In 1861 he joined Meredith Townsend, recently returned from India, as a joint editor of the *Spectator*. In this liberal weekly – which espoused the cause of the North in the American Civil War at a time when it was distinctly daring to do so – Hutton fought against what he conceived to be the dangerous agnostic views of those who were supporting Huxley in his powerful attacks on Victorian complacency and hypocrisy. One of the founding fathers of the Metaphysical Society (1869), Hutton wrote a history of the movement. As an anti-vivisectionist, he served on a royal commission in 1875, and helped to draft the final report that, within a year, stirred Parliament to pass a law seriously limiting experiments on living animals. He died in 1897.

So much for the facts of Hutton's life, which suggest, though barely, the hard work, dedication, and high quality of his contributions to a number of journals. It is difficult to find personal marginalia in these essays; Hutton is not autobiographical in the same sense as Bagehot or Lewes; but one way of approaching his work is to remember the friendship between himself and Bagehot, for one's choice of friends inevitably defines the kind of person a young man becomes. Bagehot's questions, put to a professor of mathematics at University College, 'showed that he had both read and thought more on these subjects than most of us', as Hutton wrote in a Memoir attached to an edition of Bagehot's *Literary Studies* (2 vols, 1879).[1] Hutton, anxious to know more about this lad 'with large dark eyes and florid complexion',[2] made his acquaintance, and began a friendship that lasted for thirty-five years. Hutton quoted Bagehot's grim verdict on Oxford, recorded in an essay on Shelley: 'A distinguished pupil of the University of Oxford once observed to us, "The use of the University of Oxford is that no one can overread himself there. The appetite for knowledge is repressed".'[3] Hutton remembered, with the pleasure that always accompanies the sense of time usefully spent, the fierceness of the debates that raged in 'Gower Street, and Oxford Street, and the New Road, and the dreary chain of squares from Euston to Bloomsbury . . . .'[4] Once, he recalled, 'in the vehemence of our argument as to whether the so-called logical principle of identity (A is A) were entitled to rank as "a law of thought" or only as a postulate of language, Bagehot and I wandered up and down Regent Street for something like two hours in the vain attempt to find Oxford Street . . . .'[5]

What Hutton remembered about his educational years, in particular, was the manner in which he acquired a love of 'fastidious taste' and 'exquisite nicety in treating questions of scholarship',[6] and he developed a liking for the 'caustic irony, accurate and almost ostentatiously dry learning, and profoundly stoical temperament'[7] of one of his professors. It was an exciting decade, for the 1840s saw widespread agitation on behalf of Free Trade and against the Corn Laws. 'To us this was useful rather from the general impulse it gave to political discussion, and the literary curiosity it excited in us as to the secret of true eloquence, than because it anticipated in any considerable degree the later acquired taste for economical science.'[8] With Bagehot he roamed (or 'scoured') through London, looking for opportunities to hear Cobden, Bright and W. J. Fox; he studied 'the declamation of Burke and the rhetoric of Macaulay'.[9] Bagehot was, by instinct and in religious matters, more conservative than Hutton, who at the time was a firm believer in Unitarianism. But Bagehot provided a luminious example of the value of restraint: of doing less, and shying clear of unnecessary responsibilities.

> Lord Melbourne's habitual query, 'Can't you let it alone?' seemed to him, as regarded all new responsibilities, the wisest of hints for our time. He would have been glad to find a fair excuse for giving up India, for throwing the Colonies on their own resources, and for persuading the English people to accept deliberately the place of a fourth or fifth-rate European power – which was not, in his estimation, a cynical or unpatriotic wish, but quite the reverse, for he thought that such a course would result in generally raising the calibre of the national mind, conscience, and taste.[10]

Hutton admired Clough for his imperturbability in treating 'most of the greater problems of life as insoluble, and enjoining a self-possessed composure under the discovery of their insolubility',[11] a poise which annoyed Emerson sufficiently to describe thus the Oxford of his day: ' "Ah," says my languid Oxford gentleman, "nothing new, and nothing true, and no matter." '[12] Bagehot's distrust of the 'ruinous force of the will' and of any 'excess of practical energy' was – with necessary modifications – one of his more valuable legacies to Hutton, who (one tends to forget the fact) was almost exactly his age.

Hutton needed years to appreciate the need for occasionally standing still. Moreover, it would be unfair to imply that Bagehot's attractiveness to Hutton lay in his frosty reception of innovative ideas, in a desire to render cool judgements on all issues. It is true that in his last work Bagehot preached the value of a 'cake of custom', one 'just sufficiently stiff to make innovation of any kind very difficult, but not quite stiff enough to make it impossible', as 'the true condition of durable progress'.[13] But in his late teens and early twenties Hutton appreciated the sheer zest of Bagehot's style:

Hunting was the only sport [Bagehot] really cared for. He was a dashing rider, and a fresh wind was felt blowing through his earlier literary efforts, as though he had been thinking in the saddle, in effect wanting in his later essays, where you see chiefly the calm analysis of a lucid observer.[14]

Hutton's characterisation of Bagehot is self-revealing in that it enumerates those qualities Hutton admired most, and praised most heartily whenever he discovered them operant in the works of other writers: 'high-spirited, buoyant, subtle, speculative. . . . gay and dashing humour which was the life of every conversation in which he joined. . . . visionary nature . . . .'[15] The source of many of our best memories of Bagehot's wit is Hutton's sketch: the remark, for instance, that Bagehot made to his mother when she expressed some anxiety about his delay in marrying, 'A man's mother is his misfortune, but his wife is his fault.'[16] Or his disdain of sherry at a dinner: 'tasted as if L— had dropped his h's into it'.[17] Or, perhaps best of all, his remark to a friend, who had a church in the grounds near his house: 'Ah, you've got the church in the grounds! I like that. It's well the tenants shouldn't be *quite* sure that the landlord's power stops with this world.'[18]

Bagehot's friendship for Hutton was based on respect for intelligence and editorial talents; and Bagehot saw in Hutton the kind of young Englishman he thought might build the new Jerusalem. Indeed, on reading Hutton's essays, many of them but suggestions of a line of thought, and most of them briefer than the critiques that Bagehot wrote during his busiest period as literary reviewer, one is struck by Hutton's interest in the specific passage needed to demonstrate a point, and his exploitation of opportunities to characterise a style by means of a few quoted lines.

Hutton, who admired Sir Walter Scott almost without qualification, and who regarded Scott's final years of travail as an epic of courage, wrote a model biography of his hero for the English Men of Letters series edited by John Morley. A point for speculation, of necessity considered at an early stage in Scott's career, was why Scott should have received £769 for *The Lay of the Last Minstrel* when Dr Johnson had received only fifteen guineas for *The Vanity of Human Wishes* (and even less for his *London*) but fifty years earlier. What led to a popularity so disproportionate – and even more so for any later poems that Scott might pen? (Constable paid Scott 1500 guineas for one-half of the copyright of *The Lord of the Isles*.[19]) It was easy enough to respond by noting the 'high romantic glow and extraordinary romantic simplicity' of the *Lay*'s poetical elements.[20] Pitt, dying in the year of Ulm and Austerlitz, was particularly impressed by the old harper. The lines in which Scott described the embarrassment of the harper when first urged to play produced in Pitt a reaction which was more to be expected from a painting than from a poem. To illustrate the reasons why, Hutton quoted more than fifty lines from the *Lay*, and conceded that, in fairness, a shorter quotation could hardly document 'the particular form of Mr Pitt's criticism, for a quick succession of fine shades of feeling of this kind could never have been delineated in a painting, or indeed in a series of painting at all, while they *are* so given in the poem'.[21] This study of 'a mood of feeling' is not classical, 'for there is no severe outline, – no sculptured completeness and repose, – no satisfying wholeness of effect to the eye of the mind, – no embodiment of a great action'.[22] Scott's interest lies, rather, in catching

> an emotion that had its roots deep in the past, and that is striving onward towards something in the future; – he traces the wistfulness and self-distrust with which age seeks to recover the feelings of youth, – the delight with which it greets them when they come, – the hesitation and diffidence with which it recalls them as they pass away, and questions the triumph it has just won . . . .[23]

Scott's manner is neither subtle nor complex, but its saving grace is swiftness. Hutton recognises that Scott's simplicity ('almost to bareness'[24]) had much to do with winning him an enormous public; but he also puts his finger squarely on the problem of Scott's deficiency, a thinness, particularly as compared to the variety, richness and lustre of the effects created by Byron – a poet who, Scott admitted, 'bet' him.[25] When Hutton speaks of the 'hurried tramp of [Scott's] somewhat monotonous metre', or Scott's 'special feeling for the pomp and circumstance of war', he points to Scott's 'stern patriotic feeling' in the description of the battle of Flodden Field, in *Marmion*.[26] To counter the damaging argument against Scott's anachronisms in a supposedly accurate historical reaction, he first identifies more lapses from grace than one might have imagined are strictly necessary.

> In *Kenilworth* he represents Shakespeare's play as already in the mouths of courtiers and statesmen, though he lays the scene in the eighteenth year of Elizabeth, when Shakespeare was hardly old enough to rob an orchard. In *Woodstock*, on the contrary, he insists, if you compare Sir Henry Lee's dates with the facts, that Shakespeare died twenty years at least before he actually died. The historical basis, again, of *Woodstock* and of *Redgauntlet* is thoroughly untrustworthy, and about all the minuter details of history, – unless so far as they were characteristic of the age, – I do not suppose that Scott in his romances ever troubled himself at all . . . .[27]

Hutton entertained serious reservations about Scott's humour, the Scottish 'wut' which led to 'rather elaborate jocular introductions, under the name of Jedediah Cleishbotham', as well as the writing of letters to his daughter-in-law (Lockhart regarded them as 'models of tender playfulness and pleasantry', but Hutton dismissed them as 'decidedly elephantine'); Dalgetty bored him almost as much as he would do in real life, 'which is a great fault in art'; Bradwardine became a nuisance, and Sir Piercie Shafton was 'beyond endurance'.[28]

To document his assertion that Scott was a poet of the people, deriving his inspiration from them and earning their trust in turn, Hutton cites two lovely cases of how the memorable lines of Scott's poetry became the permanent legacy of a nation. Thomas Campbell is quoted by Lockhart as having so loved 'Cadyow Castle', one of the ballads of *Border Minstrelsy*, that he repeated its lines on the North Bridge. The whole fraternity of coachmen knew him as he passed: 'To be sure, to a mind in sober, serious, street-walking humour, it must bear an appearance of lunacy when one stamps with the hurried pace and fervent shake of the head which strong, pithy poetry excites.'[29] To this anecdote Hutton adds the story of two old men, complete strangers, passing each other on a dark London night, when one of them happened to be repeating to himself the last lines of the account of Flodden Field in *Marmion*. 'Charge, Chester, charge', when suddenly a reply came out of the darkness, 'On, Stanley, on', 'whereupon', Hutton continues, 'they finished the death of Marmion between them, took off their hats to each other, and parted, laughing. Scott's is almost the only poetry in the English language that not only runs thus in the head of average men, but heats the head in which it runs . . . .'[30] Lockhart tells the story of how Sir Adam Fergusson, 'posted with his company on a point of ground exposed to the enemy's artillery', perhaps on the lines of Torres Vedras, read aloud to his men – while they lay prostrate on the ground – the battle description in canto VI of *The Lady of the Lake*; the listening soldiers 'only interrupted him by a joyous huzza when the French shot struck the bank close above them'. Hutton, ever on the look-out for such apposite anecdotage, adds, 'It is not often that martial poetry has been put to such a test; but we can well understand with what rapture a Scotch force lying on the ground to shelter from the French fire, would enter into such passages as the following'[31] – and follows his story with the quo-tation of some fifty-odd lines of poetry.

This notorious habit of Victorian critics – allowing quotations to run on so long that they make points quite unrelated to those of the surrounding context – is not unknown in our century, though publishers and editors, more conscious of space-costs, have reduced the self-indulgence of critics. At any rate, part of the rationale for quoting at such length has to do with the cumulative force of poetical description; it takes time to illustrate the weight and power of a particular passage in Scott, whose greatness lies less in the individual line than in a gathering or configuration of effects. Elsewhere, Hutton's quoted excerpts tend to be briefer, and tend to be especially happy in relation to the larger point he wants to make.

One of the most perceptive tributes in Victorian criticism to the genius of Nathaniel Hawthorne was written by Hutton, who admired the singleness of effect that Hawthorne wished to create in the mind of his reader. In *The Scarlet Letter*, for example, 'the deranging effect of the sin of adultery' is developed in three, or perhaps even four, 'scenes of great power'. 'Throughout the tale every one of the group of characters studied is seen in the lurid light of this sin, and in no other.' Every incident of *The Blithedale Romance* is intended to delineate 'the deranging effect of an absorbing philanthropic idea on a powerful mind, – the unscrupulous sacrifices of personal claims which it induces, and the misery in which it ends.' *The House of the Seven Gables* shows us how 'both personal character, and the malign influences of evil action, are transmitted, sometimes with accumulating force, even through centuries, blighting every generation through which they pass'. Hutton notes that even the little shop which 'old maid Pyncheon' reopens in the dark old house is not new; nor are the 'half-effaced picture of the ancestral Pyncheon which hangs on the walls, the garden-mould black with the vegetable decay of centuries, the exhausted breed of aristocratic fowls which inhabit the garden'.

Perhaps as fitting an excerpt as any is the one selected by Hutton to demonstrate his thesis that Hawthorne's power derives from his fascination with combinations of emotions that are, at one and the same time, 'abhorrent to nature and true to life'. In *Transformation* (known in the United States as *The Marble Faun*), a novel for which Hutton entertained little liking, since in its 'distended' form it contained only 'one powerful scene',[32] there comes a moment when Donatello discovers and seizes a 'half-madman, half-demon' who has been tormenting Miriam, 'a lady artist of warm and passionate nature, high powers, and mysterious origin'.[33] Donatello holds this nagging, much-disliked creature over a precipice, 'catches Miriam's eye, reads it in eager and fierce assent to the act he is meditating, and drops him down'. Miriam, who up to now has felt nothing but pity for Donatello, is now, for the first time, shocked to discover that 'horror and love are born together in her breast, and the monstrous birth, the delirium of love born in blood, is thus powerfully described'.[34] However finely conceived the scene, Hutton confesses that he finds it 'revolting', and adds, in some wonderment, 'Have I not reason for saying that Hawthorne's chief power lies in the delineation of unnatural alliances of feeling, which are yet painfully real, – of curdling emotions that may mix for a moment, but shrink apart again quickly, as running water from clotted blood?'[35] The characterisation of Hawthorne's technique is quick, nervous and just. Hutton's insight explains a good deal of the perversely strong fascination that Hawthorne's style has exercised over readers who, at times, may be unwilling to define the nature of their attraction to reading about the unspeakable, and the hitherto unimaginable.

Hutton identified a number of limitations in Hawthorne's vision of human nature, in the American's abnormal compulsion to write about 'certain outlying moral anomalies, which are not the anomalies of ordinary evil and sin, but have a certain chilling unnaturalness of their own'.[36] In some ways Hawthorne's imagination failed to go so far as that of Poe, who could, and did, create images of superlative physical horror. But Hutton responded to that imagination as to a 'lonely wistfulness', a superstitiousness (not quite a credulity) that wondered about ways of dramatising 'imaginative inquisitions into morbid subjects'.[37] After citing a number of ideas for sketches contained in the *Notebooks*, Hutton writes, 'Hawthorne seems to have illustrated his contemporary and friend Dr Holmes's theory that we are each of us a sort of physiological and psychological omnibus for bringing back our ancestors in new shapes and under different conditions to this earth.'[38] To some extent Hawthorne's genius was fertile, but cold and restless. 'It was used more to help him to explore mysteries than in obedience to the glowing creative impulse that cannot choose but paint.'[39] The hero of *The Blithedale Romance*, a Mr Coverdale, speaks of a 'cold tendency between instinct and intellect, which made me pry with a speculative interest into people's passions and impulses', and which 'appeared to have gone far towards unhumanising my heart'.[40] To be sure, Hawthorne's heart was tender. But, adds Hutton with some darkness of tone, 'no doubt, he was led by the speculative bias of his mind to steep his imagination in *arcana* on which it is scarcely good to gaze at all'.[41]

Despite its moral emphasis, Hutton's criticism is making the point, by means of numerous examples, that Hawthorne deliberately suppressed the facts which have given rise to the situations he describes, and for good reason. Hawthorne knew that

> people of a matter-of-fact turn of mind attach more value to knowing the exciting causes than to knowing the state of mind which results. If they hear what seems to them an insufficient cause for a heroine's misery, they set her down as feeble-minded, and give up their interest in her fate. If they hear a *too* sufficient cause, they say she deserved all she suffered, and for that reason discard her from their sympathies.[42]

Since Hawthorne saw the difficulty 'of inventing facts that would exactly hit the shade of feeling that he desired to excite in his readers' minds', he would frequently refuse 'to detail the facts distinctly at all'.[43] Hutton defined the essence of Hawthorne's method in the following sentence: 'He often gives us our choice of several sets of facts which might be adequate to the result, declines to say which he himself prefers, and insists only on the attitude of mind produced.'[44]

Before one may judge the degree of success achieved by Hawthorne in each of his fictions, the strategy pursued by him must, it seems to me, be defined in some such way. Hutton's analysis was sound, and early on the critical scene. This is not to suggest that Hutton, in understanding, was willing to forgive all. 'The predominance of moral colouring over the definite forms of actual fact in Hawthorne's novels is to me, I confess, unsatisfactory', Hutton wrote before going on to rank the novels by their willingness to provide a 'solid basis of fact'.[45] By such a scale, *The Scarlet Letter* stands at the top of the list, and, in descending order, there follow *The House of the Seven Gables*, *The Blithedale Romance* and *Transformation*.

Hawthorne is an artist within a narrow spectrum, though what he knows he knows thoroughly, and can express with wit and undeniable conviction. Yet Hutton did not much care for 'the melancholy of a man with a rather slow flow of blood in his veins, and almost a horror of action'; he did not much relish the spectacle of a man's mind exhibiting 'a sort of capillary repulsion' against the society in which he mixes.[46] Perhaps Hawthorne did not know enough about deep pain.

> He pictured real anguish, but more as an anatomist would lay bare a convulsive movement of the nerves, than as a poet would express passion. You feel that you are reading a *study* of human pain, rather than feeling the throb of the pain itself. The melancholy is the meditative and microscopic melancholy of a curious and speculative intelligence; there is little of the imaginative *sympathy* with pain which is at the heart of all true tragedy.[47]

Hutton's sympathy with Hawthorne's separation from both the world of voluntary action and the world of impulsive passion was necessarily circumscribed. Hawthorne, who spent most of his talents on the delineation of chronic suffering or sentiment, 'in which all desire to act on others is in a measure paralysed', liked 'to get past the rapids any way he can. . . . he not seldom introduces you to his tale with only the distant rush of them still audible behind you, his delight being to trace the more lasting perturbations which they effect for winding miles below.'[48] The sentiment on which he lavished his powers was often 'unhealthy', and his characters were 'necessarily very limited both in number and in moral attitude'. Hutton could discover in Hawthorne's novels only two characters with 'any active bent', Hollingsworth in *The Blithedale Romance* and Phoebe in *The House of the Seven Gables*.[49] A moral ideal lying behind such imaginative creations deserves, and receives, close scrutiny, for, as Hutton rightly says, Hawthorne should be regarded 'as something more than a mere writer of fiction'. His writings were widely read. 'He may safely be considered almost the first, and quite the highest, fruit of American culture.'[50]

But the close, even symbiotic, relationship between life and art which every major Victorian literary critic believed in meant – for Hutton – that Hawthorne's fascination with characters who possessed 'no impulse to help or to hinder', who cared only 'to look on, to analyse, to explain matters to themselves', fed his political and social convictions, and marked him as 'a democratic quietist; one might almost say a fatalist'.[51] Hutton, like Arnold, held reservations about 'the preacher of one-sided action and over-strained vigilance'. Highly strung energies might well look forward to a period of rest. But Hawthorne's quietistic creed disturbed Hutton, who expected more from the American writer's interpretation of the actual political world in which he lived. There was, after all, a connection between the kind of fiction Hawthorne wrote, the kind of character he created over and over again, and the biography he volunteered for the campaign of Franklin Pierce in 1852. Hawthorne understood clearly that General Pierce 'represented the party of conciliation to the South, – the party of union at almost any sacrifice of Northern principles'.[52] Pierce had come out in favour of enforcement of the Fugitive-Slave Law, and, as Hutton interpreted his politics, 'the whole system of which it was a part'.[53] Hawthorne sought to justify Pierce's pragmatism by arguing, in his electioneering volume, that slavery might well be 'one of those evils which Divine Providence does not leave to be remedied by human contrivances, but which, in its own good time, by some means impossible to be anticipated, but of the simplest and easiest operation, when all its uses shall have been fulfilled, shall vanish like a dream'.[54] In brief, Hawthorne thought that Providence would ultimately remove slavery from the land, and General Pierce should be supported as 'the man who dared to love that great and grand reality – his whole united native country – *better than the mistiness of a philanthropic theory*'.[55] Hutton's snort of disdain was loud and clear: 'This is the most immoral kind of political fatalism.'[56] He added, 'Measured by Hawthorne's standard, there would be no criminal national custom, however oppressive, with which it would be our duty to proclaim open war. He might denounce the political advocates of any such war as sacrificing the national peace to the "mistiness of philanthropic theory".'[57] The question is not to be avoided by casuistry: 'Was the duty of restoring moral freedom to a whole race to be classed as one of the doubtful visionary philanthropies of modern times?'[58] Hawthorne was not duty-bound to be an anti-slavery agitator, but Hutton felt himself obligated to say, sternly, that Hawthorne 'prostituted the noblest speculative faculties, when he attempted to perpetuate a fearful national sin on the dishonest plea that those who strove to resist its extension and to limit its duration were endangering the Union for the sake of a "misty philanthropic theory".'[59]

Hutton proceeded to his peroration:

> The fatalism which Hawthorne rather suggested than advocated in *Transformation*, when he presented sin as the necessary condition of moral growth, received a terrible elucidation when he calmly deprecated all impatient criticism of the providential 'uses' of slavery as if they were the affair of Providence alone. In the great civil war, his sympathies, as might be expected, were with the trimming Buchanans and Douglasses of the hour, not with Mr Lincoln, of whom he spoke slightingly as a man incapable of true statesmanship. . . . If he had cultivated a deeper sympathy with action and its responsibilities, he would not only have taken some interest in the removal of wrongs that were gloomy enough, whether picturesque or not, but might have widened greatly the range of his artistic power, and deepened considerably the spell of the great fascination which he wielded over his countrymen.[60]

Hutton's doctrine, pursued throughout his active editorial career, was dedicated to the twin propositions that words have consequences, and that the imaginative life is meaningless without some consideration of moral and ethical beliefs. It is also the product of a serious, intensely felt faith in the higher culture; for Hutton, as for Bagehot, literature helps to shape the better man, because the best literature is produced by human beings with superior insights, greater zest for living, and a more exhilarating sense of how to handle language. Above all, Hutton's criticism is original – a curiously angled approach to literary works that never quite adopts a conventional stance, or an ordinary moral attitude. Not a single essay by Hutton ever goes in exactly the anticipated direction, and even those essays which take up again, and still a third time, the same literary creation do not seem to repeat themselves; there is always something new to say.

But Hutton's criticism is surprisingly, and in some respects disappointingly, narrow in its concentration on domestic literature. Apart from his extended essay on Hawthorne and a surprising encomium to Lowell's *Biglow Papers* (scarcely 'surpassed in either kind or scale of humour since the world began'[61]), Hutton acknowledged only the rise of 'a totally new school of humour of the most original kind' in Artemus Ward's various lectures, Hans Breitmann's ballads, and Bret Harte's 'Heathen Chinee';[62] expressed a limited appreciation of Emerson's genius (his verse is 'laborious', and 'gives one that sense of uphill straining, as distinguished from flight. . . . very little indeed of genuine poetic passion', though his criticism is stimulating, and 'his gnomic wisdom will live long'[63]); evaluated justly the merits of the novel *Democracy*, though he did not know the identity of its author;[64] and saw in Longfellow, if not a very great or original poet, a writer whose less showy, more restful productions exhibited greater talent than such poems as 'Excelsior', 'A Psalm of Life', and 'The Light of Stars', written about common-place or conventional subjects 'with a pretty patch of colour that does not redeem them from common-placeness, but does make their common-placeness agreeable to the popular mind'.[65]

Nor does Hutton have even that much to say about Continental literature, though there is the obligatory bow to 'Goethe and his Influence'. To some extent Goethe was more interesting than Shakespeare, for the latter's impersonality prevented a reader from seeing clearly 'what kind of individual influence he put forth'.[66] On the other hand, an 'imperturbable self-possession and Napoleonic *sang froid* of judgment . . . underlay in Goethe all storms of superficial emotion',[67] and were no little embarrassment to him in many of his literary moods. They 'prevented him, we think, from ever becoming a great dramatist. He could never lose himself sufficiently in his creations . . . .'[68] Hutton admired Lewes's biography of Goethe, and agreed with the judgement that *Götz von Berlichingen* had suffered during the process of revision: 'No doubt something is cut away that needed cutting away, and more appearance of unity is given by the condensation of Adelheid's episode. But this is the part on which Goethe's imagination had really worked with finest effect, and the gain to unity is a loss to poetry.'[69] Like Hawthorne, whose frustratingly amorphous characters bore witness to their creator's failure to concretise experience, Goethe's picture of a mist seen from inside (*Werther*, and the works of fiction that followed) made it impossible to catch a glimpse of firm land.

> We believe the extraordinary want of outline in his characters to be greatly due to this entire absence of any attempt at moral proportion in all his later works ... Werther's mind is so dissolved that he can only feel and grope his way in the dark, as it were, to grace of form. .... Outline is a result of comparison, – moral outline of moral comparison. You cannot compare without an implied standard. The heroes in *Werther, Wilhelm Meister, Tasso, Faust*, are such cloudy, shadowy pictures, because they are essentially sketches of moral weakness without any relief in characters of corresponding power. Albert, Jarno, Antonio, are *not* foils to them – they have not the force which the others want, but are simply deficient in the moral qualities which make the former characters problems of some interest.[70]

This, Hutton suggests, provides a sharp contrast with Shakespeare's practice, for the English dramatist always gives his character 'some clear vision of the nobleness and the strength above it' even when he fails to provide a foil to the character whose weakness he is delineating.

> Hamlet knows what he could do and dare not. Lady Macbeth knows what she should do, and will not. Antony knows what he would do, and cannot. But Faust has no glimmering of salvation; Werther has no gleam of what he might be; Wilhelm is a milksop pure and simple; and Tasso's character is then, and then only, a fine picture if it be granted that he is supposed insane.[71]

Hutton thus delivers a home thrust against the theory that art is morally indifferent. Goethe's writings are impressive – nay, perfect –

until dramatic action, which relies on moral actions and moral faith, reveals the emptiness of the supposedly superior indifference of an uncommitted artist. Hutton cites Niebuhr's characterisation of *Wilhelm Meister* as 'a menagerie of tame animals', and adds that this might not have been the case 'if Goethe had not lost the (never strong) moral predilections of younger days, but had purified his eye and heart for their insight into human weakness by reverent study of nobler strength'.[72]

Perhaps in a major sense Hutton does not go beyond Lewes's insights, and the notion that an outline of a character is strengthened by the presence of an implicit moral estimate does not take us very far. But moral judgements are essential not simply because they provide the rich humus of circumstantial detail, but also because they make possible the forging of links between different periods of history. We are most intelligently moral when we know whence we have come and the direction in which we wish to travel.

Werther's uneasiness grows organically; but it grows as a tree puts out its branches, without memory or reference to its past stages. Egmont does not grow at all. Faust does not grow. Tasso undergoes changes; but only those of a sensitive plant, drawing in with every touch, expanding at every sunbeam. All Goethe's feminine creations grow; but usually it is the growth of affection only. The only portions of a coherent drama that Goethe ever wrote are the Gretchen elements in *Faust*. That is the highest drama in every sense, and one of the most essential elements in it is a deep and true remorse.[73]

Hutton is, of course, the classic case of a Victorian critic whose dedication to an informed moral judgement has undermined, for later critics, the value of his aesthetic pronouncements. Those who admire Swinburne's battle for artistic licence in the 1860s and 1870s are probably aware that Hutton kept a sharp eye out for breaches of decorum committed by Swinburne and his admirers. Hutton became impatient with Swinburne's 'petty resentments' and the 'intricate innuendoes inspired by a whole host of unintelligible literary animosities' that disfigured his essays; such defects interfered with 'the lucid beauty of genius';[74] yet the quarrel lay deeper.

Once, in writing of *In Memoriam*, Hutton recognised the presence of 'a definite teaching', one that came from the very depths of Tennyson's soul.[75] Two questions had to be considered before any judgement might be made as to whether such 'teaching' injured the poem. First, Hutton wrote, one had to decide if the message 'obtruded didactically instead of merely shaping and turning his song': did it mar the music, or was it of the essence of the music? 'For any one may spoil a song or a poem of any kind by incorporating with it fragments of a sermon.' Second, the important question was, 'Is it true?'[76] If Tennyson preached an unsound (i.e. untrue) doctrine, 'it must injure the poem, as well as the morality of the poem'.[77] Swinburne maintained that 'the only absolute duty of Art is the duty she owes to herself'. (Hutton was quoting Swinburne directly.[78]) For Swinburne 'the worth of a poem has properly nothing to do with its moral meaning or design'.[79] But for Hutton art must acknowledge the supremacy of the moral emotions – of the conscience – that shapes it. Hutton conceded that Swinburne did not prohibit art from taking a moral aim, 'so long as the aim does not so protrude as to injure the art'.[80] But Swinburne's refusal to admit that the character of the morality involved is even an element in the matter deeply angered Hutton.

It is this position, defended by Hutton primarily in the pages of the *National Review* and the *Spectator*, that led to an increasingly intemperate set of charges against writers whose tastes often seemed fleshly and decadent. The writers whom Hutton attacked, in turn, were savagely contemptuous of the kind of genteel humanism that they thought Hutton represented. To some extent Hutton was not well prepared to wage this war. His failure to consider in detail the developing trends in French realism, German critical theory and Scandinavian drama meant that his criticism, restricted largely to the productions of Englishmen of his own time, was needlessly provincial, and often too restricted in its points of reference.

For example, the only Romantic poets Hutton treated in any depth were Wordsworth and Shelley, and, though his reflections on the significance of their contribution to English letters were provocative then, and are still filled with good sense, comparable full-scale treatments of other Romantic poets would have forced Hutton to see the Victorian years as part of a longer century. Even the criticism of Wordsworth gave scanty recognition to the possibility that Wordsworth's poetry had created a revolution in poetic standards which Victorian literature had barely adjusted to; Hutton's major emphasis lay on an attempt to reconcile the two lines of argument that Wordsworth was, on the one hand, 'too transcendental', and on the other 'ridiculously simple', making 'an unintelligible fuss about common feelings and common things'. Hutton's solution to the dilemma ('He drew uncommon delights from very common things') may please us by its neatness of formulation, but it does not grapple with the real problem.[81] More searching, perhaps, is Hutton's thesis that Wordsworth, unlike Tennyson, withdraws his imagination from the heart of his picture to contemplate it in its spiritual relations, while Tennyson continues in the same strain of emotion as he begins. The two poems contrasted are 'Tears, idle tears' and 'The Fountain', and there is no question that Hutton admires Wordsworth's 'quiet, steadfast, and spiritual lights' more than he does Tennyson's 'self-consuming aspirations'.[82] But the bill of indictment against Wordsworth is weighty. If Coleridge's criticism of Wordsworth's tendency to indulge in 'thoughts and images too great for their subject' is misapplied to poems about Nature ('The daisy and the daffodils breathed a buoyant joy and love into Wordsworth's simple nature which Coleridge could but half understand'[83]), it is all too true about poems of incident, in which Wordsworth gives way to an unfortunate tendency 'to erect a meditative dome over an inadequate pedestal'. Wordsworth's mind lacks 'structural power'.[84] The 'voluntary, frugal, contemplative character of Wordsworth's intellectual nature'[85] is quite unequal to the task of blending a variety of elements into a single picture. Hutton's analysis builds inexorably toward an accusation:

> There is no whole landscape in all Wordsworth's exquisite studies of nature. There is no variety of moral influences in all his many beautiful contemplations of character. There is no distinct centre of interest in any but his very simplest narratives. Indeed, he can deal with facts successfully only when they are simple enough to embody but a single idea: as in the case of Peter Bell and the Idiot Boy.[86]

Worse yet is to follow: Wordsworth also lacked a good ear. It was not (as some critics and biographers had stated) the finest of his senses. 'There is no indication that he had any fine faculty for music . . . .' Rather, 'vision absorbed him, and would not allow his "inward eye" to see until sight was exchanged for memory. . . . It was not easy for him to macadamise his poetry with little abrupt matter-of-fact sounds.'[87] The reason that Hutton liked Hazlitt's description of Wordsworth's speech ('a deep guttural intonation, and a strong tincture of the northern *burr*, like the crust on wine'[88]) well enough to quote it in more than six different essays was that it defined so well those 'little disfiguring specks of incongruous material' in Wordsworth's poems that so often annoyed him, those 'unshaped half-human thoughts' that Wordsworth located in the mind of his Peter Bell; that he himself knew all too well. If the rigidity of Wordsworth's mind was a fact well agreed-on by those who knew him, and indeed confessed to by Wordsworth (who called it a 'tendency to hardness'[89]), it explained for Hutton Wordsworth's 'great deficiency in humour, which cannot exist without a certain flexibility of both feeling and thought, allowing of rapid transitions from one point of view to another'.[90] Wordsworth lacked ease and delicacy 'in the lesser movements of his intellectual nature'. He introduced jarring terms such as 'machine' to the language of that most lovely poem, 'She was a phantom of delight'.[91] Hutton ascribed this preservation in poetry of 'the smallest memoranda' to Wordsworth's egotism, to 'a kind of blind faith that they have a universal meaning'. Indeed, 'half Wordsworth's weakness springs from the egotistical self', while 'all his power springs from the universal self'.[92]

To some extent this reading of Wordsworth's genius may seem more dry and unenthusiastic than Hutton intended, for Hutton's admiration of the Cumberland poet's 'pure, deep well of solitary joy',[93] a spring that Hutton described as 'something even fresher than poetic life', was genuine enough. Still, these charges lead ultimately to the judgement that Wordsworth's concentration on single influences harmed his ability to apprehend general Truth: 'His genius was universal, but was not comprehensive; it did not hold many things, but it held much.'[94] Wordsworth's unwillingness to humanise the spirit of natural objects was related to his sense of realism; Nature was a tributary to Man, 'sending him influences and emanations which pass into the very essence of his life',[95] but they did not constitute that life because they were not like in *kind* to humanity.

It is unlikely that we shall ever again think of 'Ode to Duty' as containing, in essence, 'nearly all the truth that Wordsworth anxiously gleaned from a life of severe meditation',[96] or as a poem that constitutes one of Wordsworth's 'sublimest' statements on Nature, free will and God; and twentieth-century evaluations of the best that Wordsworth achieved may not concur with Hutton's admiration of 'The Song at the Feast of Brougham Castle' as 'the

last, perhaps, the most perfect effort of his genius'.[97] Hutton lacks
sympathy with the experiments in poetic diction that meant so much
to Wordsworth, and is unwilling to consider the historical context
against which the *Lyrical Ballads* rebelled. Altogether, Hutton's essay
'The Genius of Wordsworth' is too remote, because it deals with a
man whose best work had been produced long before Hutton's birth
(even 'Ode to Duty' is dated 1804), and Hutton's concerns were
almost entirely focused on the second half of the century.

A sense of tension also runs through the other important essay on a
Romantic figure, for in 'Shelley and his Poetry' Hutton makes an
unexpectedly strong point of the irrelevance of Shelley's life to the
poetry he wrote. While acknowledging the importance of Professor
Dowden's biography, Hutton felt constrained to remark, 'Shelley's
poetry is in a different plane from human life of any kind'.[98] Hutton
was baffled by the exceptionalness of Shelley's natural disposition; it
had gone too far beyond the range of 'ordinary experience'. He
could not be sure that any judgement he might pass on Shelley's
conduct was fair, though, like many others of his era, he was
confident that Shelley had 'wandered very far indeed from the right
track'.[99] Shelley 'held no creed which imposed upon him as a duty
what was not the teaching of impulse'. Hutton could not refrain
from deploring Dowden's account of Shelley's flight with Mary
Godwin, and of the cold-blooded letter that he wrote to his wife; this
was lawless conduct; yet (Hutton may almost be seen biting his lip)
'Shelley could never see in all these troubles any shadow of guilt.'[100]
Shelley's guilt was shared by others:

> We may say that all his worst griefs were due to the lawlessness of
> love either as illustrated by himself or as taught to others by those
> who taught it to him. . . . Two terrible suicides, one lifelong
> shame, and several years of painful shrinking from public
> criticism, were the direct fruits of those doctrines. And when
> Shelley had to remonstrate with Byron on Byron's much more
> deliberate wickedness, he must have felt his authority lessened, if
> not extinguished, by the knowledge that Byron in his cynicism
> would regard his friend's remonstrances as due rather to pruden-
> tial than to moral feelings.[101]

Reconciling such knowledge with a love of the poetry, a love
acquired at an early age, was no easier for Hutton than for Bagehot.
Hutton's awkwardness manifested itself, as usual, in a lavish, and

often excessive, praise of the short lyrics at the expense of most of the long poems ('*The Cenci*, of course, is full of power and grandeur, but the subject is too revolting, as well as one which admits too little scope for pure song, to exhibit Shelley's genius in its most characteristic light'[102]). Hutton may have created an antithesis more stark than a balanced assessment required; he found himself forced to explain Shelley's passion as aerial and sweet – a travesty of interpretation, though it was a standard Victorian view of Shelley, and Arnold subscribed to it – while denying merit to Shelley's more complex conceptions. He denied Shelley's interpretation of a notable passage in Wordsworth,

> But in the very world which is the world
> Of all of us, the place in which, in the end,
> We find our happiness, or not at all.

(Shelley believed that Wordsworth was 'launching a blow against the school of the Unsatisfied', or, as Hutton interpreted Shelley's meaning, 'As if, after sixty years' suffering here, we were to be roasted alive for sixty million more in Hell, or charitably annihilated by a *coup-de-grâce* of the bungler who brought us into existence at first.'[103]) Yet it is easier to see where Shelley derived his view of Wordsworth's meaning than where Hutton found his argument: that 'if the springs of infinite joy are not so some extent discoverable in man *here*, as he was sure that they were, they can scarcely be inherent in human nature, and can hardly be confidently expected in the world to come'.[104] Surely Hutton makes Wordsworth too easily content with 'the spiritual opulence of this homely earth',[105] and does so because he cannot bear to have, even for a moment, Shelley and Wordsworth sharing a heresy.

It is too easy, in taking account of Shelley's failures, to ascribe some portion of the responsibility to the largeness of the poet's ambitions. Shelley, Hutton writes at one point, 'was essentially the poet of intellectual desire, not of all emotion'.[106] He pursues a fugitive feeling, often in vain, or acknowledges that it 'has just slipped through his faint intellectual grasp'.[107] Later, Hutton rephrases the doctrine: 'Other lyrical poets write of what they feel, but Shelley almost uniformly of what he *wants* to feel.'[108] It hardly matters that Hutton believes in the close connection between these unfulfilled desires and the creation of some of Shelley's finest poems;

there exists a too-convenient nexus between such desires and the poems that do not come alive in the reader's mind.

Thus, one can anticipate why Byron's 'mere acts of intellectual impertinence' – performed by 'a grown-up schoolboy, with a keen pleasure in playing practical jokes on mighty Powers in which he half believed'[109] – should occupy a lower level than the feelings testifying to the awelessness of Nature (Hazlitt called it 'curiosity') which Shelley displayed. It was not that Shelley sought new *truth*; what he wanted was 'a new effervescence of nature half way between knowledge and feeling'.[110] As a consequence, Hutton denied an oft-made claim that Shelley was a mystic, because he believed that the poet reconstructed the spiritual universe rather than – as a true mystic might – halt on the edge of the spiritual world and bend before its mighty mysteries. Shelley's genius vibrated in suspension between 'the world of living reality' and 'the world of unseen strength', wielding 'a wonderful power over ideal essences, but neither giving him a strong hold on life nor reaching their root in God'.[111] The criticism in some ways is reminiscent of what Hutton had already said about Wordsworth: 'His intellect, subtle as it was, had no vigorous grasp in it. . . . it had no integrating power.'[112] A poet who fails to enjoy reality is an idealist, opposed to the major direction of the pre-Raphaelite school of art, and unimpressed by the claims made by others for 'the infinite significance of actual ties'.

One may argue that this view of Shelley as an abstractor of Beauty, as the possessor of a conscience showing 'the finest feminine qualities of disinterestedness and even fortitude',[113] but also recoiling abruptly 'from all aggressive exploits against the coarse jumbled evils of the world',[114] tells us far more about Hutton than about Shelley. It bespeaks a curious unwillingness to consider some of the most significant evidence gathered by Edward Dowden to show how often Shelley directed his arrows against real injustices and social problems created by overweening institutions. Shelley's minimising of the need for government grew from a strong conviction that the governments of the world had been tried and found wanting; and who, reviewing the sorry history of most European dynasties in the hundred years preceding Shelley's coming to manhood, would want to contradict the generalisation? *The Revolt of Islam* may be called (it has been called) the last great poem of the Enlightenment, and Shelley's polemics against Church and State have links with the diatribes of Rousseau, who figures so prominently in *The Triumph of Life*. In a major sense the essay on Shelley, like that on Wordsworth, disappoints because it proceeds so unerringly to its concluding platitude.

Even so, Hutton's conclusion, which cites as the height of sublimity a speech of Beatrice Cenci when she suddenly suspects that there may be no God after all, is unexpected:

> Sweet Heaven, forgive weak thoughts! If there should be
> No God, no Heaven, no Earth, in the void world, –
> The wide, gray, lampless, deep, unpeopled world!

This suspicion, Hutton writes, may be at the root of Shelley's restlessness.[115] (Hutton denied that Shelley was an atheist.) What if, behind the painted veil, there lay 'a dreadful phantom of possible emptiness'? What if the One who remains is 'a thinner, fainter, less living thing than the "many" which "change and pass"', – that there is nothing substantial at the heart of the universe, – no Will behind the fleeting beauty, no strength of self-sacrifice behind the melting love'?[116] What if – the rhetorical question is vibrant with a personally-felt anguish – 'we were to find even behind the fresco of universal loveliness nothing but a "wide, gray, lampless, deep, unpeopled world"'?[117] Hutton does not answer the dread question.

Hutton's admiration of Shelley's purest strain prevented him from descending to bathetic commentary. A second essay, 'Shelley as Prophet', took a clearer look at Shelley's sense of the future. The concluding lines of *Hellas* suggest not only that good and evil alternate, but that the future contains too much bitterness 'to admit of anything like steady contemplation'.[118] It is unwise to enlist Shelley as a prophet of the inevitable triumph of good over evil, and, since Shelley had no faith in the existence of an evil inside himself, the blame for evil lay at the feet of God.

> No doubt [Shelley] held willing suffering to be the greatest of all healing influences; but then he thought the mere existence of willing suffering a great blot on the holiness of the Ultimate Power by which it is permitted. Martyrdom was to him the great redeeming power, but then it was also the great arraignment of the Creative Spirit. Shelley's mind vibrated between a passionate admiration of Him who could suffer to save others, and passionate resentment that suffering to save others should ever be needful at all.[119]

But Hutton did not seek to conventionalise Shelley's religion: 'He never even admitted for a moment the idea of a suffering God, and therefore he never admitted for a moment the root-idea of the Christian revelation and of all true prophecy.'[120] Hutton saw no prophet in Shelley, but rather a credulous believer in the 'divinity of desire'.[121]

An awareness of evil is essential if we are to define a hierarchy of moral truths. Before we dismiss such a notion as truistic, we should recall how often the romantic writers of the turn of the century had defined evil in precisely the terms that Hutton used for the description of Shelley's verse: as an external force, as something that priests and kings had superimposed upon an all-too-credulous mankind. Hutton found himself an uneasy reader of Emerson because of what John Morley had noted, a 'marked dislike of disease in any form',[122] and a helplessness in the face of sin. (Hutton defined *sin* as 'a conscious and voluntary revolt against a moral authority to which we owe obedience',[123] and knew of no better name for the phenomenon.) Not for Hutton was Emerson's 'pale moonlit world of ideality',[124] no matter how much pleasure he derived from Emerson's style. Hutton's love of moral truth was always within beck and call of his appreciation of literary values, as when, in reviewing Leslie Stephen's life of Dr Johnson, he remarked that 'the hearty old man would have been a most valuable ally during the American Civil War of seventeen years back, when English society got quite sentimental about slave-drivers who were yelping their loudest for liberty to drive slaves'.[125]

Hutton's concentration on Victorian writers led him to write important essays on Browning, Tennyson, Arnold and Carlyle, and some less important pieces on Clough, George Eliot, FitzGerald and Dickens. An ingratiating feature of these critiques lies in the fact that Hutton rarely compared one author with another; comparisons usually led to minimising the merits of one writer as opposed to another, and although on occasion Hutton might argue that Carlyle was a finer transcendental thinker than Emerson, equity compelled him to indicate immediately that Emerson in some respects – magnanimity, patient possession of his own soul, a willingness to commit himself to such practical movements as anti-slavery, an abiding sanity, and reverence toward man – was a more attractive person than Carlyle.[126] If Arnold were to be compared with Wordsworth, the linking would show that Arnold's message, 'Endure', could best be understood by seeing it as a modernisation of

Wordsworth's exhortation, 'Rejoice'.[127] George Eliot was second only to Sir Walter Scott; her stories, Hutton believed, were 'richer than Fielding's, as well as far nobler, and vastly less artificial than Richardson's';[128] but this kind of comparison is rarely drawn, and Hutton's primary concern is discovering the particular essence of a writer's contribution to letters, what makes him (or her) worth reading. Hutton seldom, if ever, wrote a critical review designed to turn away the reader from the text he was considering. He enjoyed sharing insights, and, on occasion, enthusiasms.

For Hutton, poetry of the purest kind was to be found in Isaiah, Aeschylus, Shakespeare and Shelley (though, as we have seen, Shelley's lengthier and more ambitious poems lacked *grip*).[129] Poetry of the highest quality was being written by his contemporaries, particularly by Tennyson and Arnold. The knowledge that this was so cheered Hutton tremendously as he surveyed the contemporary landscape. Tennyson in particular repaid close attention. Hutton modified Coleridge's remark, in *Table Talk*, that Tennyson had begun to write poetry before he knew what metre was: 'that remark applied, of course, only to his very earliest publications',[130] and Tennyson's mastery of metre after what Hutton called his 'pre-poetic period', before 1832, could not be questioned. The magical year of 1832 – when Tennyson not only composed the first poem of his new period, 'The Lady of Shalott', but also began to draft the first of the lyrics of *In Memoriam* – saw the infusion of a soul into poems that hitherto had been empty. Tennyson then understood, for the first time, 'the utter satiety which compels any true imaginative nature to break through the spell which entrances it in an unreal world or visionary joys'.[131] Not that Tennyson found it easy to break away from 'the emptiness of the life of fancy', inasmuch as several of his poems of the 1830s and 1840s began with a picture or a narrative rather than the more successful genesis of a thought or feeling. 'Whenever Tennyson's pictorial fancy has had it in any degree in its power to run away with the guiding and controlling mind, the richness of the workmanship has to some extent overgrown the spiritual principle of his poems.'[132] But Tennyson, perhaps more than any other poet of mid century, possessed a power to compel the external world 'to lend him a language for the noblest feelings', or, in terms of a recurring concern of Hutton, to master 'the power of real things', to a degree unknown since the time of Shakespeare's dramas.

Hutton defined Tennyson's range as one that moved with surety through certain kinds of characterisation: 'the smarting and not very deeply wounded heart of a grandiose and somewhat bumptious lover dismissed like the rejected of Locksley Hall';[133] the half-delirious St Simeon Stylites, who has triumphed 'over the half-dead body which had in great measure dropped away from him before he died';[134] 'the intolerable restlessness of the wanderer born and bred', Ulysses;[135] the feelings of a Tithonus who confronts 'the awful prospect of a solitary eternity of decay'.[136] Tennyson was not a dramatist, because he could not depict with sure strokes the variety of moods within a single person, and his plays failed to convince an audience when they were produced. Still (the thought is piquant), Tennyson's genius for the depiction of single moods was superior to that of Browning, for the latter would have made Tithonus, Ulysses, St Simeon Stylites, and the Northern Farmers 'all talk Browningese'.[137]

Tennyson in many ways is a model for a kind of decorum that later generations characterise by the term 'Victorian', used in a denigrating sense. Hutton, on several occasions, protested against Tennyson's 'tendency to over-express any morbid thought or feeling' that he wished to resist.[138] Hutton's example, Tennyson's characterisation of Nature as being 'red in tooth and claw', was labelled 'hysterical', because 'Nature is very much besides the teeth and claws of beasts of prey, and the "shrieks" of her victims can hardly be fairly represented as her voice.'[139] Hutton also disliked the effusiveness 'beyond what a perfectly simple taste admits' that marred such an image as the one in which Tennyson imagines that Hallam might return alive from the ship that bears his corpse, and 'strike a sudden hand' into that of the poet: '*strike* is surely too pronounced, too emphatic a word for the occasion, especially as the idea is conveyed by the word "sudden"'[140]

Perhaps the most signal contribution made by Hutton to the debate over the characterisation of Arthur in *Idylls of the King* lay in his imaginative return to the original dilemma confronted by Tennyson as he worked through his source materials. On the one hand, King Arthur was depicted as a great and near-perfect sovereign, a man touched by a spiritual halo; on the other, he was seen as a medieval Oedipus, afflicted by the consequences of voluntary sin and involuntary incest, and ultimately murdered by the hand of his own son. Tennyson had to choose between inconsistent elements; shame and retribution could not be retained along with an element of 'mystic spiritual glory', and the latter alone was consistent with 'the Christian mysticism of the San Grail legends'.[141] Swinburne insisted on Arthur's guilt, and on Guinevere's shared complicity; but Hutton showed that Tennyson's reading was consistent with Malory's recension. Tennyson's poetic instinct was sure when he attributed to Arthur a 'reluctant assent to the search for the San Grail',[142] reluctant because he had committed himself and his knights to the 'higher though humbler task' of 'restoring order on earth'.[143] The argument between Hutton and Swinburne – the echoes of which have not wholly died – turned on the question of whether Tennyson should have tainted the life and character of Arthur in the manner of a Greek dramatist. Tennyson's decision, to keep the spiritual glory of Malory's Arthur, 'not only raised the character of his poem, but connected it with some of the most prominent and distinctive threads in our modern spiritual life'.[144] By this Hutton means that Arthur, like many Victorians, is torn between the ideas of chivalry and 'the ideas of an age of hesitating trust, an age of a probing intellect and of a trusting heart'. *Idylls of the King* brings us, in more glory than Swinburne thought seemly, a king who incarnates spiritual authority. The charge that Arthur is 'an impeccable prig' depends on the unspoken postulate that all sinlessness is didactic; Hutton adds, with some grimness, that sinlessness is 'therefore jarring to those who are not sinless'.[145] *Idylls of the King* is not the most perfectly finished of Tennyson's poems; but, Hutton concludes, it 'has a grander aim and larger scope than any, and paints the waste places of the heart and the strength of the naked soul with a stronger and more nervous touch'.[146]

This view of Tennyson as a poet who understood clearly the reasons for the despair of his contemporaries – and never shook off his own profound doubts – prefigures much of twentieth-century criticism. Hutton's line of argument, to sum up, is that Tennyson did not speak for the dominant beliefs of the nineteenth century so much as he reacted, vigorously, and with the full powers of his genius, against what he conceived to be false ideas. Tennyson repudiated a mindless democracy, utilitarian doctrine and unprincipled Free Trade. He was never a confident optimist. 'Tennyson', wrote Hutton in an essay on Tennyson's 'Despair', 'seems to me always to be greatest when his thought is moving in a resisting medium.'[147] Like the persona in *In Memoriam*, Tennyson earned whatever faith he enjoyed only by achieving a difficult triumph over grave misgivings, 'faith that no longer perhaps "faintly", but certainly not in any dogmatic or positive attitude of mind, "trusts the larger hope".'[148] Tennyson's poetry is most noble when 'it gives the reader the impression that the poet is stemming the current of the age, and convinced that the age is all astray'.[149]

In the 1880s this was not fashionable doctrine; it gave higher status to the quality of the poems written during Tennyson's last phase than many Victorian critics were willing to concede. Hutton's emphasis on Tennyson's resistance against 'false assumptions and degrading creeds'[150] provided a convenient means of seeing the unity in Tennyson's choices of subject-matter over a half-century. There may well have been a crankiness in the aging poet's temperament to which Hutton responded, for the defence of 'Locksley Hall: Sixty Years After' against critical neglect or downright misunderstanding was based on Hutton's conviction that no one should expect age to be full of 'the irrepressible buoyancy of youth':[151] age 'is conscious of a dwindling power to meet the evils which loom larger as experience widens'.[152] Tennyson's poem conveyed brilliantly 'the natural pessimism of age in all its melancholy, alternating with that highest mood of "old experience" which, in Milton's phrase, "doth attain to something like prophetic strain" '.[153] Nevertheless, the younger and the older Tennysons were recognisably the same man in all of Hutton's forcefully written essays and reviews.

Of Matthew Arnold, the other Victorian poet for whom Hutton entertained the highest respect, Hutton said, more than once, that his subject-matter was singularly limited, and could be described as 'the divorce between the soul and the intellect, and the depth of spiritual regret and yearning which that divorce produces'.[154] From Goethe, Arnold took his definition of spiritual unrest; from Wordsworth, the remedy, communing closely with Nature.[155] But Arnold transcribed what he saw in Nature, unlike Wordsworth, who gave us 'a newly-created meditative universe'. For Hutton, this restfulness of Arnold's verse – this determination to keep an eye on the object itself rather than on the spiritual lesson it discloses – amounts to a limitation of talent. Despite his admiration of Arnold's simplicity of taste, Hutton sees it as a somehow inadequate response to the modern world of 'change, alarm, surprise'. 'He has not caught from his fine studies of Homer the exquisite music of the Homeric wave of rhythm', Hutton writes in his essay 'The Poetry of Matthew Arnold'; 'but he has caught his clearness of atmosphere, what he himself has so finely termed "the pure lines of an Ionian horizon, the liquid clearness of an Ionian sky" '.[156] There seems to be an excessive calculation in poems that amount to *recitatives*, 'usually a train of thought rather than feeling, and very frequently a train of very directly hortative or argumentative thought'. Arnold's verse can be, and is more often than Hutton likes, 'cold', 'grandiose', even 'obscure'. In addition, Arnold's longer poems – 'The Sick King in Bokhara', 'Sohrab and Rustum', 'Balder Dead' and to some extent the fragment 'Tristram and Iseult' – are limited successes, though 'The Sick King in Bokhara' comes closer to satisfying Hutton's expectations of an organic whole than any of the others,[157] which tend to run down rather than properly conclude, as if before their final lines Arnold had exhausted his interest in the subject-matter.

Perhaps these are less damaging criticisms than at first they appear to be. Arnold's contribution to his century lay in his ability to diagnose a spiritual illness, even if, as Hutton hastened to add, only from the intellectual side – 'sincerely and delicately, but from the surface, and never from the centre'.[158] Hutton regarded religious faith as a matter for individual decision. Subscribing to Christ's doctrine took place 'in a spiritual plane far deeper than that where the dialogue with Doubt, which Mr Arnold so leisurely dramatises, takes place'.[159] But Hutton, a Christian humanist who seldom used the vocabulary of Christian faith to make his critical points, never wavered in his admiration of Arnold's poetry, despite what he considered to be that poetry's 'erroneous spiritual assumptions'.[160] Drama is not the worse, as drama, 'for delineating men as they seem to each other to be, and not as they really are to the eye of God',[161] nor should readers be distracted from the fineness of Arnold's lyrics by religious considerations.

In 'The Poetic Place of Matthew Arnold', Hutton, reviewing Arnold's selection of his own poems, praised their purity of taste and feeling, elements comparable in their strength only to similar elements in the writings of Dr Newman. Arnold is also, for Hutton, a thinking poet, whose elegies are worth far more than all his prose essays; whose pity for the fallen is passionate and generous; and who so rigorously controlled his output that any selection 'necessarily excludes what it seems almost barbarous to exclude'. Indeed, Hutton's study of Arnold's poetry must have been close and painstaking from the very beginning, as if something were being sought therein which amounted to more than a lofty and calm regret at the state of things – for example, the line, in 'To Marguerite – Continued' (1852), 'The unplumb'd, salt, estranging sea'. Of it Hutton writes, it shadows out to you the plunging deep-sea lead and the eerie cry of 'no soundings', it recalls that saltness of the sea which takes from water every refreshing association, every quality that helps to slake thirst or supply sap, and then it concentrates all these dividing attributes, which strike a sort of lonely terror into the soul, into the one word 'estranging'.[162]

This is well said, and moving.

Hutton wrote on Arnold's letters, his poetic place, his poetic charm, his elegies and his popularity; it is not surprising, therefore, that he should also have something to say on Arnold's critical essays. As might be expected, Hutton admired Arnold's 'sureness as well as confidence of literary judgment',[163] and paid due homage to his judgements on 'the finer taste'. Arnold delivered his unpopular judgements with aplomb. Hutton cited Arnold's verdict on the Burns poem 'A man's a man for a' that' as lacking 'the accent of high seriousness', and the ranking of 'The Jolly Beggars' as a poem infinitely superior to 'The Cotter's Saturday Night'.[164] Arnold, who called for poetry to deliver a higher criticism of life, wanted more precision of outline than such a poet as Shelley was prepared to give. Arnold did not lack sympathy for Shelley, but, Hutton added, he lacked a standard by which to judge him. Arnold was so intensely concentrating on what a poet meant to convey, 'and whether he had really succeeded in conveying it', that he found himself baffled in dealing with Shelley's 'evanescent lights and shadows and essences and potencies of melody'.[165] Sometimes, to be sure, Arnold benefited from his positiveness:

> He knew what was false and true to life, and hardly ever failed to point out where the truth was, where the falsetto note came in. But his confidence in this positive ear of his was a disqualification for criticising those unique efforts to supply both the world to be criticised and the standard of criticism, in which once and again strange spirits like Shelley's have attained success.[166]

Best of all, perhaps, in these critical essays was Arnold's style, whereby literary assessments were dressed in sincerity, confidence and clear authority, the kind which gives 'to true criticisms almost all their charm and half their finality'.[167] Hutton concluded that Arnold rendered Milton's poetic style into prose in a noble manner, and no man could do it more appropriately than he who had

celebrated duly the grand style of Milton.[168] It was the same
standard of translation to which Hutton aspired, and to which he
occasionally rose.

Of Hutton's importance on the Victorian scene there can be no
question; partly his influence derived from the fact that authors
trusted his interest in discovering praiseworthy elements in their
attitude toward life and partly from their conviction that he paid
serious attention to their uniqueness of idiom and style. One
characteristic anecdote is related to Anthony Trollope's *Nina
Balatka*, 'the story of a maiden of Prague', the composition of which
Trollope began in September 1865. George Smith, despite his
knowledge of Trollope's authorship, decided not to print it in
Cornhill Magazine; Trollope, determined to publish the work
anonymously, brought it to J. M. Langford, the London manager of
the Edinburgh publishing firm of Blackwood. *Nina Balatka* was
accepted, and began to appear on 1 February 1867, as the first of
several novels to be serialised in the pages of *Blackwood's Magazine*.
Mr Blackwood believed that its style would not give its authorship
away, but (as Trollope wrote in his *Autobiography*)

> it was discovered by Mr Hutton of the *Spectator*, who found the
> repeated use of some special phrase which had rested upon his ear
> too frequently when reading for the purpose of criticism other
> works of mine. He declared in his paper that *Nina Balatka* was by
> me, showing, I think, more sagacity than good nature. I ought
> not, however, to complain of him, as of all the critics of my work
> he has been the most observant, and generally the most
> eulogistic.[169]

Hutton may be studied, in all his strengths and weaknesses, in
*Essays on Some of the Modern Guides of English Thought in Matters of
Faith* (1887). The essays on Thomas Carlyle and Frederick Denison
Maurice were reprinted from *Good Words*, and the essays on
Cardinal Newman, Matthew Arnold and *George Eliot's Life and
Letters* (edited by her husband, J. W. Cross) from the *Contemporary
Review*. The long essay on George Eliot had been collected first in
Literary Essays; it came originally from the pages of the *British
Quarterly Review*; Hutton withdrew it from the second edition of
Literary Essays because he 'perceived that George Eliot at that time
had still to publish some of the most striking and characteristic of her
works', as he wrote in his prefatory note, even though the essay

covered George Eliot's career past the publication of *Middlemarch*.
As a critic of her creative fictions, Hutton gave generous praise:
Eliot, he maintained, was better than the society-novelists (Jane
Austen, Mrs Gaskell, Anthony Trollope, William Makepeace
Thackeray), 'possessed great shrewdness and range' in her miscellaneous observations of life,[170] a Shakespearean sense of humour, and
'a great fertility in illustrative analogies which go to the very heart of
a one-sided view of any question'.[171] He admired *Adam Bede*, her
most popular work, as 'a story of which any English author,
however great his name, could not fail to have been proud'. It was
'the simplest possible unfolding of a tragedy'. And of *Middlemarch* he
could write, 'Richer and more abundant humour there has not been
in any book of our own day . . . .'[172]

He knew that her art was, in some damaging ways, pinched. She
borrowed too frequently the devices and even the point of view of
that master satirist Thackeray, and they did not often suit her
talent. She never overcame her stiffness in reproducing social
conversation among 'the uncultivated and the philosophising
classes'.[173] *The Mill on the Floss* was 'painfully inferior' to *Adam Bede*,
and in part its problem lay with the kind of people she depicted;
even *Middlemarch* had, as its 'general drift', the showing-up of 'the
petty moral scale of the life depicted'.[174]

Essentially Hutton's criticism moved outward from ethics rather
than aesthetics, though his analysis of her poetry (which he believed
wanted 'spontaneity'[175]) was as alert and just as that offered by any
contemporary. It is Huttonian to an extreme when, in a consideration of how George Eliot avoided 'smothering' a character in
society, or in incident, he mentions Hetty's cry, in *Adam Bede*, for
divine mercy, a cry that is directed at Dinah rather than God, and
bursts out, 'How strange and painful it is to realise that the great
author who painted this for us did not herself believe in the divine
mercy which she makes Dinah proclaim!'[176]

The complexity of George Eliot's character baffled him, even
while he acknowledged her literary genius. 'To me', he wrote in a
review of the *Life* prepared by her husband, 'the character and
works of this remarkable woman seem one of the most startling of
the moral phenomena of our time . . . .'[177] Perhaps, he speculated,
the irony contained in the German works she read and translated
undermined her faith, and led to her renunciation of Christianity in
the early 1840s. 'She certainly took the moral law into her own
hands with very unhappy results in forming what is euphemistically

called her "union" with Mr Lewes . . . .'[178] And again, with infinite sadness: 'She tried to do for herself all that religious people rightly leave to God, as well as all that religious people rightly do for themselves.'[179]

The relationship of our moral judgements of human conduct in the real world to our perception of how best to 'read' a novel was, understandably, a problem of greater concern to the Victorians than it has ever been since, or may ever be again. Hutton could not dissociate what he knew of her life from what he read in her novels, short stories and poems.

From one perspective, this may seem to be a failing of sensibility, or no more than a hope for reconciliation with a divine power superior to the power of human intelligence that George Eliot worshipped; a hope against hope, in other words, defeated by George Eliot's death and the publication of an official biography. But, from another perspective, Hutton's critiques of her art provide ample documentation of how, even with some unwillingness, his basic honesty about the nature of genius, and the need for encouraging its manifestations, had to express itself. Hutton's 'moral criticism' is far from being a contradiction in terms, an oxymoron; at its best, this self-questioning, ethically based humanism proposes for our examination and approval the highest standards for the practice of both literature and life.

4 Leslie Stephen

It is difficult to think of a serious literary critic of the Victorian Age who wrote fewer ambiguous or obscure sentences than Leslie Stephen. In part his emphasis on logic and clarity derived from an abiding love of the eighteenth century; approximately half of the 378 articles that he wrote for the *Dictionary of National Biography* (DNB), the massive reference work for which he more than any other individual was responsible, dealt with literary figures of that period. Of Leslie Stephen's views on the nature of biography, and on the responsibilities of a biographer, I shall have much to say, for the relationship between a man's life and the literature that he created was Stephen's paramount concern for more than four decades.

In a lecture given before the members of the Students' Association of St Andrews on 26 March 1887 Stephen declared,

> The true object of the study of a man's writings is, according to my definition, to make a personal friend of the author. You have not studied him thoroughly till you know the very trick of his speech, the turn of his thoughts, the characteristic peculiarities of his sentiments, of his imagery, of his mode of contemplating the world or human life . . . . [1]

Addison may have ridiculed the reader who wanted to know whether his authors were short or tall, black or fair; but Stephen did not feel that he really knew an author till he almost believed that he should recognise him if he met him at a railway station.[2] He admired Walter Bagehot's attempt to discover the human being behind the books: 'It is this interest in character, the comparative indifference to the technical qualities of books, which he values as bringing us into relations with living human beings, that gives a special quality to Bagehot's work.'[3] Much as he disliked Laurence Sterne the man, he so loved *Tristram Shandy* that he found ways of evading his own categorical imperative: 'I confess that I at any rate love a book pretty much in proportion as it makes me love the author.'[4]

The range of Stephen's interests is astonishingly wide. It covers mountain-climbing, travel, philology, philosophy, religion, the American Civil War, and 'social rights and duties' (the title of a two-volume collection of addresses to various ethical societies); but from the beginning his interests were primarily literary. Those interests often expanded to consider a large number of the areas of human thought and endeavour treated by literary texts (the sociology of literature).

It is not my intention, therefore, to seek to 'explain' Stephen. His essays were full, clear explanations of the lure that serious literary texts cast over his imagination. Stephen often trod familiar ground, repeated his critical theses, enjoyed returning to old favourites (Boswell's *Johnson*, read and almost memorised when he was young, supplies for his essays as many quotations as Shakespeare) and in general avoided writing about books or authors he disliked. (It is not often given to critics, this gift of finding room and time only to consider one's enthusiasms.)

It seems appropriate to relate to Stephen's own life the observations made briefly in his article 'Autobiography', and more extensively in an article entitled 'Gibbon's Autobiography', observations noting the delicious congruity of the fit between the circumstances of Gibbon's early life and his resolve to write the one history for which he was qualified. Gibbon assessed correctly what he could do, and what indeed his opportunities enabled him to do. As Stephen noted, 'Gibbon had the additional good fortune that even his distractions seem to have been useful'.[5] What were some of these distractions? Gibbon seems to have occupied middle ground so far as wealth was concerned; he was not a denizen of Grub Street (what denizen of that cheerless region would have had the necessary time to reflect on the significance of his materials, or to acquire the languages essential to the unlocking of texts?); his grandfather, ruined by the South Sea speculation, and his father, unable to retrieve the family fortune, prevented him from swimming in luxury. He was delicate in health, which prevented him from indulging in boxing and cricket; perforce he read. For others his age, neglect and 'the incapacity of his schoolmasters' might have proved fatal; for himself, these elements turned out to be salutary; they helped him to develop latent abilities. 'It gives one a pang to think of the probable fate of a modern Gibbon', Stephen wrote more than a

century after Gibbon's aborted formal education. 'Even ill-health
would hardly save him from the clutches of the crammer; or prevent
so promising a victim from being forced upon the reflection that a
knowledge of Turks and Tartars would not pay in a competitive
examination.'[6] Oxford, with its bias for sweetly doing nothing,
could not have turned Gibbon into a model pedant – and did not
try. Gibbon learned neither to cherish a 'decaying Jacobitism in
comfortable, common rooms', nor to sink into what he called 'the fat
slumbers of the Church'.[7]

As for his religious conversion, Stephen understood that it was
unlikely that a single argument, which had brought Gibbon into the
Catholic religion, could last as long as a conversion based upon
aesthetic appeal or surfeit with other religions and ways of life.
Gibbon's attraction to Catholicism was based, in large part, on a
conviction that the Protestant view of things – the Catholic Church
had once owned an authority based on miraculous powers, but had
lost it 'at some date which it was rather difficult to fix'[8] – was
logically unconvincing. Gibbon showed by the nature of his
conversion his faith in the continuity of history, and by the brevity of
the same conversion his willingness to consider anew the grounds of
any belief, including his own.

The exile of Edward Gibbon to Lausanne was the best possible
thing that his father could have done for the embryonic historian,
for he was thus removed from the sybaritic and lazy temptations of
Oxford as well as from the errors of Rome. He read philosophy; he
met Voltaire; and, moving among the circles of cultivated Swiss and
French intellectuals, he became cosmopolitan in the best sense. He
was 'initiated into the freemasonry of the most enlightened circles of
Europe'.[9] His passion for classical literature was uninhibited by any
narrow set of dogmas. He prepared abstracts, and considered in
advance what benefits he might derive from the author of any new
book he might wish to read. He readied himself for an Italian
journey by writing his own handbook, based upon classical texts
dealing with the geography of the land. It was of enormous benefit
to himself to begin casting 'a long paragraph in a single mould',
preplanning its length and cadences before writing down a single
word. 'Most of us, I fear,' wrote Stephen with a sigh, 'think that we
have done enough when we begin a single sentence with an
approximate guess at the way of getting out of it.'[10] The man who
composes by paragraphs will also frame his chapters with a view to
their position in an organic whole.

Nor was Gibbon allowed to drift down the path of solitariness, to indulge for long in the pleasures of scholarship, of books read in the study that bore no visible connection to real events and current history. Gibbon's passion for Mlle Curchod entangled him with real life. 'She was beautiful and intelligent enough to rouse Gibbon to an apparently genuine devotion; and yet as she was a foreigner, without a penny, it was quite clear that the elder Gibbon would never take her for a daughter-in-law.'[11] We are all familiar with the notorious formulation wherein Gibbon 'sighed as a lover and obeyed as a son'. If we do not agree with Rousseau, who denounced Gibbon as unworthy of her, as a man who could only have made her 'rich and miserable' in England, we still can detect something less than heroic in Gibbon's willingness to renounce the flame of his youth. 'Perhaps Gibbon was not of the finest human clay', Stephen summarised his view of this somewhat untidy episode, 'but the problem, I repeat, was not how to make a perfect man, but how to make a great historian.'[12] Gibbon could not have done what he needed to do, what he was born to do, if he had become entangled in the financial demands inherent in the married condition. He might have accepted an appointment in the Excise (the thought of doing so crossed his mind); he might have become a five-day-a-week official. He was little suited to enact the role of Romeo. The net gain for the chronicler of Justinian and Athanasius more than compensated for his tepid depictions of the erotic impulse in the *History*. As he wrote to his father soon afterwards, no longer would he be distracted by romantic follies.[13]

Other elements contributed to his becoming an historian rather than anything else: his experience in the Hampshire grenadiers ('of some use', as Gibbon complacently recorded in his *Autobiography*, 'to the historian of the Roman Empire'), his political career ('I went into Parliament without patriotism and without ambition, and all my views tended to the convenient and respectable place of a lord of trade'), and his common-sense views on contemporary issues such as those of the corruption of government ministers, the American War, and the foundation of the British Empire in the East. His views accepted the unlikelihood of his personal intervention making any difference; to a later generation they smacked unpleasantly of cynicism. Stephen understood well the ways in which disinterested considerations of current history were compatible with a longer view of the 'vast drama of human history on the largest scale',[14] and argued that for Gibbon to have appreciated (and to have acted on the basis of) such ways 'would in his time have required almost superhuman attributes'.[15] Nor was Stephen regretful that Gibbon failed to take more positive stands on pressing human and social issues of the late eighteenth century, or that, midway through his *History*, he failed to secure a bureaucrat's post that would have constituted a 'semi-suicide'.[16]

It is strange to read, in Stephen's resolutely modern and quizzical prose, these references to 'fate' in the sense that any man of the fourteenth century – Chaucer or Langland, say – would have understood. But Stephen admired the manner in which Gibbon, aiming at less than the highest mark, managed so unerringly to hit the bull's-eye. Gibbon, fitted for his task, was first turned out 'of the quiet grooves down which he might have spun to obscurity',[17] and then felt the goad applied to him – judiciously – 'whenever he tried to bolt from the predestined course'.[18] Fate was responsible for both kinds of action. Gibbon, 'with singular felicity', came 'at the exact moment and found the exact task to give full play to his powers'. Again and again Stephen reverts to the inevitability of Gibbon's playing the role he did, not only because the ironic stance was the only one suitable to an historian who found himself unable to believe in 'a sudden revelation of Reason' or 'the advent of a new millennium', but because he saw as his obligation the delineation of how the puppets of history had evolved. He left to later generations of historians attempts to show 'the hidden strings that moved them'. 'Happily for us,' Stephen concluded his essay of 1897, 'the man came when he was wanted, and just such as he was wanted . . . . It is only when the right player comes, and the right cards are judiciously dealt to him by fortune, that the great successes can be accomplished.'[19]

Fortune, fate . . . . It may be that Noel Annan, in his biography of Stephen, exaggerates the importance of his subject's having been born into an aristocracy of intellect who, 'pre-occupied with the intellect', often 'respond uncertainly to beauty'.[20] A man is to be judged by his mental and moral attributes, according to those who belong to this aristocracy, rather than by his birth or his wealth. The implication that birth and wealth become, if not actually irrelevant, uninteresting, would hardly be borne out by closer examination of the texts or the conversation of the members of this class. Nevertheless, Annan's argument hits dead centre when the significance of the Clapham Sect – those Evangelicals who fought for humanitarian causes and contributed generously to philanthropic causes – is stressed.[21] Stephen's father belonged to the sect. James Stephen was an MP who enjoyed close relations with William Wilberforce before the latter became his brother-in-law; he fought furiously on behalf of the slaves. While labouring as a civil servant, he created images of rectitude, knowledge and power that his son could never forget. He worked hard, and exhibited ability, insight and conscience; as a role-model he was formidable. Suspicious of pleasure, decorous in behaviour, and reluctant to expose his emotions to a world assumed from the outset to be prurient in its interests, Sir James deliberately chose the company of fellow intellectuals rather than the society of Holland House.

What Leslie Stephen owed to his father, therefore, is a keen awareness of duty to a profession and to a code of behaviour, and a distaste for fools that manifested itself in a deliberate turning-aside rather than any head-on confrontation. If, as has been maintained by more than one critic (for example, Desmond MacCarthy in his notorious Leslie Stephen lecture of 1937), Stephen was so attracted to puritan ideals, domestic affection and moral judgements that his criticism lacked balance, we can nevertheless appreciate the inevitability of this imbalance. But those demanding more fire in Leslie Stephen's belly have never satisfactorily defined the direction from which the spark for that fire should have come. Surely not from Stephen's years at Eton, which exposed him, as a dayboy, to the disastrous bullying of his classmates. Leslie Stephen, interested in literature, and often present during the serious conversations of his father with fellow intellectuals, became – at school – the victim of raggings like those described by Thomas Hughes, and the scorned butt of brutal bullying by adolescents who would have readily claimed Thwackum for one of their own. The most important fact of Stephen's Eton experience had to do with the slovenliness of the education provided within its walls: no mathematics, a dilatory supervision of reading in the classics, no modern language, an unreformed curriculum. Fitzjames, Leslie's brother, hated it, and on his final day ripped off his white tie and trampled it into the mud. Leslie, in later years, could not find it in his heart to forgive, as Fitzjames did; unlike Fitzjames, he sent his sons elsewhere (to Clifton and Westminister), and entertained no affection for public schools in general, and little for Eton in particular. Eton, in brief, had forced Leslie Stephen back into his home for the intellectual training and sustenance that he needed, as in the acquisition of French.

Like Gibbon, whose stages of life seemed to follow a fortuitous sequence that ultimately proved preordained, Leslie Stephen's life moved next to Cambridge, and to the college of his father, Trinity Hall. It may be, as Sir James feared, that the rigours of an honours degree at Trinity College would have proved too daunting to one in frail health, as Leslie, up to 1850, had seemed to be. But the boy's health improved with extraordinary rapidity as he rose to the challenge of competing for a first or second Wrangler. In a class of over-achievers he earned after ten terms the twentieth place in the list of Wranglers, with mathematics as his specialty. The next step, exquisitely right for the kind of decision that ultimately had to be made, required him to take holy orders for the Fellowship at Trinity Hall to which he had been elected. For a young man with a strange sense of scruples, the sense of being in orders exerted a huge effect on his efforts to find himself, or, more precisely speaking, to define his own gifts as distinct from those of his brilliant elder brother Fitzjames.

Detesting physical weakness, in part because it had rendered him as vulnerable to sadists at Eton, Leslie Stephen became a dedicated athlete at Cambridge, a rower who rose to the second boat and a famous rowing-coach, one of the most famous walkers of the nineteenth century, and a runner who could do the mile in 5 minutes 4 seconds and two miles in 10 minutes 54 seconds. The consequences of this astonishing transformation of a weakling – transformed by will-power and the sense that prizes within the university system were worth competing for – were unforeseeable, but extremely important in shifting the compass-needle of Stephen's life. For his love of the river, his cultivation of rowing-men and of conversation on athletic subjects, meant that intellectual subjects were placed to one side; not to be forgotten, to be sure, but they had a place and an appropriate time; and so bumptious a sportsman did Stephen become, going so far as to write the college boating-song, that the Apostles rejected him.

Perhaps being passed over was surprising, for Fitzjames and some of his friends belonged, and he had made no secret of his aspiration to membership. But, if he had become an Apostle, his athletic appetite would surely have lessened; more important than a premature shift in the nature of his active pursuits, he would again have been cast in the shadow of Fitzjames. The *Moirai* who conspired against him were marking out the path down which he might most usefully travel. Moreover, Stephen's attempt to win for mathematics undergraduates (the poll-men) necessary and sensible changes in the curriculum ran into exactly the kind of stubborn conservatism that could convince him his career lay not in increasingly eccentric donnishness, but in another field of endeavour entirely. His reforms, proposed twenty years before their time, failed to persuade the university to open a career to talent, and even a series of four articles, written for *Fraser's* (1868–71), made little headway. Stephen's insistence on the need for a learned class of dons expressed not only his strong sense of irritation at the lack of one in his time at Cambridge, but a deeply felt, if still somewhat inchoate, need for better intellectual companionship than that which he enjoyed in mid century. Even Henry Fawcett, who led a circle of congenial conversationalists at Trinity Hall and became one of Stephen's closest friends, did not know enough or read enough to satisfy Stephen's hunger for mastering philosophy, or for establishing Christianity upon a more rational footing.

The decision to take holy orders had more than one motivation; his lack of interest in the law and his desire to achieve financial independence from his family were powerful considerations. The spiritual crisis of his life followed shortly after 1859, when he took priestly orders. By mid 1862, unable to do his duties at chapel, he resigned; a little more than two years later, he left his college and university. London, and the life of a man of letters, awaited.

F. W. Maitland, in *The Life and Letters of Leslie Stephen* (1906), has provided the sequel to this story of a resignation caused by the stirrings of conscience. The famous anecdote wherein Stephen invited Thomas Hardy to witness his formal renunciation of holy orders stresses the drama of that scene. Stephen was wearing a dressing-gown over his clothes, and, by lamplight, resembled nothing so much as a Victorian sage, which of course he was in the process of becoming. Stephen was simply formalising what he had long believed: that his concept of an intelligent man's religion was inconsistent with the responsibilities of a parson. A Broad Churchman who repudiated dogma could not retain his position as a representative of that institution. As a matter of record, the religious tests that required Fellows to be Anglicans had been repealed in 1871; Stephen's resignation, in 1864, of his Fellowship, bursarship and stewardship was the critical step; and the renunciation of holy orders late at night in the spring of 1875 provided the coda to a musical movement that had been composed, and largely completed, years before.[22]

The point of this recapitulation of Stephen's career prior to his becoming a contributor to the *Saturday Review* and the *Pall Mall Gazette* has been to show the exquisite rightness of the choices made between alternatives, time after time, by a young man who could not help seeing himself, for a long time, as a man of intelligence with changing and unfocused objectives. Being a day student at Eton (a choice, to be sure, that he had not made for himself) meant that the influence of his father as the main director of his formative years remained strong. At Cambridge he went out for precisely the right kind of rigorous training – in mathematics – that facilitated his later grasp of logical development in philosophical argument as well as the plots of novels. His passion for athletics, walking and mountain-climbing meant that his later interests in literature would be broad-minded, and masculine in the best sense. His deep involvement in university affairs underlined his heartfelt conviction that English character, trained by the university system, could be – indeed, was – superior to that of any other nation. Though there are limitations to the beefsteak-and-ale view, it was essential to Stephen's later love-affair with the eighteenth century, and to his abiding affection for hard-headed, no-nonsense clubmen such as Dr Johnson. And the decade-long dalliance with formal Christianity, ending by 1865, enabled him to judge the crises of conscience experienced by others with a becoming sense of charity, and a deeper understanding than he would otherwise have had.

No survey of Stephen's life can omit his years as an editor of the *Cornhill Magazine* (1871–82). His sound advice to Hardy – to avoid reading the critics, and to spend his time reading the writers with ideas who 'don't prescribe rules' – is not as clearly remembered as it might be, perhaps because Hardy, preternaturally sensitive to adverse criticism, gave up the writing of novels soon after the publication of *Jude the Obscure* (1895) on the grounds that he would be a fool to stand up and be shot at; in other words, he ignored Stephen's advice, and continued to read the critics. But Stephen's advice was sensible in terms of Hardy's temperament, which needed tender care, and for its time and place. When Stephen noted that the heroine of *The Trumpet-Major* wed the wrong man, Hardy's response was that 'they mostly did'. But Stephen capped him: 'Not in magazines.'[23] The anecdote reminds us of the editorial policies which Stephen pursued in order not to offend the upper middle-class readers of the *Cornhill*; those policies were sexually decorous, frequently sentimental, always English, upbeat in their philosophy (to an extent that may have dismayed the serious thinking side of Stephen), and stolidly unwilling to move with the times. Within a decade Stephen managed, through his over-reliance on formulaic elements such as a certain kind of serialised novel, to halve the circulation of the *Cornhill*, from 25,000 to 12,000.

Nevertheless, it would be grievously unfair if we were to leave it at this. In *Some Early Impressions*, and in such essays as 'The Evolution of Editors', Stephen fought back against the notion, held by many authors, that an editor was 'a person whose mission is the suppression of rising genius', or a traitor who had left the ranks of authors to help 'their natural enemy, the publisher'. Stephen, like serious-minded editors everywhere, was 'always in a state of eagerness for the discovery of the coming man (or woman)', and, though he never found in his pile of manuscripts a new *Jane Eyre* or *Scenes of Clerical Life*, he did not *know* that he had ever rejected an angel unawares. One of Stephen's favourite quotations, Charles II's description of a preacher as a man whose 'nonsense' suited the nonsense of his audience, was employed to defend the proposition that most of the time a book succeeded because it deserved success. 'A critic has no business to assume that taste is bad because he does not share it. His business is to accept the fact and try to discover the qualities to which it is due.'[24] Stephen secured literary materials from Matthew Arnold, John Addington Symonds, Robert Louis Stevenson and Henry James, among many others of distinction; he encouraged them with shrewd and pragmatic advice about what was suitable for the pages of the *Cornhill*; and, though Arnold had to take his essays elsewhere after a time ('He wished to discourse upon topics to which we had to give a wide berth'), Stephen retained his friendship, as, indeed, he did that of Hardy, whose more daring passages he had routinely questioned or excised.

Still, like an actor who builds in snow while the sun is shining, the achievements of an editor lie buried, and largely unacknowledged, in the pages of a bound periodical seldom, if ever, taken down from the shelf. A more important assignment now became Stephen's responsibility. Sidney Lee's contributions to the *DNB* began while he was performing the functions of an assistant editor, but Leslie Stephen planned and organised the massive reference work. He got under way the publication of four volumes per year, and edited volumes I–XXVI. Lee continued on for the remaining thity-seven volumes, plus the supplements (1901, 1912). Stephen wrote only a fraction of the total of 29,120 articles; there were, after all, 654 contributions. The real question is what Stephen conceived the responsibilities of a biographer – a national biographer – to be.

In the characteristically diffident article 'National Biography', contributed to the *National Review* (1896),[25] Stephen made a number of significant observations about the role of the modern historian. Looking back nostalgically to the age of Hume, when a writer might pretend to a knowledge of all the history between the age of Julius Caesar and that of Henry VIII (and might pen his chronicle with some confidence that his sources would not soon multiply), Stephen expressed dismay at the manner in which 'innumerable sources of knowledge have been opened'.[26] 'A historian who now does his work conscientiously has to take about the same time to narrate events as the events themselves occupied in happening':[27] a remark that does a great deal to clarify the reasons why Macaulay's history of England slowed to a dogtrot pace as it approached the seventeenth and eighteenth centuries. One had only to enumerate the new sources in addition to the chronicles, and the summarisers of the chronicles, that now terrorised conscientious historians: 'ancient charters, official records of legal proceedings, manor rolls, and the archives of towns', the findings of local historians, calendars of State papers, despatches of ambassadors (they 'lie in vast masses at Simancas and Venice and the Vatican'), the Historical Manuscripts Commission, the library of the British Museum. Small wonder, then, that a nervous historian might suspect that 'no fact which has happened within the last few centuries has been so thoroughly hidden that we can be quite sure that it is irrecoverable'.[28]

One might retort that, after all, the duties of an historian are not those of a biographer, and that Stephen exaggerates the anguish of his tasks. The biographer has the lesser chore; he surveys the life of a man (or woman), whose life records are fewer in number, and are available within a smaller compass, are more easily retrieved and consulted, than those of an institution or a nation. But Stephen resisted this kind of demeaning of his life's work.

> History is of course related to biography inasmuch as most events are connected with some particular person. Even the most philosophical of historians cannot describe the Norman Conquest without reference to William and to Harold. And, on the other side, every individual life is to some extent an indication of the historical conditions of his time. The most retired recluse is the

product at least of his parents and his schooling, and is affected by contemporary thought.[29]

A biographer may ignore much of the available evidence; but an historian may also be ignorant of vital cross-connections. The biographer must reduce to order the disparate materials of his chosen subject; no less than the historian he must make sense of *disjecta membra*; he must beware of 'rhetoric or disquisition in criticism'. Stephen adds, 'Condensation is not only the cardinal virtue of his style, but the virtue to which all others must be sacrificed. He must be content sometimes to toil for hours with the single result of having to hold his tongue.'[30] Fine judgement is required before one can even write that nothing is known of a man's birth or parentage; the fact may be true, but it is not self-evident or obviously redundant; and one 'might have to consult a whole series of books before discovering even that negative fact'.[31] Stephen regretted that he often had to condense a 'charming anecdote'. Facts have to tell their own story. The writer of articles for the *DNB* 'is not to pronounce a panegyric upon heroism, but he ought so to arrange his narrative that the reader may be irresistibly led to say bravo!'[32]

In essence, the task of a biographer is to condense without squeezing out the real interest. Often he must keep his most important reflections to himself. If it seems absurd to underscore the truism that all facts are not equally important (some are cardinal, some inessential and antiquarian), one must keep in mind the observation that Stephen was confronting, for the first time, a number of problems related to a rudimentary aesthetic of biography. Toward the end of the nineteenth century, as an interest in defining genres created by a developing passion for extended prose began to grow, the art of biography, like that of the novel, received its first searching consideration from Leslie Stephen. Stephen may have defined, for the first time, what more a biographer could do for his subject beyond reproducing, warts and all, what he saw before him.

It was not as if biographers, beginning with Plutarch, had not practised their art with skill before the latter decades of the nineteenth century. But the prerequisites of objectivity, an ability to condense, and the widest possible knowledge of a great variety of disciplines and fields of knowledge had never been set down with such precision or insistence before Stephen's time. Moreover,

Stephen, well aware that he was breaking with the tradition whereby biography was taken to mean the life of a great man, one who stamped his personality on history by means of memorable actions, saw clearly that the *DNB*, for the sake of usefulness as well a's completeness, had to review the lives of less than unanimously acclaimed great men and women.

> There is also an immense number of second-rate people whose lives are full of suggestion to any intellegent reader. The life in such cases should have the same kind of merit as an epitaph, though under less exacting conditions. The epitaph should give in the smallest possible number of words the very essence of a man's character and of his claims upon the memory of posterity.[33]

If the reader of the *DNB* cultivates the art of skipping ('lying like a trout in a stream snapping up, with the added charm of un-suspectedness, any of the queer little morsels of oddity or pathos that may drift past him'[34]), and collaborates with the writer of the biographical profile by supplying something for himself, he will appreciate the riches spread before him as being the product of an enterprise that was worth undertaking, one that will not soon be exhausted, and that offers – in addition to information and edification – its share of fun.

Stephen did not regard the art of biography as an excuse for glorification, or the choice of subject as an opportunity to moralise. He was not vulgarly familiar with authors, and he traced no easy connections between intelligence or character and the success of a work of literary art. Each case provided its own interest and problems; each writer was an opportunity to consider afresh the mysteries of personality. A biography, whether presented within the compass of a few pages as in a *DNB* essay or over the full expanse of a volume prepared for the English Men of Letters series, was in at least a small measure a love-letter to the personality of the writer who had given Stephen enjoyable 'hours in a library' (the title of a series of books published by Stephen, finally reprinted as four volumes in 1907). In an age of psychobiographies that explore 'darker secrets' and of debunking studies that diminish a writer's achievement to an often uninteresting level, Stephen's honest admiration of achievement, and of the human being who had produced it, is worth remembering.

Emerson, with his all-too-facile optimism and his American

innocence, would appear, at first blush, to be a dullish subject for a writer who, by his mid twenties, had mastered the main currents of English philosophy, and who, in 1861, became one of the first examiners in the Moral Science Tripos (Stephen was twenty-eight at the time). Beyond his sympathetic response to the fine rapture which sings through much of Emerson's prose, Stephen found of particular interest Emerson's recommendation, in a lecture upon books, of a number of writers who stressed biography as providing an insight into character: Plutarch, whose *Lives* and *Morals* 'should be in the smallest library';[35] the confessions and autobiographies of Augustine, Benvenuto Cellini and Rousseau; the table talks of Luther, Selden and Coleridge; books of anecdotes; and, among historians, Hume, Goldsmith and Gibbon.

> History represents merely the background in which the great lives are set; and what you should really want is to be brought into contact with inspiring minds, not to get up dates and external facts. Emerson is weak in criticism, if the critic is to give a judicial estimate of a man's proper position in the development of poetry or philosophy; but he can say most clearly and forcibly what is the message which any great writer has delivered to him personally.[36]

Stephen, admitting the right of the poor 'Lockish' or 'average common-sense mortal' to be bewildered by the 'mere theosophical moonshine' of much of Emerson's writing, added that this emphasis on biography shows how we 'may approach one secret of reading Emerson himself'.[37]

One of the more extended comments on the values of biography may be found in an article written for the *National Review* (1899)[38] upon the occasion of the publication of the Browning correspondence. The claims of men of genius to the right of posthumous privacy were being challenged by such 'biographies' as Froude's *Carlyle*, a work which dismayed those who loved the Victorian sage and hardened the prejudices of those who did not. Stephen might not have agreed with the legal position that it is impossible to libel the dead. Even so, he found disturbing the doctrine that the 'many-headed beast'[39] had no legitimate interest in discovering after a man's death what he would have 'jealously guarded from publicity in his lifetime'. Who would willingly have surrendered the discovery that, after all, 'old Johnson's love for his Tetty' humanised the

Doctor, and informed an ignorant generation of 'the sweetest element of his character'?[40] The position of Stephen is clear enough. But the poet's washing-bills and the early drafts of great works[41] are interesting only in so far as they illuminate character, and illustrate 'the concentrated personal essence of the mind'. A biographer is not an antiquary, and not all scraps and fragments are worth sharing with subsequent generations. On truly important matters, more-over, not enough is known, and the means for retrieving from an undocumented past the data that would settle large questions is faulty at best. 'Biography, alas! even the biography of intimate friends involves, as soon as one tries to penetrate the inner life, a great deal of guesswork', Stephen wrote in an essay on John Donne. 'How are we, judging from fragmentary records and ambiguous utterances and rose-coloured sophistications, at a distance of some three centuries, to speak with any confidence?'[42]

Stephen was impressed by the newness of the interest shown by readers of his own age in the memorabilia of a man's life. He was struck, for example, by the way in which John Milton's perform-ance as a poet was judged, in his own time and for a full two centuries after, by the standards previously applied to Homer and Virgil. The older critics, Stephen wrote, made no more reference to Milton's personality than to Homer's. 'Biography had not formed an alliance with criticism. Though Johnson's admirable *Lives* marked the growing importance of biographical data, he still keeps the two subjects apart.'[43] (Stephen's essay, entitled 'New Lights on Milton', used as its point of departure the appearance of books by Walter Raleigh and Robert Bridges, as well as three new editions of Milton's poems.)

By this reasoning a biography is always at one remove from the autobiography; even the lies which an author of an autobiography employs to disguise his past become revelations of character. 'Nobody ever wrote a dull autobiography', he declared unequivo-cally in the opening sentence of an essay written for the *Cornhill Magazine* (1881). 'If one may make such a bull, the very dulness would be interesting.'[44] At its best, autobiography is more than a book written about a subject in which the author is 'keenly interested', more than about a topic on which the author is the highest living authority. Rousseau and John Stuart Mill are only two of the authors who, compelled by an inner longing to confide in someone, anyone, have 'laid bare to us the working of their souls in the severest spiritual crisis'. Some writers of autobiography, such as

Augustine and Bunyan, are more concerned with great religious and philosophical questions than with their own individual problems. *Grace Abounding*, for example, 'was worth writing' because Bunyan's heart, 'like the allegorical Mansoul, had been the scene of one incident in the everlasting struggle between the powers of light and darkness, not because the scene had any independent interest of its own'.[45]

Stephen's life was a heroic attempt to define the narrow limits of human knowledge, and to achieve wisdom; but, as he wrote in his consideration of Bunyan's merits to later generations, 'the greatest [man] should be penetrated with the strongest conviction of his own insignificance. The higher we rise above the average mass of mankind, the more clearly we should see our own incapacity for acting the part of Providence.'[46] But there is an inevitability about the way in which some great figures, reacting to the flattery that surrounds them, record their life stories as an act of vanity. 'A man who expects that future generations will be profoundly interested in the state of his interior seems to be drawing a heavy bill upon posterity. And yet it is generally honoured.'[47]

It might seem that autobiography, by bringing Stephen closer to the man behind the book than a novel or drama could ever do, would derive its major interest from the drama of the man's life. But the vanity which provokes a man to record his life for the sake of that as yet unborn readership he hopes to claim is related to his general philosophy of life. 'The autobiography takes so much the form of a philosophical sermon on the true principles of conduct, that we quite forget that the preacher is his own text.'[48]

The example chosen to document this point is Mill's *Autobiography*, which, to be sure, revealed much about its author's character, but also provided an exposition of a definite theory of life. Mill's father preached a stern morality, the sole objective of which was to produce happiness; but, if he himself did not believe in happiness, if he regarded human life as 'a poor thing at best after the freshness of youth and unsatisfied curiosity had gone by',[49] feelings could be denounced as a sentimental distraction from the business of living, and one would be well advised to become a reasoning machine, a 'simple logic-mill grinding out the materials supplied by the father and Bentham'.[50] Mill's solution (working for some external end and not meditating upon your own feelings') is too familiar to be repeated here in detail. Nevertheless, Stephen's mention of the importance of philosophy in so distinctively a literary genre as autobiography brings us to the issue responsible for the diminished reputation of Stephen in this century.

For Stephen was maintaining, in numerous contexts and at moments when such declarations were unnecessary, that literature as an aesthetic experience was somehow less worthy, less defensible, than literature seen as related to moral and ethical issues, than literature based upon a philosophical premise. We have heard before the notion that one main interest in reading 'is always the communion with the author'. Stephen's stress on biographical concerns – whether incidental or quite irrelevant to the main purpose of a book – suggests that often he is less concerned with art, with the shaping of form or with the relationship between form and content, with the aesthetic principles that were becoming so critical to a large number of men of letters in the final decades of the century, than with elements of literary works not always uppermost in the minds of their creators. A literature that depends for acceptance on its reader's approval of the man behind the work or of the doctrine held by the writer is being judged on extra-literary principles.

Is literature in itself important enough to Stephen to justify Stephen's choice of vocation? Stephen often enough considers the possibility that it is not. A sensible man, such as Stephen thought himself to be, and such as he portrayed himself to others, is not necessarily the guide we choose for ourselves when wandering through the labyrinths of art; and matters are not improved when Stephen employs repeatedly, and perhaps in a more idiosyncratic sense than is justifiable, the term of 'Cynic' for himself. (For example, he wrote twelve essays for the *Cornhill Magazine* in 1869–70, and signed them 'A Cynic'; Stephen was ridiculing various forms of sentimentality and cant; but the notion that he was cynical and sneering in all his views, self-deprecating and unconvinced of the importance of his reviewing, damaged his reputation for fully a century.)

Stephen did not enjoy some kinds of literature, those written by authors he could not like personally: Walt Whitman ('I am hopelessly unable, for example, to appreciate Walt Whitman. . . . The shortcomings still stick in my throat . . . '[51]); Ossian ('I cannot read him. Nobody can read him'[52]); Matthew Arnold's melancholic heroes, the Obermanns and Amiels of other writers as well as the protagonists of his own poems ('excellent but surely effeminate persons, who taste of the fruit of the Tree of

Knowledge, and finding the taste bitter, go on making wry faces over it all their lives; and, admitting with one party that the old creeds are doomed, assert with the other that all beauty must die with them'[53]); the quarterly reviewers ('a mere combatant in a series of faction fights, puffing friends, and saying to an enemy, "This will never do" '[54]); the second part of Goethe's *Faust* ('intolerably allegorical'[55]); and a discreetly brief list of writers, many of them poets. One inevitably comes to suspect that Stephen's dislike of what he called the 'mere moonshine' element in poetry, an element that bulked large in the poetry of his century, prevented him from writing at length about most of the Romantics, and many of his contemporaries, though the shyness which had afflicted him as a day student at Eton and as an undergraduate in Trinity Hall undoubtedly contributed to his desire not to give needless offence.

He had serious reservations about the right of a critic to legislate. Though he seriously doubted that art had ever been 'perfectly spontaneous', or had ever lacked critics to bother the artist who sang or recited by instinct, he was convinced that Spenser and Shakespeare had thought about the principles of their art as much, or almost as much, as their modern critics. 'But as the noxious animal called a critic becomes rampant', Stephen wrote in an essay on Gray,

> we have a different phase. . . . The distinction seems to be that the critic, as he grows more conceited, not only lays down rules for the guidance of the imaginative impulse, but begins to think himself capable of producing any given effect at pleasure. He has got to the bottom of the whole affair, and can tell you what is the chemical composition of a 'Hamlet', or an 'Agamemnon', or an 'Iliad', and can therefore teach you what materials to select and how to combine them. He can give you a recipe for an epic poem, or for combining the proper mediaeval or classical flavour to your performance . . . .[56]

The only improvement that modern critics offered over the 'noxious animals' of previous ages was a useful emphasis on 'the necessity of an historical study of different literary forms'. Stephen was rendering judgement on Addison's criticism of Milton; Longinus, Aristotle and M Bossu wrote for different audiences in different centuries; surely, Stephen implied, there were many different types of art; surely, too, a critic must study how they evolved before he could argue that they needed to live up to an 'absolutely correct and infallible code of art, applicable in all times and places'.[57] The changeability of genres and artistic interests means, inevitably, the fallibility of a critic who assumes he speaks not merely for his own or for his contemporary audience's taste, but for all posterity. In commenting on Ruskin's critical judgments, which Stephen politely noted were 'certainly not always right', Stephen went on to say, 'No critic can always judge rightly, unless at the cost of being thoroughly commonplace.'[58] Ruskin's discussion of the 'theoretic' faculty or imagination might not pass muster with later psychologists any better than his theory of the beautiful with professors of aesthetics. The message, therefore, was that critics in general would do well to cultivate humility. As Stephen says elsewhere (in an essay on Johnsoniana), a critic who defines his duties as those of finding fault ('shortcomings') will never be guilty of unprofessional conduct, or (horrors!) an unbecoming enthusiasm.[59]

This variety of modesty did not arise from the fact that Stephen had much to be modest about. But what may have endeared the critic of the Victorian Age, who after all was simply repeating the common refrain of his profession, has more than a slightly chilling effect to modern readers. In fairness, Stephen concentrated on his subject-matter rather than on himself as the peculiar sensibility through whose filter any writer's talent had to pass; he did not conceive his duty to be remaking the writer's achievement in terms of what might be suitable for a cultural context decades or even centuries removed from the era in which that writer worked; nor did he cull flowers of selected passages at the expense of their contexts. It is therefore unrewarding, for the most part, to read Stephen hoping to learn more about the whims and biases of the critic; Stephen's eye is usually on the sparrow.

Still, there are moments that one might wish extended. We can gather from an essay on Godwin and Shelley that Stephen despised extremism in all its forms; the comment that Shelley was, 'in one aspect, a typical though a superlative example of a race of human beings, which has, it may be, no fault except the fault of being intolerable',[60] leads inevitably to the conclusion that Shelley, had he not been a poet, would have been 'an insufferable bore'.[61] Shelley had 'a terrible affinity for the race of crotchet-mongers, the people who believe that the world is to be saved out of hand by vegetarianism, or female suffrage, or representation of minorities, the one-sided, one-ideaed, shrill-voiced and irrepressible revo-

lutionists'.[62] Unlike Bagehot, who admired Shakespeare for understanding and sympathising with the stupid and the boring elements
of England's population, Stephen, with a very deep-rooted distaste,
confessed, 'I believe that bores are often the very salt of the earth,
though I confess that the undiluted salt has for me a disagreeable
and acrid flavour.'[63] Moreover, the din arising from the devotees of
some of Shelley's 'pet theories' had become 'much noisier' in
modern times; in much of Shelley's poetry one could hear 'the
apparent echo of much inexpressibly dreary rant which has
deafened us from a thousand platforms'.[64]

Many modern readers agree with Stephen's argument that an
effort to separate the poet from the man 'as though his excellence
were to be measured by a radically different set of tests' is 'either
erroneous or trifling and superficial'.[65] Stephen is simply paying
homage to a view expressed by Carlyle: 'The poet who could merely
sit on a chair and compose stanzas could never make a stanza worth
much. He could not sing the heroic warrior, unless he himself were
an heroic warrior, too.'[66] But the line drawn by Stephen between his
own opinion and that of Carlyle is worth stressing. Carlyle
emphasised conscience as 'not only the supreme but the single
faculty of the soul', and morality as not only a necessary but the sole
condition of all excellence; and an ethical judgement as 'the sole
essence and meaning' of any aesthetic judgement. The view,
Stephen believed, is too harsh; it has 'a certain stamp of Puritanical
narrowness'.[67] The distance measured here may be taken as witness
to a saneness or wholeness of spirit. Although we of the late
twentieth century have no Carlyle-like figure to repudiate in quite
the same way, Stephen's position provides useful documentation
against the view, widely accepted by readers bemused at Virginia
Woolf's portrait of her father as Mr Ramsay in *To the Lighthouse*,
that Stephen could not divorce ethical considerations from aesthetic
judgements.

There is also in Stephen's writings a rueful, rather attractive
willingness to write himself down as someone who failed to make the
most of special occasions, and one who perceives clearly enough the
chasm between personal ambition and worldly achievement. In an
essay on Matthew Arnold, Stephen confessed that he had known
Arnold personally, though he could not honestly say that he could
pass on 'reminiscences'. 'At one of my meetings with him, indeed, I
do remember a remark which was made, and which struck me at the
moment as singularly happy. Unfortunately, it was a remark made

by me and not by him. Nothing, therefore, should induce me to report it . . . .'[68] This honesty carries over to his description of the way in which Tennyson's poems became the centre of an admiring circle of undergraduates at Cambridge. Stephen memorised large swatches of his work: 'It was delightful to catch a young man coming up from the country and indoctrinate him by spouting *Locksley Hall* and the *Lotus Eaters*.'[69] For Stephen, 'poet' in those years turned into a phrase equivalent to 'Tennyson'. He knew then that such enthusiasm, though partly obligatory, was in large measure 'warm and spontaneous'. 'For that one owes a debt of gratitude to the poet not easily to be estimated. It is a blessing to share an enthusiasm . . . .'[70] This could be said without elevating to a height higher than their merits deserved such later poems as *Idylls of the King*. Stopford Brooke's admiration of the *Idylls*, accompanying such hosannas as those heard from Thackeray, Macaulay and Gladstone, was 'cordially reverential'. But Stephen failed to appreciate Tennyson's best-seller, despite his careful study of Brooke's critique.

> Even a knowledge that one ought to be enthusiastic is a different thing from enthusiasm. Not to recognise the wonderful literary skill and the exceeding beauty of many passages would, of course, imply more stupidity than any one would willingly admit; but I am afraid that from the publication of the *Idylls* I had to admit that I was not quite of the inner circle of true worshippers.[71]

That may, of course, be no more than the declaration of independence that a mature man makes after reviewing the fad-following excitements of his adolescence; still, there is wistfulness in the admission.

Nevertheless we seldom find in the essays of literary criticism the vigorous outburst of personal feeling – the admiration for 'the heroes of the river and the cricket-field' of Stephen's youth who are still surrounded by the halo 'who surrounded them in the days when "muscular Christianity" was first preached and the whole duty of man' was said 'to consist in fearing God and walking a thousand miles in a thousand hours',[72] a remark that enlivens the essay 'In Praise of Walking' – and the autobiographical candour that Stephen enjoyed in the writings of other men. We may well ask, therefore, for a review of the legacy that Stephen has left behind over and beyond an abiding sense of earnestness, a conviction that good writing matters, and a pellucid style. The thousand pages or more than he contributed to the *DNB* deliver 'endless judgments in a brief Tacitean manner without a touch of arrogance',[73] as one critic has noted; but one may read steadily for hours, and at a later time recall no more of the personality of the chronicler than that he dislikes excess and uses 'fancy' in much the same derogatory sense as Bagehot (whose hard-headedness he admired). What a reader will remember is judgement, and an appreciation of humane values. Articles on Addison, Burns, Charlotte Brontë, Byron, Carlyle, Coleridge, Defoe, Dickens, Dryden, Fielding, George Eliot, Gibbon, Goldsmith, Hobbes, Johnson, Landor, Macaulay, the two Mills, Milton, Pope, Scott, Swift, Adam Smith, Thackeray, Warburton, Wordsworth and Young remain compactly written models of articles that illustrate the complex relationships between life and art.

We have, too, Stephen's brief but excellent books on George Eliot,[74] Hobbes, Swift, Pope and Johnson, written for the English Men of Letters series; three volumes in a series entitled *Hours in a Library* (1874, 1876 and 1879); a collection, in four volumes, of largely literary essays, *Studies of a Biographer* (1907); some charming works about personal interests (*The Playground of Europe*, 1871, has often been reprinted as a classic mountaineering book, and *Some Early Impressions*, 1924, is perhaps better reading for the information it supplies about Stephen's undergraduate years than *Sketches from Cambridge, by a Don*, 1865); a number of works on philosophy and ethical questions as well as an unexpected historical study of the way in which *The Times* covered the American Civil War (1865); a life of Henry Fawcett, another of his brother Fitzjames, and still another of J. R. Green; editions of J. R. Green's letters and W. K. Clifford's lectures and essays (Sir Frederick Pollock was co-editor of the latter); a three-volume history of the English Utilitarians (1900) that was considered good enough to be worth reprinting, by the London School of Economics, fully half a century later; and approximately two hundred articles, most of them substantial in length and content, still uncollected from their original appearances in the *Alpine Journal*, *Cornhill Magazine*, *Fortnightly Review*, *Fraser's Magazine*, *Macmillan's Magazine*, *Mind*, *National Review*, *Nineteenth Century* and a number of other journals. Even this list does not include all of Stephen's contributions to various books edited by others.

The work by which Stephen is best known, however, is the

collection of Ford Lectures that he prepared for delivery at Oxford
in 1903. Illness prevented him from reading them, and Herbert
Fisher of New College, who read them as his deputy, also reviewed
the proofs for the press. *English Literature and Society in the Eighteenth
Century* (1904) offers, perhaps on a more extended scale than
elsewhere in Stephen's writings, a view of the function of the literary
critic. It is a mistake to say (as some of Stephen's detractors have
said) that Stephen saw no use for the literary critic, a role that he
himself played to perfection. Still, as we have seen, he regarded
literature as a relatively minor activity of the human race,[75] and
criticism, in its turn, as 'a nuisance and a parasitic growth upon
literature'. He saw that writers who preened themselves on being
famous deceived themselves both as to the extent of their fame and
of their influence. 'The reading class is at most times a very small
part of the population. A philosopher, I take it, might think himself
unusually popular if his name were known to a hundredth part of
the population.'[76] And Stephen went on to tell the story of how
Thackeray, at the height of his fame, found that many persons knew
nothing about him, and soberly believed that the author of *Vanity
Fair* was named John Bunyan.[77]

If this is somewhat chilling, Stephen could note, still one more
time, that the development of an historical attitude toward literary
genres and literary works was the most notable improvement in the
craft of criticism during his own century. Older attitudes had been
dogmatic, and often unreasonable; the modern critic (Stephen
considered himself one) 'speaks like the liberal theologian, who sees
in heretical and heathen creeds an approximation to the truth, and
admits that they may have a relative value, and even be the best
fitted for the existing conditions'.[78] A critic now must be inductive,
and begin with the experience of reading a particular text
unblinded by preconceptions handed down from Aristotle's disciples or Voltaire's admirers. He will want to appreciate the
individual talent, the special characteristics of the writer of the text.
But he must not ignore, and could not if he tried, the 'existing stage
of social and intellectual development'. Dante is a distinctive poet;
but a modern student of his work must set it against what he and
others know of the Middle Ages.[79] Tennyson and Browning are
individual poets, but they are also 'organs of a society'. This, in
brief, is a sociological view of literature, which Stephen correctly
regarded as the innovative contribution of Victorian critics. It was
sufficiently flexible that it could balance the value of the ideas of an

age against the worth of the literary vehicle (complete with passions and convictions) within which those ideas were encased. The critic now had to take into account 'the political, social, ecclesiastical, and economical factors, and their complex actions and reactions', before he could be satisfied that he had fully appreciated a particular literary production.

This is not a stridently argued case. To the obvious objection that emphasis on the succession of literary species as part of a grander developing pageant minimises the value and function of genius – Cervantes, Shakespeare, Molière – Stephen responded that the other extreme had already been staked out as a position. 'Carlyle used to tell us in my youth that everything was due to the hero; that the whole course of human history depended on your Cromwell or Frederick.'[80] A reaction had inevitably set in against such hyperbolic rhetoric. 'Our scientific teachers are inclined to reply that no single person had much importance, and that an ideal history could omit all names of individuals.'[81] This view, Stephen reasoned, applied more to history, to the possibility that without Napoleon the French Revolution and the days of the Terror would still have developed along much the same lines, than to literature: 'I see no reason to suppose that if Shakespeare had died prematurely, anybody else would have written *Hamlet*.'[82] Shakespeare gave full utterance to the characteristic ideas of his contemporaries, and exploited the resources of the stage of his time; but we understand him better because, in studying the works of his fellow dramatists, we appreciate more fully the direction in which Shakespeare was travelling. 'Even the greatest man has to live in his own century.' Hence, although we do not define Shakespeare's genius (genius being, by definition, indefinable), 'we can learn something from studying the social and intellectual position of his contemporaries', and the general characteristics of the school to which he belongs – to which any genius belongs – 'may be tolerably intelligible'.

More than a series of truisms, Stephen's main line of argument commends to our consideration a convenient means of differentiating between artistic and scientific progress. In science a truth that has been discovered remains true, 'and may form the nucleus of an independently interesting body of truths'.[83] But in art a special form or a school may arise, flourish and decay, without our being able to say that its successor is superior, or that we have witnessed progress develop as the inevitable consequence of the natural evolution of species. Moreover, although literature and the general social condition of a nation are closely interrelated, great works may be produced in a time of ugly political developments, and inferior literature may be all that writers create in an age of genuine material and moral improvement; simple generalisations will not explain the way in which literature functions. If we understand that literature is a by-product of civilisation (this is part of Stephen's diffidence about claiming too much for the role of the man of letters), we shall not be distressed at the observation that it can never become 'a complete indication of the many forces which are at work, or as an adequate moral barometer of the general moral state'.[84]

Two further considerations, however, are important. The English Renaissance during Elizabeth's reign reached its flowering shortly after the repulse of the Spanish Armada, and ended with Shakespeare's retirement from London, a period of approximately fifteen years. If the Victorian theory of the growth of literary schools is related to a reader's understanding of the political and social context, we are led to generalise on the opening-up of new intellectual horizons, which served as the necessary prerequisite for the kinds of creative activity that marked the end of the sixteenth and the beginning of the seventeenth centuries. The growth of new forms became more possible when the old were seen to be decaying: 'The development of new literary types is discontinuous, and implies a compromise between the two conditions which in literature correspond to conservatism and radicalism.'[85]

Stephen's second point has to do with a change in audience. Any such change seriously affects the content as well as the quality of the literature addressed to its tastes. In Milton's time the readers of serious literature were mainly in London, and belonged to certain classes of society. Shakespeare's theatre, which appealed to all classes, had been genuinely popular. But the accession of James marked 'the time at which the struggle between the court and the popular party was beginning to develop itself',[86] and the Puritans should not be blamed for the decay of the theatre that had already begun when they were the victims rather than the inflictors of persecution (as in the closing of the theatres). The dramatists, in Shakespeare's time, had spoken for the nation; in James's reign, they adhered to their patron, but the old heroic touch had gone, and the Restoration stage 'became simply the melancholy dependent upon the court of Charles II, and faithfully reflected the peculiar morality of the small circle over which it presided'.[87] A particular literary genus, hence, can easily be related to the general national movement. Plays written for the Restoration stage (to put it as simply as possible) were markedly inferior to those of the Elizabethan stage because the national consensus had been shattered, and because the audience had become more narrow in its interests.

Other examples of cultural 'placing' may be cited; indeed, Stephen's essays and reviews attempt, with varying degrees of success, to define sociological parameters affecting most of the writers he is considering. It would be unfortunate, however, if this observation obscured the second lasting contribution that Stephen made to literary criticism – namely, his taking seriously the aesthetics of the novel as a literary genre, and his attempting to define the criteria whereby excellence in the novel might be judged. He did not look further back than Richardson. The romances of the seventeeth century were wildly out of touch with the realities of life, and, though Lady Mary Wortley Montagu and Dr Johnson enjoyed reading some of them, and Chesterfield had to note, for his son's sake, that Calprenède's *Cassandra* had 'become ridiculous', the eighteenth century, almost without recognising it, was ready for the development of a kind of narrative fiction closer to Defoe's realistic stories than to Horace Walpole's *Castle of Otranto*, Clara Reeve's *Old English Baron* and Oliver Goldsmith's *The Vicar of Wakefield*. It is likely that the shift to the novel resulted from the decline of opportunities to write for the stage, partly accelerated by the licensing-system introduced by an Act of Parliament in 1737. Whatever the cause, a new reading public was emerging, one that did not regard theatre-going as its highest priority (some Puritan prejudice was surely at work here); and Richardson, preaching his popular sermons, discovered its identity and catered to its interests. The latter he shared so completely that he could not even recognise the merging of his own identity with that of 'the middle-class cockney'. Richardson 'looked upon free-thinkers with such horror that he will not allow even his worst villains to be religious sceptics; he shares the profound reverence of the shopkeepers for the upper classes who are his customers, and he rewards virtue with a coach and six'.[88] Stephen harboured reservations about Richardson's sentimentalism ('I will confess that the last time I read *Clarissa Harlowe* it affected me with a kind of disgust'[89]), and understood completely the basis of Fielding's disgust: 'Richardson seemed to be a narrow, straitlaced preacher, who could look at human nature only from the conventional point of view, and thought that because he was virtuous there should be no more cakes and ale.'[90] But the genius who moved readers in England, Germany and France to tears, and who became the prime mover in Rousseau's fictions, was not a 'realist' in Stephen's sense: an artist whose vision of the world corresponds to the genuine living convictions of his time. Such an artist will cease to be a realist 'when he deliberately affects beliefs which have lost their vitality and uses the old mythology, for example, as convenient machinery, when it has ceased to have any real hold upon the minds of their contemporaries'.[91] Richardson was such an artist, and Fielding was another kind of artist altogether. Although Stephen regarded Taine as overmechanically applying preconceived theory to the English literary scene, he borrowed from Taine the convenient phrase 'good buffalo' to describe the essence of Fielding's character: 'the big, full-blooded, vigorous mass of roast-beef who will stand no nonsense, and whose contempt for the fanciful and arbitrary tends towards the coarse and materialistic'.[92]

These characterisations of Richardson and Fielding have become standard in our understanding of the eighteenth-century novel. But Stephen was not praising realism at the expense of idealism. The value of Stephen's criticism lay in his ability to see, and to write essays on the basis of a sympathy for, the two directions toward which *all* literary art should be directed. If realism deals with actual life and the genuine beliefs of its time, idealism commands that a novelist should see 'the most essential facts' and utter 'the deepest and most permanent truths in his own dialect'.[93] If we examine closely what emotions and thoughts are, we can see that for both Richardson and Fielding the novels that they write are limited in perspectives. Fielding believed that Locke and Hoadley had 'said the last words in theology and philosophy', and Richardson never understood that there could be any speculation outside the Thirty-Nine Articles.[94] Both men belonged to a class that was 'in many ways worthy and domestically excellent', but they were men of the eighteenth century, and no man, as Stephen has told us elsewhere, can live out of his century, or ahead of it; and they were determined 'not to look too deeply into awkward questions, but to go along sturdily working out its own conceptions and plodding along on well-established lines'.[95]

Stephen's observations on the nineteenth-century novel are equally liberal in their willingness to recognise the right of a creative artist to pursue his or her *donnée*. In commenting on the obvious fact that George Eliot's achievements and reputation had been, to some extent, related to her interests in philosophy, Stephen said, still again, what he had been saying in his critiques of many other novelists:

> Novels should, I take it, be transfigured experience; they should be based upon the direct observation and the genuine emotions which it has inspired: when they are deliberately intended to be a symbolism of any general formula, they become unreal as representative of fact, and unsatisfactory as philosophical exposition. George Eliot's early success and the faults of her later work illustrate, I have said, the right and wrong methods.[96]

Such remarks may seem platitudinous, but they represent a straightforward and reasonably stated verdict, the refutation of which will involve any hostile critic in some ingenious redefining of what a novel should be up to; and they express a view consistent with a large number of other very late Victorian opinions on the relationship between literature and life that were focusing on the novel-genre for the first time.

Though we cannot forget the statement that *Treasure Island* was the one story which Stephen could admire 'without the least qualification or reserve',[97] an admission that Stephen himself labelled a 'confession', we can at least characterise it as an anomalous remark, and append the footnote that Stephen recognised how often Stevenson's fictions involved 'the omission of a great many aspects of life which have been the main pre-occupation of novelists of a different class'. Stephen rarely confessed to an enthusiasm so sweeping, to a pleasure so unalloyed by more somber considerations of the responsibilities of craft. It is striking that Scott, the one novelist to whom Stevenson is compared, emerges as the more serious artist because one of his aims was to illustrate the conflict between feudal ideals and the modern commercial state.[98] Waverley as hero was far less interesting to Scott than Fergus MacIvor, 'the type of a chief modified by modern civilisation'. Story-telling often assumed a subordinate role in lengthy stretches of Scott's novels. But Stevenson was *always* a story-teller, conscious of and indeed obsessed by problems of style (Scott was 'audaciously indifferent' to these problems), and, as Henry James once wrote, the love of youth was the beginning and end of Stevenson's message:[99]

perhaps a stern dictum, and one written before Stevenson had finished his career with *Weir of Hermiston*; but not one that Stephen found himself prepared to contradict.

Scott in some respects provided an object-lesson to later generations, as Stephen wrote in a review of Andrew Lang's biography of J. G. Lockhart (1897).[100] Scott himself was 'an anachronism', and Abbotsford 'a sham'.[101] But Lockhart, Stephen believed, was correct in his assessment of Scott as a novelist (no less than as a man) who passionately desired to carry on the old traditions 'and preserve the ancient virtues of his race'.[102] To a large extent, of course, Stephen shared Scott's simultaneously held love of literature and covert suspicion that literature, a 'harmless amusement', might best be regarded as an 'ornamental appendage'.[103] Still, for Scott, as for all serious novelists, real life is the material of art; the uncultivated express 'higher sentiments' than any found in books; and authors must 'consider everything as moonshine compared with the education of the heart'.[104]

Stephen's essay 'The Late Lord Lytton as Novelist' (1873)[105] summarises a number of views about the mission of the novelist that Stephen expressed in essays on Hawthorne, Kingsley, Charlotte Brontë and Disraeli. Stephen, who appreciated the second-rate nature of Lord Lytton's talent, felt moved to write a qualified encomium. Perhaps bulking as large as any other factor in Lord Lytton's favour was the fact that he toiled hard in the vineyard: 'He was a thoroughly good workman.'[106] Too many writers of mid century had written too much, and written down for the benefit of an audience seeking only amusement; but Lord Lytton respected the intelligence of his public. Still, Stephen hestitated to express 'a distinct opinion'[107] upon *The Last Days of Pompeii*, because, having encountered it as a schoolboy, he retained faith in its excellence while preferring not to return 'in the colder spirit of mature life to the haunts of one's boyhood'. Other productions could be judged more dispassionately. Like Scott, Lord Lytton knew the world, had taken his part in serious business, and was familiar with all the wheels of the great machinery of life. Yet he had designs on his reader, and these were often insufficiently disguised in the raiments of art.

The most palpable defect of his novels is their extreme self-consciousness. The writer is evidently determined that we shall not overlook his claims to be a teacher of mankind. . . . His

1   George Henry Lewes, by Anne Gliddon, 1840

2 Walter Bagehot

3 Richard Holt Hutton

4 Leslie Stephen, by W. Rothenstein

5   Andrew Lang, by H. Furniss

6   George Saintsbury, from a painting by Sir William Nicholson

7   George Saintsbury

8   Edmund Gosse, by J. S. Sargent, 1886

moral is not embodied in his work, but exhibited with all the emphasis of sententious aphorisms. He aims at the Ideal, and very rightly, but the Ideal and the True and the Beautiful need not always be presenting themselves with the pomp of capital letters.[108]

Spontaneity and vigour are the signs of genius; here, however, artifice has replaced art; the plots are too carefully constructed, the scenes too judiciously balanced. *Eugene Aram*, because of its excessive ingenuity of design, is markedly inferior to Godwin's *Caleb Williams*, a novel treating a similar subject, and one about which Stephen wrote admiringly several times.

> We can see how [*Eugene Aram*] is put together. Aram must fall in love with a beautiful young lady, to make his fate more disagreeable. The young lady is contrasted with a sister, after the conventional fashion of Minna and Brenda or the inevitable pair of young women in Fenimore Cooper; and is provided with an admirer to act as rival and counterpoise to Aram. Having got thus far, the plot is worked with infinite dexterity . . . .[109]

Nevertheless, the novel is 'barely readable', though 'no French dramatist could have worked out the problem more neatly'.[110] Stephen is expressing irritation at 'all this ingenious byplay', the large number of irrelevant characters, the poor humour, the woodenness of the main character, the reprchensible habit of apostrophising the heavenly bodies and talking sham philosophy about the true and beautiful.

> The problem is, given a man in intellect and amiable temper, to account for his committing a murder. Lord Lytton's answer would suggest, not that he was driven to desperation by poverty or jealousy or sense of unrequited merit, but that his mind had run to seed owing to an unfortunate habit of talking twaddle, till he had lost all sense of reality and fancied that a few fine words would convert a murder into a noble action. And yet the creator of this mere wooden dummy in philosophical robes takes him for a living human being.[111]

Stephen's tenacious grip on what he conceived to be reality – the psychological plausibility of dialogue and motivation – forced him to reject Lord Lytton's complacent estimate of the merits of *Eugene*

Aram. Nor was Stephen's largely negative verdict devoid of an impish streak of humour:

> Our wonder is, not that such a good man should have had the heart but that such a prig should have had the heart to commit a murder. The extraordinary delight with which he pours out his pinchbeck philosophy upon his father-in-law, and his mistress, and his accomplice, may be venial in a man who has long led a solitary life; but one cannot be seriously annoyed at his execution. Hanging is too good for a man who could address the lady to whom he has just become engaged after this fashion: 'Oh, Madeline! methinks there is nothing under heaven like the feeling which puts us apart from all that agitates and fevers and degrades the herd of men . . . .'[112]

The genius of the novel at its best does not work this way, and Lord Lytton, for all his palpable merits, was no George Eliot (who also had moral and ethical messages to deliver), no Scott (whom Stephen persistently describes as 'manly'), no Stevenson. Trollope wrote, like Lord Lytton, with more method than art, in accordance with a schedule, and without bothering to wait for inspiration; his fictions inevitably suffered. Stephen tells the melancholy anecdote of how, passing time at an inn 'where the literature consisted of waifs and strays from the Tauchnitz reprints', he discovered, much to his chagrin, that a Trollope novel he had taken up with eager anticipation had lost all its charms, and seemed to him 'as insipid as yesterday's newspaper'.[113]

Even so, Trollope at his best wrote swiftly, and with mounting excitement over what his characters, driven by their inner natures, might do. He lived with his characters, and believed in them. His ideal architecture might be prosaic and humble, but he always kept to the probable, and 'his imaginary world was conterminous with that in which he lived'.[114] Trollope, as a consequence, could not create a Maggie Tulliver or a Jane Eyre: such characters were simply beyond his artistic capabilities.[115] Another claim, that the Barsetshire novels were a 'marvel of fidelity', was seriously modified by Stephen's stern correction – namely, that they omitted or attenuated the element of religion. But Trollope's fictions were, in terms of their commonplace subject-matter and their truthful manner of execution, remarkable for what they were, and a fair enough index of the Victorian Age to deserve the respect of subsequent generations. They were not the whole story, by any means; they excised 'all that is energetic, or eccentric, or impulsive, or romantic';[116] and in them 'we see the world as it was, only in a dark mirror which is incapable of reflecting the fairer shades of thought and custom'.[117]

Stephen's aesthetic theory of the novel is, therefore, remarkably flexible, and able to accommodate different kinds of talent, and different messages about the nature of virtue and the ultimate goals of life. He approved of experiment, and believed that the final word about an ideal form had not been written. He acknowledged the power of ordinariness; perhaps more of his criticism deals with the kind of fiction that records its endless minutiae than even he realised; but always he sought for some 'suggestion of the depths below the surface of trivial life' (as he wrote in his chapter on *Scenes of Clerical Life* in the study of George Eliot).[118] He spoke often of the power of attractive characters, those who embodied noble and tender sentiment; and his distaste for the clouding of ignoble deeds with torrents of rhetoric is a constant in his criticism. A concomitant line of argument was that insipidity in itself was no recommendation; a reader could not enjoy reading about a character who was all-pure, all-virtuous; some contamination by (or at least sympathetic understanding of) the baser elements of instinct was essential. He disliked novels that aimed too obviously at impressing him with their own cleverness, and he had little good to say about novels that were disguised allegories. Like Fielding, one of his heroes, he was contemptuous of the artificial and the conventional, and irritated by the sentimentalism which had spoiled so many of the novels of the eighteenth century; but he had more enthusiasms, and made more people interested in wanting to read novels, than his later detractors appreciated.

Perhaps most important of all is his repeated argument that a novelist can convert by example. 'A formal lecturer upon the evils of intolerance', Stephen wrote in his essay on Sterne,

> might argue in a set of treatises upon the light in which such an employment of sacred language would strike the unsophisticated common-sense of a benevolent mind. The imaginative humorist sets before us a delicious picture of two or three concrete human beings, and is then able at one stroke to deliver a blow more telling than the keenest flashes of the dry light of the logical understanding.[119]

His example – the manner in which Trim drops his hat at the peroration of his speech upon Master Bobby's death – illustrates Sterne's art, the endowing of a simple gesture with a radiating eloquence; and Stephen's power as a critic often derives from his ability to cite a telling example for each of his writers. In Charles Kingsley's *Yeast*, a novel for which Stephen entertained little affection, there occurs the moment when a gamekeeper, wounded during a poaching incident, rises in his bed, holds out 'his withered paw with a kind of wild majesty', and shouts, 'There ain't such a head of hares on any manor in the country! And them's the last words of Harry Verney!'[120] This outburst characterises the social disease which has afflicted the peasant community: Verney's pride, such as it is, is the only 'higher feeling' left. Again and again Stephen chooses the right quotation, focuses on the right phrase, and directs our attention to the idiosyncratic excellence of a given scene. Unlike Bagehot, who delighted in the opportunity to cry 'Off with his head!' at failed literature, Stephen much prefers to praise (when he can, in good conscience) the writers who have given him pleasure.

We come, finally, to the most interesting aspect of Stephen's long career, which is related in an odd but crucial way to his sheer productivity. Despite the fact that most of his literary essays are out of print, and over half of them were not collected during his lifetime, the *DNB*, a classic of the biographer's art and a standard for all such works prepared in other lands, will be forever associated with his name. Stephen's influence on his contemporaries and juniors grew primarily from the fact that he was so often correct in his judgement on the virtues and weaknesses of writers. Though not as witty as Bagehot in his assessment of Shakespeare, Stephen's essay seems closer to the truth of the man. *English Literature and Society in the Eighteenth Century* was not only a pioneering clearing-away of rubble, enabling Victorians to see the full dimensions of what the preceding century had accomplished; it remains today the most readable and informative introduction to an age that provided one of England's richest intellectual feasts. In his evaluations of nineteenth-century writers, the emphasis on the human being behind the art is firmly grounded on considerations of form and content. For example, Stephen may announce that Charlotte Brontë is the heroine of all her novels, that Lucy Snowe 'is avowedly her own likeness, and Lucy Snowe differs only by accidents from Jane Eyre; whilst her sister is the heroine of the third novel';[121] but Stephen then goes on to define, with almost scientific care, the nature of the realism to be found in her fictional portrait-painting. He may have thought more highly of Grant Allen and a few others than subsequent generations have done. Still, it is difficult to find in the pages of the many volumes of *Hours in a Library* or *Studies of a Biographer*, or of the periodicals to which he contributed so frequently, literary judgements that have since been overturned or seriously modified, despite the accumulation of data, and despite the devising of new critical methodologies. He wrote with vigour, style and intelligence about the kinds of literature that he enjoyed reading. His critical essays retain to this day their power to interest, and to convince.

5 Andrew Lang

The versatility of the Victorian man of letters has never been more marked than in the case of Andrew Lang. Though Lang himself thought that his primary work lay in the realm of anthropology, many readers, remembering with some gratitude their first acquaintance with the fairy tales that Lang so gracefully retold, can still see in mind's eye the bindings of the volumes in which those stories were printed: *The Blue Fairy Book* (1889), and, as the *New Cambridge Bibliography of English Literature* puts it, 'Further collections under colours': *Red* (1890), *Green* (1892), *Yellow* (1894), *Pink* (1897), *Grey* (1900), *Violet* (1901), *Crimson* (1903), *Brown* (1904), *Orange* (1906), *Olive* (1907) and *Lilac* (1910). He was also responsible for a stirring version of *The Arabian Nights Entertainments* (1898), *The Book of Romance* (1902), and *The Red Romance Book* (1905). These are substantial volumes; but they are chips in the forest of a much larger production record. What would have made the name and fortune of many other writers proved to be a single category of works turned out by one of the busiest, most happily occupied writers in the world of London journalism.

Roger Lancelyn Green, defying Lang's injunction against a biography, has written a most remarkable and graceful life (1946), in which he corrected George Saintsbury's estimate that a 'library' edition of Lang's works would run to two hundred volumes.[1] Green's computation put the total at nearer three hundred, and he noted that, even then, such an edition would omit 'the great amount of Lang's work that is lost to us in the anonymous files of forgotten daily papers'. But the Keeper of Printed Books at the British Museum pointed out to A. Blyth Webster (compiler of the Andrew Lang lectures delivered at the University of St Andrews, 1927–37, and printed by Oxford in 1949) that in the BM Catalogue there were 215 books wholly by Lang, fourteen books written in collaboration, eighteen books translated by Lang, and 105 works edited or with introductions or contributions by Lang.[2] Green's

short-titled bibliography is supplemented by a list of more important uncollected magazine articles; this appendix to his biography
runs for nineteen closely printed pages.[3]

Before concentrating on Lang's literary criticism, which in its
time made reputations and sold books in a way not to be equalled
until the height of Arnold Bennett's reviewing-career, I should like
briefly to review the more scholarly areas of Lang's work. (My
assessments of Lang's mastery of these non-literary areas draw
heavily, of necessity, on statements made by authorities who
delivered the Andrew Lang lectures.) Lang, despite his self-
acknowledged biases and occasional failures to review all the
available evidence, wrote well, and with judicious intelligence, on a
large number of extra-literary fields. His poems on Greek topics
(including *Helen of Troy*, 1882) grew from an abiding interest. *Homer
and the Epic* (1893) was a frontal assault on the notion, made popular
by a school of German scholars, that 'Homer' was a convenient
name for countless poets who had transmitted fragments and
separate poems down through the centuries. Lang, who knew the
early literatures of many lands, was outraged by these disintegrators
of the text, by the insect criticism of Wolf (and, in later decades,
Wilamowitz and Murray); he believed that Homer was a man, an
individual who really had composed his poems, and an artist of the
highest order; and the Wolfian school offended his sense of the
homage due the greatest poet who ever lived. Lang's argument,
daring for its time because it challenged authorities who claimed to
be using scientific method, pointed out, with devastating effect, how
personal and subjective their arguments were. Later, in *Homer and
his Age* (1908) and *The World of Homer* (1910), Lang developed
important arguments on the unity of Homeric culture, the Achaean
nature of that culture (he believed that it originated on the Greek
mainland), the complexity of the character of Achilles, and the
ways in which Homer, rejecting the 'mere folk element', consistently chose the 'noble, heroic, possible and human' modes of
conduct for his two epics.

Alexander Shewan, in his Andrew Lang lecture (1928), concluded that recent scholarship has confirmed Homer's descriptions
of both the geography and topography of the west of Greece. The
Catalogue of the Ships has turned into a 'genuine ancient gazetteer
of Mycenean Greece'.[4] The tablets discovered in a royal Hittite
library connect with Greek prehistory in startling and significant
ways, so that we now believe the Homeric poems to have been (in

the words of Wace) 'an epitome of the last stage of the Minoan and Myceanaean culture'.[5] Shewan concludes that 'everything tends to show that Lang was right in his view of Homer and his age. . . . Those who agree with Lang can await further developments without misgiving, indeed with confidence that, in Pindar's words, the days to come will prove the wisest witnesses.'[6] Part of Lang's legacy is the substantial contribution he made to the translation of the *Odyssey*, worked out with Butcher (1879), and of the *Iliad* in collaboration with Walter Leaf and Ernest Myers (1883), among the most noble (and most widely read) versions in the English language.

Lang was fascinated by the problems of methodology, as his quarrel with the German text-disintegrators indicated. He was disturbed by the way in which these scholars disregarded passages that inconveniently contradicted, or might challenge, their overall readings. He marvelled at their creation of new meaning for words that classical scholars believed they already understood well. He could not agree with the concept of 'Expurgation' (i.e. early poets recorded barbaric customs; later poets eliminated them as much as possible; but 'traces' remained); over a period of centuries – and even the length of time needed for such a process was vaguely fixed by those who advocated as a fact the existence of such a process – it would have proved impossible for a small army of improvers of the text to establish and maintain a tone-consistency. Lang did not appreciate the process whereby guesses were made as to what might have been in Homer's text before the 'expurgations' were made; from his point of view, those suppositions created difficulties where none had existed, and sometimes even ludicrous readings. Lang's cheerful and vigorous counter-attack disposed of battalions of 'Expurgators', 'Harmonisers', and 'Interpolaters'; one need not agree with all his lines of reasoning to see that such an attack had become necessary in the declining years of the century; that if Lang had not written his three books, the Wolfian school – with Gilbert Murray as perhaps its most distinguished English champion – would have enjoyed a much longer reign.

Lang's work on anthropological matters placed a similar emphasis on the evidence: for example, many primitive religions did not promulgate animistic beliefs. He was no iconoclast; he believed in 'Mr Tylor's Science'. But Tylor's stress on animism in *Researches into the Early History of Mankind* (1865), *Primitive Culture*

(1871) and *Anthropology* (1881), seemed excessive, particularly in relation to the Greeks; animism explained much, but not all; and Lang's *The Making of Religion* (1898) introduced a new concept of the High Gods. It continued a line of inquiry that Lang had begun in the early 1860s with his consideration of the way in which myths and fairy tales kept exploiting common elements. Lang was directly opposed to the work of Professor Max Müller, an Oxford philologist who taught, in a dogmatic and influential way, that myths and fairy tales had originated, at some remote time, among the members of an Aryan race dwelling in the Himalayas, and that their dissemination to European cultures was at least partially attributable to the 'disease of language' that had overtaken the human race. Müller also preached a related doctrine, that myths originated from metaphors describing natural phenomena. Lang, dismayed by Müller's concentration on the *Veda* as the basis of his mythological system, began his crusade for a fuller, more enlightened view with 'Mythology and Fairy Tales' (*Fortnightly Review*, May 1873); continued with *Custom and Myth* (1884), *Myth, Ritual and Religion* (1887, rewritten in 1899); introductions to Grimm (1884), *Cupid and Psyche* (1887), Perrault (1888), and Kirk's *Secret Commonwealth of Elves, Fauns and Fairies* (1893); *Magic and Religion* (1901), *Social Origins* (1903), *The Secret of the Totem* (1905) and *Method in the Study of Totemism* (1911). Historians of anthropology believe that Lang won a clear decision in his arguments with Müller. It is less clear that Lang's conviction about the lateness of the appearance of *mana* in human language ('The *mana* business appears to me to be an hypothesis invented after magic was a going concern') really touches the question of the importance of *mana* among primitive peoples. R. R. Marett has suggested, kindly, that Lang's unwillingness to 'wallow more freely in the refuse heaps of prehistoric archaeology'[7] certified his gentlemanly nature, but inhibited his understanding of the 'humble and even sordid past' of religion. Lang investigated the topics of great concern to anthropologists at the turn of the century – the High Gods, animism and *mana* – and attempted to establish a rational basis for our understanding of the origins of man. He quarrelled with James Frazer over the issue of totemism; he thought that classical scholars didn't understand particularly well the significance of the concept of fertility ('Fertility is becoming a match for the Dawn or Mr Casaubon's *Key to All Mythologies* . . . .'[8]); and he sought to define more sharply the aspects of the still-developing discipline that he could handle with authority. In Marett's view, 'One may say that he wore himself out by attempting all things at once.'[9]

Cultural anthropology – the interest taken by scientists in how men adapt to cultural systems at the same time that they reshape those systems to suit their needs – has become far more important in this century than Lang could have anticipated. But Lang repented of his use of the phrase 'High Gods of Low Races' at a fairly early point after the publication of *The Making of Religion*. His respect for the facts, as soon as they might be ascertained, would have kept him in touch with developing trends, and might have shifted his interest from religious polemics (in which, sometimes, it seems that no one wins debating points permanently) to matters more directly intersecting with his literary interests. If he could have made a living out of it – so Lang confessed to Marett – he might have become a great anthropologist. He had the right attitude toward comparative studies. He understood the need for patience and the systematic accumulation of information, the value of languages, the importance of taste and sensibility. He appreciated the human core of the discipline, in a manner and to a degree not always shared by those who studied artifacts.

Lang also accumulated impressive credentials as an historian. These were all the more impressive because they were earned in unravelling a number of knotty, obscure and ancient problems in a way that did not fully satisfy the academic communities of Scotland and England, and that certainly did not reward Lang sufficiently for the time invested. It is possible that Lang conceived of his travails as some sort of repayment to his Scottish heritage, for his historical investigations dealt largely with the past of his beloved nation, and the writing of his works in this line occupied much of his final fifteen years.

What might have happened if Robert Louis Stevenson's health had enabled him to work on the Pelham Papers? (Lang had sent to Samoa copies of portions of these, transcribed at the British Museum, at Stevenson's request.) These excerpts became the basis of a full-scale detective story after Stevenson's death, and after they had been returned to Lang. Stevenson would have completed his romance *Dyce of Ythan*; he might have respected the anonymity of the spy who for more than a century and a half had remained unknown to all save a very small number of Scottish historians (Scott's allusion to the existence of such a spy, in his preface to

Redgauntlet, does not clearly establish whether Scott knew who he was). In Stevenson's letter to Sidney Colvin, dated 9 March 1892, Stevenson's approach to the materials dealing with Prince Charlie's life '*after* the '45' is clearly uninterested in fidelity to the facts. Stevenson would have reintroduced the Master of Ballantrae; the hero would have been 'a melancholy exile', whose wife, a young woman, would have interested the Prince, and there would have been 'the devil to pay'. Perhaps the Master would have killed him in a duel, or at least wounded him, and then the Master would have played *deus ex machina*; and so forth.[10] Lang, understandably, junked all that, and worked away diligently on the problem of who, for six years, had spied upon Prince Charlie within his own camp. He was determined not to expose himself to the criticisms, many of them just, which had been provoked by the publication of the inaccuracies and inadequate research of his history *St Andrews* (1893). He identified the informer – in a way that has not been shaken, or even censured save by those who preferred (in Green's phrase) 'a sentimental silence to a plain statement of unpleasant truths'[11] – as Alastair Macdonell, thirteenth Chief of Glengarry. *Pickle the Spy, or The Incognito of Prince Charles* (1896) was followed by *The Champions of Pickle* (1898). Both works suggested the truth of various unpleasant rumours about Prince Charlie; this truth-saying was further expanded into the biography, prepared for the Goupil Series, *Prince Charles Edward Stuart* (1900); and, although Lang sketched a better image of the Old Chevalier, James III and VIII, than Thackeray had done in *Henry Esmond*, his portrait of the prince's limitations ('He failed utterly, failed before God and man and his own soul . . .') represented an astonishing victory of his own scholar's integrity over nationalistic sentiment. Once more, in *The King over the Water*, written with the collaboration of Alice Shield (1907), Lang took up – for the last time – the character of Prince Charlie. His kindest words were reserved for those who loyally and without question had followed the banner of the feckless Prince. 'We fools', Lang wrote in his concluding paragraph of that work,

esteemed their life madness, and their end to be utter destruction, but they are numbered among the heroes of all time. They stood with great constancy against those that afflicted them, and made no account of their sufferings; and they shone as sparks among the stubble of their sordid, self-seeking age. As gold in the furnace were they proved, and in time there has come respect to them. In

the sight of the unwise they seemed to perish in misery, but they
who were faithful in love now rest in honour, and their names live
for evermore where loyalty and faith are crowned.

To the cause of Scottish historiography Lang contributed his
most substantial work, a four-volume *History of Scotland from the
Roman Occupation to the Suppression of the Last Jacobite Rising* (1900–7).
He had a healthy sense of scepticism about the murky basis for the
legends of Scotland's prehistorical past (lasting until the ninth
century). Without reducing his argument to special pleading, he
assayed the grains of truth in the English claim to sovereignty over
Scottish affairs, and found them few indeed. He was remarkably
frank about the character flaws of the Scottish bishops in the critical
fourteenth century; fascinated by James III as an enigmatic
'princely amateur'; and aware of the dangers implicit in his
challenge to orthodox opinion, a balanced judgement of the
Reformers who fought, and often enough died, for the cause of
Scottish freedom. He published the monographs *The Mystery of
Mary Stuart, James VI and the Gowrie Mystery, John Knox and the
Reformation* and *Mary Stuart*, as well as a number of 'Studies in Secret
History' and 'Historical Mysteries'; the main findings from these he
incorporated into his longer *History*. Of Knox he wrote, with intense
emotion, that the Reformer treated 'Mary of Guise in the spirit of a
thoroughly damnable Society journalist. . . . He had the right end
of the stick, he gave a shove in the right direction, so blindly, so
clumsily, so hypocritically and so antichristianly, so to speak – and
probably a Christian could not have done the job.' He would not
cast Nelson's blind eye upon the sins of either the Reformers or the
Covenanters. They persecuted with too free a hand, too strong a
relish, when provided the opportunity; and Mary Queen of Scots
could not be exonerated before Lang's bar. His *History* resonates
with due acknowledgements of chivalry and generous gesture; he
dared to be interesting, as Robert S. Rait pointed out in his
summation of Lang's qualities as historian.[12] Lang scanted
Scotland's constitutional history prior to the seventeenth century,
loved the manoeuvrings of real men and real women ('our honest
old plots and dirkings'), and presented history as a structured
narrative with strong elements of causation and effect. He was a
story-teller who had little patience with recapitulating the history of
institutions.

It may be, as some historians argued, that his love of an original thesis led him to reverse, with excessive vigour, the conventional opinions on the 'poor old Mr Misfortunate' (the Old Chevalier), or the earlier James II, whom he distrusted, or James VI, whom he actively disliked. If Lang sought for a more sympathetic under-standing of the Stuart contribution to Scottish progress, his delight in presenting evidence hitherto overlooked or misunderstood may have arisen as much from the certainty that he was discomfiting English historians as from the likelihood that he was changing the minds of members of the lay public. He was – one hardly needs the assurance or authority of J. D. Mackie[13] to confirm two strong impressions – master of an art 'which was sometimes forensic rather than historical', and he was 'plainly a partisan as well as a romantic'. But Mackie concluded that Lang was not a mere sentimentalist, and that he 'had a genuine regard for truth'.[14] Lang could be convinced by the evidence: 'That is why, despite his openly admitted prejudices, he takes his place as a great historian.' And Mackie quotes Lang's reply to a bitter critic: 'We are all fallible, but I sincerely believe that we are all honest, doing our best to find out the truth.'[15]

Lang's interest in Joan of Arc, which produced an extraordinary run of essays, fiction, and books over a fifteen-year period (1894 to 1909), is of much the same quality as his interest in the House of Stuart: its concern is with the evidence, but its temper is whole-heartedly romantic because the evidence permitted him to idealise his central figure. Lang's obsession (for such it surely became) originated years before the publication of Anatole France's debunk-ing biography in 1908. He had written several poems about Joan, who had led a Scottish force at Lagny; whose banner had been painted by a Scot; who was accompanied in her campaigns and at her martyrdom by a monk from Dunfermline; who saw only once her own portrait, at the time in the hands of a Scottish archer; and who benefited from the services of two archers ('of the name of Lang, Lain or Laing') about 1507. He wrote a popular novel, *A Monk of Fife* (1896), which purported to tell the full narrative begun by the monk from Dunfermline, a narrative never completed in actual fact.

Lang believed in Joan, and in her powers. He recoiled with dismay from those critics who thought of her life as some kind of charlatan's imposition on a credulous public; and, more specifi-cally, from Anatole France's *Vie de Jeanne d'Arc*, which dismissed her voices as 'evidence' of hallucinatory behaviour, and her trials as the record of the victory of corrupt priests over a manipulated young woman. France, a realist, spoke to an important mood in his reading public. His biography, with its admittedly mordant interpretation of the data, proved immediately, and hugely, popular. But it outraged Lang. Within three months he had written a stirring defence of Joan's honour, *The Maid of France* (1908). It was devastating; France's changes in a new edition of his *Vie* (1909), designed to accommodate somehow the more serious charges, proved useless; within the same year Lang produced another book, *La Vie de Jeanne d'Arc de M Anatole France*, which proved even more deadly with its evidence of irrelevant documentation and misused sources. France had impugned the honour of the Maid, but his work, methodologically suspect, could not be trusted. France saw no mystery in Joan's successes, no miracles, no leadership, no true 'saints'. However, he was not by training an historian. He could not read fifteenth-century French as well as Lang, who, it should be recalled, published his first book (1872), a collection of poems, under the title *Ballads and Lyrics of Old France, with Other Poems*. These translations of Villon, Ronsard and Du Bellay, along with the versions of poems by nineteenth-century Romantics, certified his intimate knowledge of the language and poetry of France. Several later books developed this interest, notably a translation of *Aucassin et Nicolette*. Not for Lang the coolness implicit in his adversary's attempt to 'place' or 'explain' the Maid.

In his most unfair moments Lang thought that the rationalising in France's *Vie* emanated from a deep-grained hostility. But, as Louis Cazamian scrupulously pointed out, France's emotion 'is the glow of an intellect ranging freely over a course of history from which the rank growths of supernatural explanations have been weeded out'.[16] It may be, as Cazamian adds, that France's mood is substantially that of Voltaire and Gibbon, seemingly dry but at bottom suffused by an imaginative ardour, and always bearing impatiently the burden of demonstration and proof.[17] Lang writes roundly, and with feeling; the Maid's career is – in Lang's words – 'the most marvellous episode in our history, and in all histories'; if France will not admit to that because his philosophical detachment prevents him, why, so much the worse for philosophy.

Lang emerged the clear victor in this, as in a number of other historical controversies marking his final years. Anatole France's shoddy handling of the facts prevented his French peers from rallying to his defence, and there existed not only in England but also in France the sense that some vital elements of the story had been omitted; that the Maid's denigrator knew too little of the actual conditions of Domrémy, the birthplace of Joan, and of the importance that inspiration and leadership can have to disheartened warriors; that there was no legitimate way in which the character of 'fraudulent priests' could be inferred from the surviving documents; that psychopathology diminished Joan's achievement, and demeaned the biographer who used it as a key to the visions of Joan.

Had we world enough and time, we might examine a larger number of the controversies into which Lang cheerfully waded. As a fisherman he loved the trout, and deprecated the salmon.[18] As an admirer of the John Gibson Lockhart who had done so much to tell the world about the true character of Scott, Lang felt compelled to defend the Lockhart who had manipulated evidence, excised damaging texts, and slandered the Ballantynes in order to distract attention from the financial manoeuvrings of Scott.[19] He was perhaps basically a Jacobite; as John Buchan once pointed out, his sympathies went to the little against the big, the one against the multitude, the men and women who faced impossible odds: 'the dying Gretir the Strong and Gunnar of Lithend and Hereward the Wake and Bussy d'Amboise; Joan of Arc at the stake, Montrose at the gallows' foot, Lochiel in his lonely loyalty, Gordon at Khartoum'.[20] To argue that Lang was the historian of lost causes overstates the case; but those who achieved victories without peril to both life and immortal soul did not seem to have staying power in his imagination.

One final brouhaha, however, seems, well-nigh a century later, to be worth discussing. The echoes of the controversy have not completely died. *Shakespeare, Bacon, and the Great Unknown* was completed in 1912, and published posthumously. It was dedicated to the Shakespearean scholar Horace Howard Furness; and it is doubtless the most readable of the many works published as part of the catalogue of a half-century of frequently tendentious, silly and unimpressive works. Lang did not dignify his own critical position by claiming for them more than they were worth, either as scholarship or as entertainment. But he was understandably alarmed at the attractiveness of the Baconian hypothesis to otherwise sober and respectable judges such as Lord Beaconsfield, Lord Palmerston, Prince Bismarck and John Bright. (He had already demolished in the *Pall Mall Magazine* of July 1902 the claim of Mrs Gallup that Queen Elizabeth had a stake in the controversy because – according to Mrs Gallup – she was Bacon's mother, and that hence royal blood flowed in the veins of the true author of Shakespeare's plays.) Perhaps of all those who had gathered beneath dubious banners Lang regretted most seeing there Samuel Clemens, who was 'no mean literary critic', an analyst of Dowden's *Life of Shelley*, and a conscientious investigator of the life of Joan of Arc.[21] It was easy enough to observe that both Shakespearean and Baconian 'scholars' were deeply divided against themselves on such questions as the extent of Shakespeare's classical learning; the printing-history of the quartos and the *First Folio*; the basic facts relevant to the Stratford monument; the cryptograms (what they said, or how to decipher them, or even where they might be found); the extent of Bacon's contribution to the plays of Kit Marlowe; Bacon's Rosicrucianism; the possibility that he may have written thirteen plays before 1593; or for that matter whether Bacon might not turn out to be a convenient name for the great unknown Bungay ('I use Bungay as an endearing term for the mysterious being who was the Author if Francis Bacon was not. Friar Bungay was the rival of Friar Bacon . . .'.[22]).

Lang's book is insidiously compelling and a good read, even though a casual reader soon infers that Lang is more concerned with following the argument in any direction it might lead rather than in considering the patience of his audience, or the suitability of such a detailed analysis to the given subject. (Though he complains of the length of George G. Greenwood's *The Shakespeare Problem Restated*, a volume of '503 pp.',[23] his own work runs to 314 pages, and, despite the caution of his widow, contained in a prefatory note, that the work was not corrected even in its first proofs, his lifetime practice was not to cut, but rather to expand as new ideas and new evidence turned up.) It was, of course, impossible to 'consider every argument' or 'traverse every field'. He disclaimed serious knowledge of the philological situation: 'I am all unlearned, and cannot pretend to discuss the language of Shakespeare, any more than I can analyse the language of Homer into proto-Arcadian and Cyprian, and so on.'[24] He did not want to speculate about which parts of which plays were genuinely Shakespearean, and which were not, adding that 'About them different views are held *within* both camps.'[25]

Nevertheless, as a patient man who had learned a great deal from his investigations of the even thornier *Quellen* having to do with

Scottish history, his method was carefully preplanned. He needed to ascertain the degree of truth in the legends and traditions surrounding 'our Will'. To do that, he had first to discover the original sources, 'and the steps by which the tale arrived at its late recorders in print'. Next, he knew that 'each man's view as to the veracity of the story will rest on his sense of probability; and on his bias, his wish to believe or disbelieve'.[26]

Lang found that the evidence as to who Shakespeare was, or what kind of personality he exhibited to his friends, was severely limited by the indisputable fact that in the poet's lifetime literary gossip was not deemed sufficiently important to be recorded save in rare instances. 'The public does not care a straw about the author's name', Lang wrote ruefully, referring to the Edwardian Age, 'unless he be deservedly famous for writing letters to the newspapers on things in general; for his genius as an orator, or in any other extraneous way.'[27] Playgoers in Shakespeare's time cared no more about an author than they did in the first decade of the twentieth century.

Lang preferred whatever positive evidence he could find for the affirmative, rather than the negative evidence from silence which the Baconians found so attractive. Those contemporary with Shakespeare never doubted his existence or his authorship of the plays attributed to him. 'It is incredible to me that his fellow-actors and fellow-playwrights should been deceived, especially when they were such men as Ben Jonson and Tom Heywood.'[28] Why modern lawyers should have been so quick to join the Baconian camp, Lang was unable to guess. But the Baconians did not emerge with their volumes stuffed with polemical demonstration until the years 1856–7. Lang did not absolutely deny the possibility that Bacon wrote two plays a year in addition to all his other activities. But a physical possibility was easier to credit than an intellectual miracle, inasmuch as Bacon's scientific preoccupations were well attested, not to mention his political concerns, his pamphlet-writing, his private time-consuming problems, and his schemes for the reformation of learning. 'To this burden of Atlas', Lang writes in mild amazement, 'the Baconians add the vamping-up of old plays for Shakespeare's company, and the inditing of new plays, poems, and the Sonnets. . . . Talk of miracles as things which do not happen!'[29]

Shakespeare's erudition is best understood in the context of what 'cheap and common books' were available to a young man after his years of formal education had ended. Lang, here as elsewhere, asks for an unjaundiced look at the available evidence. But the question of who wrote Shakespeare's plays was not trivial, even if some were willing to settle for the plays themselves; the answer mattered; and the Baconians, Lang concluded, were indulging in fantastic pedantries. Their guesses were 'contrary to the nature of things'. He himself wished 'to give love and praise and gratitude where they were due; to that Achaean "Father of the rest"; and to "friendly Shakespeare" '.[30]

Shakespeare, Bacon, and the Great Unknown is written with light irony, but the absurdities of Baconian-school logic have never been more devastatingly traced. Lang did not rest with an assessment that some anti-Willians had exhibited traces of senility (their years being so advanced when they became partisans of Bacon), or in other cases betrayed a self-defeating ignorance of history as well as Elizabethan texts; he did not, in other words, burn straw dummies; and Greenwood, his chief example of a Baconian, impressed him as a learned barrister who could judge evidence in an intelligent manner, and who knew more about Elizabethan literature than he himself did. His counter-brief, or rebuttal, was presented with respect, and perhaps was all the more effective because it allowed Greenwood full marks for an essentially negative argument. The book contained much good sense, and more information about the state of turn-of-the-century Shakespearean scholarship, than one might expect.

All of this so far amounts to an elaborate prologue, suggesting that Lang's importance as a literary critic in the late nineteenth century does not derive primarily from the conspicuousness of his column, 'At the Sign of the Ship', which ran in *Longman's Magazine* for two decades (January 1886 to October 1905), and the ubiquitousness of his reviews in almost a dozen periodicals as well as several newspapers. It is not a matter of personality. Though Lang's personal love of literature shines in all he wrote, he seldom titillated his readers with personal revelations, and Roger Lancelyn Green is quite correct in insisting that Lang was one of the 'most reserved of men'.[31] Younger writers who hoped to be noticed in the *Morning Post* or the *Daily News* by a Lang essay could not be assured of his favour, for Lang, with relatively few exceptions, found experiments in contemporary literature distasteful. He distrusted those writers who were preparing the way for modernist perspectives: Henry James, for one; George Moore and almost all the participants in the Celtic Twilight movement; Thomas Hardy (who never forgave

Lang for his review of *Tess* in the *New Review* of February 1892); Max Beerbohm and Theodore Watts-Dunton; and practically all the French naturalists and Russian realists whose works were so controversial, and alive, for serious readers in the last quarter-century of Lang's life. Moreover, Lang suffered from a shyness that gave to those unused to his ways a darker view of his personality than the facts warranted. Perhaps it was best that his bemused attitude toward current letters made his columns seem increasingly like a lament for a Golden Age that would never come again, thus putting off a number of writers who hoped to make his acquaintance, and reducing the strains of social intercourse. It was obvious by mid career that Lang's admiration of the romantic strain in literature not only turned him away from the major work of Zola, Ibsen and Tolstoy as 'full of squalid horrors',[32] as basically humourless, as too depressing for a sensitive critic to contemplate, but enlisted him in the writing of one encomiastic essay after another overpraising the romances of Stanley Weyman, Anthony Hope, S. R. Crockett, Maurice Hewlett, A. E. W. Mason and other writers now long forgotten. Of his attitude toward the greater romantics – Rider Haggard, Robert Louis Stevenson and Rudyard Kipling – more needs to be said; but at this point an admission needs to be made that an important element in Lang's personality responded to the claymores of second-rate romances more sympathetically than their merits deserved.

Lang's scholarship as a student of the classical world, as an anthropologist and folklorist, as an historian of Scottish and French events (often enveloped in a murk that had defied previous generations of historians) and as a well-informed arbiter of literary controversies demonstrated many times over that his understanding of the humanities helped to compensate for a number of deficiencies in taste or personality. This generalisation is valid quite apart from his achievements as redactor of the world's fairy tales, balladist and lyrist, creator of a sizable sports literature, fiction-writer, and author of that extraordinary tale for children, *The Gold of Fairnilee* (1888), which alone might preserve his memory. The most important problem confronting any effort to judge Lang's labours as a literary critic is the fact that he never wrote the major book he should, and could, have written. The energies he expended on literary detection may not have been wasted on frivolous causes, but the one extended effort in this direction – his book on the Baconian controversy – came at the end of his life, and was not, even when rated most generously, an exploration of an issue of burning importance to the creative writers of his generation. Too much of his time was expended on literary trifles; wittily recounted, to be sure, but on a lower level than the work of Bagehot or Stephen.

Typical of the sort of work which Lang produced, with a gracefulness and zest wholly disproportionate to the possible gains involved, was *Letters to Dead Authors* (1886). Sixteen of the twenty-two letters had appeared in the *St James's Gazette*, and the others appeared for the first time in the American edition of 1893. In his letter to Byron, written in the dogtrot rhythm that Byron occasionally employed for satiric purposes, Lang noted that Byron's books had entered 'on an age of iron'. Lang further protested that he hated to indulge in personalities, or current slang:

> I loathe the aimless, reckless, loose dispersion,
> Of every rhyme that in the singer's wallet is,
> I hate it as you hated the *Excursion* . . . .[33]

Of the quarrel between Arnold and Swinburne over the question of Byron's merits, Lang protested that he was not a poet himself 'to judge of right or wrong', and added,

> But of all things I always think a fight is
> The most unpleasant in the lists of song[34]

and this idealised self-portrait, of a critic who occasionally wrote in imitation of Byron but knew his own work was inferior, who would not willingly shift his allegiance from a 'Titan fairer than the gods'[35] despite the new fashion of mocking Byron's manners and morals, and who disliked literary controversy, is consistently sketched in other letters. For example, when Lang addressed Edgar Allan Poe, his primary concern was with the 'incredible and heeded slanders'[36] that clouded Poe's reputation. Lang's admiration of Poe ('the greatest poet, perhaps the greatest literary genius' of America) was not seriously qualified by his reservations about the critical dicta which seemed to suggest that the *Odyssey* was inferior to 'Ulalume', or *Le Festine de Pierre* to 'Undine'. He understood that Poe was rationalising to serve his own interests, and that Poe's theory of poetry, if accepted, would have made the American (after Coleridge, author of 'Kubla Khan') 'the foremost of the poets of the world',[37] followed closely by William Morris, author of 'Golden

Wings', 'The Blue Closet' and 'The Sailing of the Sword'. (Lang could not resist adding, perhaps not so whimsically as all that, 'and, close up, Mr Lear, the author of "The Yongi Bongi Bo", and the lay of the "Jumblies" '.) Lang's letter to Poe had been stimulated by the publication of George Woodberry's biography, 'a cold, careful, and in many respects admirable study',[38] and Woodberry's work seemed valuable because it identified the source of Poe's sagging reputation. The Daweses, Griswolds and 'smaller men' who had been offended by Poe's strictures could neither forget nor forgive, though Longfellow was more generous. Poe had knowingly risked their anger because he had written, in addition to poetry and various fictions, a number of reviews. 'How unhappy were the necessities, how deplorable the vein', Lang exclaimed,

> that compelled or seduced a man of your eminence into the dusty and stony ways of contemporary criticism! About the writers of his own generation a leader of that generation should hold his peace. He should neither praise nor blame nor defend his equals; he should not strike one blow at the buzzing ephemerae of letters.

Lang continued,

> The breath of their life is in the columns of 'Literary Gossip'; and they should be allowed to perish with the weekly advertisements on which they pasture. Reviewing, of course, there must needs be; but great minds should only criticise the great who have passed beyond the reach of eulogy or fault-finding.[39]

Hence, most of the letters are addressed to such eminent worthies of the past as Ronsard, Herodotus, Pope, Lucian of Samosata, Rabelais, Jane Austen, Izaak Walton, Sir John Mandeville, Eusebius of Caesarea and 'Q. Horatius Flaccus'. There is an odd indecisiveness of tone when literary figures closer to Lang's lifetime turn up. Thackeray is praised 'above all others', as a writer who was, and remained, 'without a rival' in his 'many-sided excellence'.[40] It is strange to read Lang's salutation:

> In what other novelist, since Scott was worn down by the burden of a forlorn endeavour, and died for honour's sake, has the world found so many of the fairest gifts combined? If we may not call you a poet (for the first of English writers of light verse did not

seek that crown), who that was less than a poet ever saw life with a glance so keen as yours, so steady, and so sane?[41]

Lang had read Dickens, but had been put off by the 'vigour' of Dickens's special devotees. He had been annoyed, moreover, by their imitation of his 'less admirable mannerisms',[42] and by the way in which 'the young lions of the Press' strained, in Dickensian fashion, 'after fantastic comparisons', and donated to people nicknames 'derived from their teeth, or their complexion'. 'Dickens was [the admission seems to come from between his own clenched teeth] the greatest comic genius of modern times.'[43] Lang's preference was for Mr Squeers, Sam Weller, Mrs Gamp, 'all the Pickwickians', Mr Dowler and John Browdie, because they linked Dickens with Hogarth, Bunbury, George Cruikshank and Gilray, not to mention Leech and Surtees 'and the creator of Tittlebat Titmouse'.[44] The unabashed hero-worship of Thackeray's talent, so complete that even that novelist's disturbing tendency to preach might be excused ('But who that loves Montaigne and Pascal, who that likes the wise trifling of the one and can bear with the melancholy of the other, but prefers your preaching to another's playing!'[45]), has no counterpart in Lang's evaluation of Dickens as a writer with too many 'grotesque' and 'gloomy' imaginations. 'To force the note,' Lang apostrophised Dickens, 'to press fantasy too hard, to deepen the gloom with black over the indigo, that was the failing which proved you mortal'.[46] Referring to Shelley's *Prometheus Unbound*, about the plot of which he entertained serious reservations, Lang quoted with approval the Cambridge critic who claimed that it revealed in Shelley 'a hankering after life in a cave – doubtless and unconsciously inherited memory from cave-man'.[47] Lang, who did admire Shelley's lyrics, felt constrained to add that Shelley's unfulfilled promise to produce a history of the moral, intellectual, and political elements in human society had been carried through by the biologists and geologists and scientists of the later years of the century. An unexpectedly strong, but thoroughly characteristic, melancholy marks the observation about Man: 'Science tells us that before becoming a cave-dweller he was a Brute; Experience daily proclaims that he constantly reverts to his original condition. *L'homme est un méchant animal* . . . .'[48]

A reviewer cannot concentrate exclusively on dead authors, though a man of letters in the late nineteenth century often attempted to persuade his readers that his personal antipathy to most of the current literary scene derived from an idealistic unwillingness to engage in controversy, petty gossip or praise that might be misunderstood as being entangled in unworthy motives, for instance, vexing a rival rather than exalting a subject, or seeking the favour of the famous). Lang did not seek to mislead his public when he chose the titles of his books of literary criticism, for the most part collections of his review essays: *The Library* (1881), *Letters to Dead Authors* (1886), *Books and Bookmen* (1886), *Letters on Literature* (1889), *How to Fail in Literature* (1890), *Essays in Little* (1891), and similar titles for a large number of essays, pamphlets, prefaces and uncollected pieces.

It was as if he had taken for guidance selected and consistently bland elements of Newman's definition of the kind of product a university training was meant to turn out: a man who knew the nature of his own opinions and judgements, and possessed 'a truth in developing them, an eloquence in expressing them, and a force in urging them'. Learning how to distinguish the sophistical from the true, and when to discard the irrelevant, Newman's idealised university graduate

> can ask a question pertinently, and gain a lesson seasonably, when he has nothing to impart himself; he is ever ready, yet never in the way; he is a pleasant companion, and a comrade you can depend upon; he knows when to be serious and when to trifle, and he has a sure tact which enables him to trifle with gracefulness and to be serious with effect. He has the repose of a mind which lives in itself, while it lives in the world, and which has resources for its happiness at home when it cannot go abroad. (*The Idea of a University*, Discourse VII: 'Knowledge Viewed in Relation to Professional Skill', 1852)

But, viewed from another perspective, this desire to avoid altercation was directly responsible for a library mustiness in some of the judgements applied to Lang's contemporaries, and perhaps an underestimation of the greatness of the Victorian contribution to English literature.

. *History of English Literature* (1912), written ostensibly to arouse 'a living interest, if it may be, in the books of the past, and to induce the reader to turn to them for himself',[49] is a decent representative of the genre. Lang would have preferred to deal with the masters only, but apparently his commission required that he treat the 'under-

wood' as well, and, for a work on an immense subject, its 687 pages
observed due proportion and moved briskly from 'Widsith' to
W. E. H. Lecky. This work is perhaps the easiest place in which a
reader may discover the full range of Lang's opinions of his contemporaries, both in England and the United States (since he
regarded American writers as contributing essentially to English
literary traditions). For example, Lang wrote that Tennyson (who
had died in 1892) was probably 'too near' for men and women of the
new century to appreciate his greatness. ' "Men hardly know how
beautiful fire is", says Shelley; the phenomenon is too familiar . . . .'[50] There is an odd unwillingness to commit himself in the
objection to Edward FitzGerald's remark that Tennyson never
regained the level of his two thin volumes of 1842: 'Perhaps we may
say that he never rose above that level',[51] an *obiter dictum* in which
the 'perhaps' seems redundant when used in conjunction with 'we
may say that . . .'. A revelation of personal concern is contained in
the remark, 'Tennyson would be more universally appreciated as a
great and delightful poet if he had never expressed any of his
personal opinions about politics, society, morals, or religion in
verse',[52] as if 'delightful' poetry without a potentially controversial
content should have been the mature Tennyson's professional
objective. The time for a tale or novel of modern life, in verse, had
passed before the death of Crabbe, and *Maud*, despite its beautiful
love poetry, suffered from being written in an age insensitive to the
attractions of its genre. Lang's praise of *Idylls of the King* is similarly
qualified ('Some critics held that Arthur preached too much to his
fallen Queen', but the best of the *Idylls* lies in Tennyson's allegiance
to the old romances rather than in any 'modern' touches).[53]

As for Browning, Lang spoke of the way in which 'The
abundance of mediaeval Italian history, – introducing, as familiar
to all, matters which were but vaguely known by few, – and the long
hurrying sentences, following trains of ideas associated only in the
poet's mind, defeated the ordinary reader';[54] he was speaking of
himself. When Browning was positive, dramatising the will to live,
he was worth praising; but Lang had no aesthetic judgement to
make on *The Ring and the Book*, and there is a swift-flowing
undercurrent of suspicion of those enthusiasts 'who value "thought"
in poetry'.[55] The obscurity which haunted Browning's manner in
his youth became more willful during his last twenty years: 'The poet
did not by any means always choose to make audible, in his verse,
the music to which, as an art, he was devoted.'[56]

Lang carefully recorded the eccentric rankings of Arnold:
Wordsworth 'was the last of our poets whom he greatly admired,
though he placed Byron (for other than Wordsworth's qualities) on
the same eminence; and preferred Shelley's letters to his lyrics'.[57]
Nor did Arnold think enough of Tennyson. 'Such', sighed Lang,
'were what most amateurs think the freaks of Arnold as a critic.'[58]
The catalogue of Arnold's deficiencies as a critic is, for the allotted
space, long enough. Arnold 'cannot always be termed "un-
affected"', and 'his banter, his "educated insolence" as Aristotle
says, was apt rather to provoke than to convert people who differed
from him, as to education, politics, social problems, or literature'.[59]
He worked a 'peculiar vein of lofty irony and academic "chaff"', as
in his *Lectures on Translating Homer*.[60] Arnold's knowledge was not
always accompanied by true appreciation, and Lang found himself
puzzled by an Arnold who slated the French for not sufficiently
admiring a Wordsworth who, he admitted, lacked inspiration after
1808.[61] Nor did Lang want to commend Arnold's somewhat sneaky
strategy ('trick') 'of taking a single line or two, perhaps of the worst,
from a poet, using this inferior brick as a sample of the building, and
contrasting it with specimens superlatively excellent from poets
whom he wanted to extol',[62] as in the comparison between
Théophile Gautier and Wordsworth, to the former's disadvantage.
Arnold did not know enough about the Celts to be warranted in
generalising about their mastery of 'general magic'[63] (Lang knew
too much about Greek, Finnish, and even savage poetry to be
considered an amateur in this field). In addition, 'Arnold was no
orientalist, and had no special knowledge of New Testament Greek,
nor of the comparative study of religions. These defects', Lang went
on, 'with surprising errors in taste, prevent his *St Paul and
Protestantism*, *God and the Bible*, and *Literature and Dogma* from
reaching a high level in their way'.[64] These flaws are hardly
overbalanced by Lang's perfunctory acknowledgement of Arnold's
'beautiful prose', or his lightly sketched praise of Arnold's descriptions of the scenery around Oxford. There is a hint of some
impatience with Arnold's avoidance of rhymed measures. 'Merope'
'certainly' avoids overstimulation of the reader, and the narratives,
in general, do not hold our attention. It is not surprising, therefore,
but somewhat anticlimactic, that Lang should speak most highly of
'Requiescat' and 'a worthy mate of the noblest "swallow flights of
song" and the *Greek Anthology*'.[65]

Of the later Victorian poets Lang might have said (as he did of

Walter Pater and John Addington Symonds) that they were 'so recently silent that they cannot here be critically estimated',[66] though that position seems less tenable for an author whose canon is complete than for one who is still writing. His notices of Edward FitzGerald ('idolised by the worst judges', the *Rubáiyàt* deserves some praise as an original work, and its stoicism is presented 'under an Epicurean wash of colour'[67]), George Meredith (a poet 'not of the centre' because he hid his meaning, and valued 'too cheaply the leisure of the reader', or valued 'too highly the reader's industry and ingenuity'[68]), Elizabeth Barrett Browning ('Her Muse is neither trimly girdled nor neatly shod'[69]), Christina Rossetti ('To institute comparisons between her and Mrs Browning is apt to cause injustice to either or to both',[70] an implied additional rebuke to Mrs Browning's Muse, inasmuch as Lang admired 'Goblin Market' and a number of Christina Rossetti's lyrics), Dante Gabriel Rossetti ('The ballads were too artificial for the ballad form, which is nothing if not simple . . .'[71]), William Morris (an uneven artist, on occasions exciting, but ill advised to attempt imitations of Homer in the post-*Beowulf* world of England[72]) and Algernon Charles Swinburne ('the skill never failed the poet, what failed more and more was the interest of his readers'[73]) are never waspish. Still, the praise is always carefully qualified, and the qualifications are often severe.

I have already indicated that Lang's personal preference for Thackeray over Dickens was based, at least partially, on dislike of Dickens's too-vociferous admirers. Lang reacted strongly (one might have expected him to do so) against Dickens's unflattering portrayal of Joan of Arc in *A Child's History of England*; and, in general, he detested the 'want of balance' in Dickens's art. Yet he had a clear appreciation of Dickens's popularity, and of his rightful claim to be admired as 'peculiarly English'.[74] One should not be surprised that the mind that delighted in unravelling knots of Scottish history should become obsessed, for fully a quarter-century, with the direction that *The Mystery of Edwin Drood* might have taken if Dickens had lived to complete it. Lang's book *The Puzzle of Dickens's Last Plot* (1905) was only one of several publications that concentrated on the problem.

It may be that Thackeray's superior education, Scott-like characteristics, humour and elegant style were stressed because Lang knew how inevitable some choosing-up of sides had become for every critic: 'But as every man is born an Aristotelian or a

Platonist, a Whig or a Tory, so men are born to take one side or other about the Great Twin Brethren of English fiction, in place of admiring and enjoying both.'[75] But the dangers of excessive praise are encapsulated in the claim made, while discussing *Vanity Fair*, that 'Fielding has not a quarter of Thackeray's variousness, does not see so wide a vision of life.'[76] For Lang, Thackeray belonged to the ages, and *Vanity Fair* had become an 'old book', while Dickens's case was still being decided.

Lang seemed uneasy with the novels of the Brontë sisters, and stressed perhaps more than necessary the autobiographical substratum of *Wuthering Heights*, *Jane Eyre* and *Villette*. He expressed some important reservations about Charlotte's 'ignorant imagination' ('borrowed romance combined with instinctive realism, bitter experience blended with the day-dreams of a life'[77]) and lack of humour that made it impossible for her to appreciate Jane Austen's novels. He could scarcely disguise his irritation with Meredith's mannerisms, though the reading public learned to like his novels. (Lang quoted Coleridge to the effect that the reading public was not to be trusted.[78]) Wilkie Collins wrote too much, had a laboured humour, and picked up from Dickens 'the mannerism of constantly dwelling on the tricks and hobbies of his people'.[79] And, even though he admired George Eliot as the best novelist after the death of Dickens, he recorded, with painful fidelity to the truth as he saw it, that from *Romola* on she preached mercilessly. As for *Daniel Deronda*, it was 'very long, and a kind of scientific jargon had been taking the place of the old rustic humours'.[80]

This conspectus of major Victorian novelists came to Robert Louis Stevenson as a climactic figure. Here, surely, were claymores aplenty, and a judicious use of psychology (that is to say, very little, oo none, since it might interfere with action). Lang believed *Kidnapped* to be Stevenson's best novel ('without a woman in it', he added[81]), and preferred poems written in the Lowland vernacular to *A Child's Garden of Verses*, though these latter poems were 'the most like himself'.[82]

These potted remarks, dealing with a millennium of English literary history, are embedded in a text much better and fairer than Henry James believed it to be; but James – in his notorious letter to Edmund Gosse – may have been reacting to the fact that his own works had been omitted from consideration rather than to what he called an 'extraordinary *voulu* Scotch provincialism'.[83] Lang's knowledge of both the major works, and what he persisted in calling 'the underwoods', came first-hand, and he had earned his right to a very large number of crotchets. *History of English Literature from 'Beowulf' to Swinburne* is more generous with its praise. The final chapters, reviewing both the Romantic and Victorian ages, are (as these quoted and paraphrased remarks suggest) relatively unsuccessful in the book's primary objective of making the reader want to return to the living texts; they may have been written from a sense of duty rather than from personal pleasure; and the occasional enthusiasms come as green oases in an expanse of sand.

Lang once declared that he ranked Scott above Stevenson, which amounted to a fairly conventional critical position for the time, but the case of Stevenson impresses us because it was based on personal contacts over a sixteen-year period, and because, in an important sense, Stevenson's talent prevented Lang's scepticism about the achievements of the second half of the nineteenth century from degenerating into cynicism. In 'Recollections of Robert Louis Stevenson', published in *Adventures among Books*, Lang described how he met Stevenson at Mentone, on the Riviera, where both men were trying to improve their health. Sidney Colvin brought them together (31 January 1874), and Lang's first impression was not wholly favourable. ' "Here", I thought, "is one of your aesthetic young men, though not a very clever one." '[84] This disdain may have been provoked partly by Stevenson's flamboyant costume. Not until Lang read and appreciated some of the early essays of Stevenson did the relationship warm. Lang's essay recounts their joint efforts to turn the periodical *London* into a successful venture, but does not say much about the thriller *Rose*, a collaborative effort that might have provided passing entertainment.

Its heroine, Rose, was a Nihilist, and its villain, 'The Whiteley of Crime', a thorough-going scoundrel *à la* Dr Moriarty ('the universal Provider of Iniquity'). One scene was set in a dungeon in Moscow. 'We'll extract information from him', Lang told Stevenson. When the latter asked, 'How?' Lang replied, 'With corkscrews.'[85] The memoir adds, 'But the mere suggestion of such a process was terribly distasteful to him . . . .' Lang believed in the narrative greatness of *Dr Jekyll and Mr Hyde*, if only because he found himself unable to continue reading the manuscript 'in a very common-place London drawing-room, at 10.30 P.M.', after he reached that point in the story where Utterson the lawyer and the butler, waiting outside the Doctor's room, heard the doctor's voice from within.[86]

Lang admitted that he could not be counted among Stevenson's intimate friends, but the reasons why he believed Stevenson's talent to have been a major one are interesting. Stevenson was, of course, a Scot who shared with Lang memories of 'our dear country', though he was unwilling to forget Burns's calloused conduct in various romances, and unable to forgive 'the *longueurs* and lazinesses of Scott, as a Scot should do'.[87] He was selflessly concerned about others, and continually inquired, in his last letters to Lang, about the health of their friend James Payn. (Stevenson rarely spoke about his own 'ill-staged fifth act of life'.)[88] He enjoyed Dickens, though perhaps he offended Lang in his evaluation of Thackeray ('Well,' Lang admitted, 'I would rather have talked to somebody else!'[89]). It is likely that Lang was alluding to Hardy's *Tess* – 'a novel dear to culture' – when he recorded Stevenson's claim, 'that he would die by my side, in the last ditch, proclaiming it at the worst fiction in the world'; Stevenson, according to Lang, dispraised any *other* book, and his dislike of *Tess* became known to Hardy as soon as he wrote back from Samoa about it.[90]

Shared literary preferences, a common heritage, a love of the picturesque and the picaresque: and there are other reasons. 'Mr Stevenson possessed', Lang wrote, 'more than any man I ever met, the power of making other men fall in love with him . . . . What was so taking in him? and how is one to analyse that dazzling surface of pleasantry, that changeful shining humour, wit, wisdom, recklessness; beneath which beat the most kind and tolerant of hearts?' He went on to answer his own questions: 'People were fond of him, and people were proud of him: his achievements, as it were, sensibly raised their pleasure in the world . . . .' Lang concluded, 'He was as unique in character as in literary genius.'[91]

'Mr Stevenson's Works', written specially for *Essays in Little*, hints at the reasons why Stevenson's work so appealed to his contemporaries, and why Stevenson has had, in subsequent decades, so uneven a reputation. 'Perhaps the first quality in Mr Stevenson's works, now so many and so various, which strikes a reader, is the buoyancy, the survival of the child in him.'[92] Lang's emphasis on Stevenson's 'fantastic' childhood, and on how Stevenson made the world 'an unsubstantial fairy place' even after coming to manhood, has distracted many readers interested in defining more precisely the nature of Stevenson's contribution to letters. However, the essay, written before *The Weir of Hermiston* became known, records views which did not significantly change in *History of English Literature*. The limitations of Stevenson's craft, as defined by Lang, were obviously not intended to be considered major: 'a delicate freakishness', a slight odour of the lamp, an occasional attempt to write 'a moral allegory', and so on. Rather, the praise, even of *Treasure Island*, begins to cloy.

> They say the seamanship is inaccurate; I care no more than I do for the year 30. They say too many people are killed. They all died in fair fight, except a victim of John Silver's . . . . A very sober student might add that the hero is impossibly clever; but, then, the hero is a boy, and this is a boy's book . . . . [93]

Again, the disturbing misogyny: 'And there are no interfering petticoats in the story.'[94] Later, in his discussion of *The Master of Ballantrae*, Lang praises Stevenson's heroine as 'the best' among his few women, and adds, with barely concealed satisfaction, 'But even she is almost always reserved, veiled as it were.'[95] To the objection tht Stevenson had not written a modern love story, Lang blusters,

> But who has? There are love affairs in Dickens, but do we remember or care for them? Is it the love affairs that we remember in Scott? . . . Love stories are best done by women, as in 'Mr Gilfil's Love Story'; and, perhaps, in an ordinary way, by writers like Trollope. One may defy critics to name a great English author in fiction whose chief and distinguishing merit is in his pictures of the passion of Love . . . . [96]

Lang's difficulty in establishing friendships with other professional writers is well known, and his sense of unease with people whom he met on social occasions became almost frighteningly intense after the turn of the century. Stevenson's appeal to Lang was basically that of a writer who moved with ease from the study to the open air, who did not seem to be circumscribed by a single subject-matter. Yet Lang's emphasis on the romantic strain in Stevenson's writing, on the boyish element, proved ultimately to render a disservice to his fellow Scot. Henley objected to the image of a 'Seraph in Chocolate' that rapidly developed after Stevenson's death, and Lang, with his admiration of Stevenson's fantasies ('The man I knew was always a boy') avoidance of love interest and women characters in his fictions, and charm, contributed to that distorted image. The emphasis on Stevenson's perfection – in his life no less than in his manner – developed from a number of complex attitudes, among them the aesthetic posturing of the late 1870s, the 'desperate search by late Victorian critics for the great writer who could follow the dead and dying giants of the previous decades', and the fear that 'vulgar people' might somehow miss Stevenson's 'True Art'.[97] The deflation in Stevenson's posthumous reputation was probably inevitable, though it should be set down that Stevenson, phenomenally popular during his lifetime, has never lost a very large readership; what he has lost are the serious critics of this century who might have carried on where Andrew Lang, Sidney Colvin and Edmund Gosse left off. But Lang lacked the art required to bring 'the living aspect of the man before those who never knew him' (an admission made toward the end of 'Recollections').[98] One realises, almost with a palpable shock, that the astonishing thing about Lang's literary criticism, despite its emphasis on biography and history, is how rarely he was able to get beyond 'literary and bookish' concerns to the human being who had actually written the book under discussion. It might not have mattered if Lang had not made so much of the importance of connecting the writer to his literary creations.

What, then, remains of Lang's contributions to serious literature, once we learn that his relationship to his own age was in some respects hostile or unsympathetic, and that he underestimated the narrative art of the best writers of his time (Hardy, James, Conrad)? It is true that Lang's recognition of Rudyard Kipling's genius was generous, and came earlier than that of any other Victorian critic. His praise of Rider Haggard, James Barrie, Kenneth Grahame and Conan Doyle aided those writers at critical stages of their careers. But he was more at home with writers of an earlier age. His writings on Homer, in particular, did precisely what was needed in an age of sometimes rancorous debate over theses and counter-theses; they suggested plausible ways of thinking about the identity of the writer behind the poetry. Lang wrote with sympathy and intelligence on the Bucolic poets and the Alexandrians; on medieval French literature and Gerard de Nerval in his own century; on a surprising number of American authors; on Fielding, Smollett and Richardson; and on Sir Walter Scott and Jane Austen. Though he had much to say about Shakespeare, his major contribution, *Shakespeare, Bacon, and the Great Unknown*, must be accounted as an extra-literary achievement. Indeed, a summing-up of Lang's best work in literary criticism returns us to the same question that Lang raised in his assessment of whether Stevenson was for the ages – that is, could Stevenson write a major novel for mature readers? Lang's collections of periodical essays, mock letters and real letters, and biographies that were no less biographies because they dealt with literary figures (John Gibson Lockhart) were aimed at popularising, and they succeeded in reaching that objective; but the absence of a sustained, major work of literary criticism is remarkable. There is no indication that Lang ever believed the production of such a work should be included among his responsibilities; the fact remains, he did not write one.

Moreover, there was always something surprising about a man of Lang's erudition, who knew so many languages, literatures and disciplines, identifying himself so wholeheartedly with 'the general reader'. At times his emphasis on the comprehensibility of a text became excessive, because it denied him the 'human pleasure' that other readers found in complicated and challenging texts. Out of sympathy with masterpieces that did not immediately yield their full meaning, and with much of the best work written between 1880 and the year of his death, Lang will be remembered – in the field of literary criticism at least – as a master of the familiar essay, an enthusiast of books and a patient analyser of one literary problem after another. Despite the fact that he wrote more often on literature than on any of his other fields of interest, it is ironic, and perhaps regrettable, that the common reader's approach was not well suited to cope with changing artistic programmes, or to ensure the continuing attention of younger writers. For all its wisdom and gracefulness of style, Lang's legacy to our age is, in this major sense, a disappointment, and less than it might have been.

6 George Saintsbury

Saintsbury was destined to write with unflagging energy about Augustinus Olmucensis as well as Schopenhauer, about Rutilius Lupus as well as H. D. Traill and R. H. Hutton; but who – in the 1870s – could have predicted his future as a scholar? Born on 23 October 1845, at Southampton – his father a general secretary and dock superintendent who died when he was fourteen – he attended a preparatory school in Westbourne Grove before going on to the lower forms of King's College School; he was in the Upper Sixth from 1860 to 1863; and at Merton College, Oxford, he took a number of classes with Jowett. His Second in *Lit. Hum.* was always a matter for rueful consideration, though, as A. Blyth Webster has noted,[1] Newman, Arnold, Pater, Creighton (the historian and churchman) and W. P. Ker also missed their Firsts. Saintsbury, unlike these, failed to get his Fellowship, though he tried five times.

He admired Carlyle; but his special love was reserved for Pusey, whom he venerated fully as much as he did Lord Roberts, and he may be set down as a Church-and-King man. For a brief period (1868) he taught English and History in the upper forms at Manchester Grammar School; approximately a decade later, after a brief return appointment, he wrote a history of Manchester.

More crucial in his life was a six-year period of teaching the classics at Elizabeth College, Guernsey (1868–74), which afforded him time and inspiration for a grand-scale reading of French literature. In Guernsey, Saintsbury wrote with wistful nostalgia in *Notes on a Cellar-Book*, 'You could get blind drunk for sixpence; a population of between 30,000 and 40,000; a garrison frequently renewed; sailors from many parts of the world dropping in; scarcely any police; *no* serious crime; hardly any minor disorder; and a splendid bill of health.'[2] This extended and useful interlude was followed by a headmastership at the Elgin Educational Institute (1874), which ended as a consequence of financial as well as personal reasons.

In 1876 he began his twenty years of journalism in London, and proved particularly active as a reviewer of the *Academy*. Much of the detritus of contemporary literary production came to him, but he gradually found ways of boosting favourites (he was especially kind to meritorious American books) at the same time that he gently dismissed third-rate novels. At an early stage, apparently, he took Thackeray as an exemplar of how a novel should be constructed and written. He went on to write for the *Fortnightly* as well, and to contribute to the ninth edition of the *Encyclopaedia Britannica* a large number of essays on French authors. The latter assignment led him, in the 1880s, to edit a collection of the masterpieces of French drama. Perhaps Saintsbury's efforts to popularise the best of French literature – its plays, novels, and lyrics – and to provide for his countrymen an intelligently proportioned *Short History* were of greater significance to his later career interests than his equally productive analyses of the masterpieces of the English novel. Contributions to the weekly *London* (that short-lived journal so hospitable to the early work of Lang, Stevenson and Henley) appeared simultaneously, or nearly so, with pieces written for the *Magazine of Art*, *Pall Mall Gazette*, *St James's Gazette*, *Macmillan's Magazine*, the *National Review*, *Merry England*, the *New Review*, *Our Times*, the *Saturday Review* and a large number of periodicals printed in Italy, India and the United States. The uncollected journalism of Saintsbury may be as bulky as the *Collected Works*.

One can only marvel, along with Oliver Elton,[3] at Saintsbury's claim that he wrote 'almost as much on politics as on literature' during his journalistic years. Saintsbury had little or no faith in democracy, the extension of the franchise, the revelations of Darwinism, the teaching of *Essays and Reviews*, 'the repauperizing of the poor; and the plundering not only of the rich but of all who work honestly and honestly save; with all the rest of what is called modernism'.[4] He might be expected to have detested Gladstone's manoeuvrings on the Home Bill question, and so he did; but he prevented the editor Harwood from printing in the *Saturday Review* the forged Pigott letters about Parnell's complicity in a murder case, and it remained for *The Times* to cover itself with shame by printing a 'facsimile letter' (18 April 1887) before it checked thoroughly on Pigott's credibility.

On the flood-tide roared: a number of studies and editions of Dryden, a history of Elizabethan literature, the popular two-volume *Essays on English Literature*, a series of studies of English prose, and much more. At the age of fifty, he offered himself in the competition for the Chair at the University of Edinburgh. (David Masson and William Minto, also with journalistic backgrounds, had been elevated to Chairs at other universities.) Saintsbury defeated William Ernest Henley in the competition; and, despite some murmurs from Southron publications (among them, rather surprisingly, the *Saturday Review*), he undertook his duties with becoming dignity and determination. He stopped reviewing, though he continued to edit reprints (a habit beginning in 1891). The number of such volumes, plus those to which he supplied introductory essays, some of very substantial length, is impressive, and a sufficient life's work for most scholars. For example, he supplied a memoir, a general criticism, and an essay on each of forty volumes in an English translation of Balzac (1895–8), begun in the same year that saw the completion of his *History of Nineteenth Century Literature*.

But even these, including the *Short History of English Literature* (1898) which provoked the perpetually provoked Churton Collins to complain of inaccuracies (though none so major that a temperate review might have been more appropriate to the scale of the 'crimes' committed), were but prolegomena to the great works that none – including, perhaps, Saintsbury himself – had predicted. These began with *Periods of European Literature*, the first volume of which involved a reconsideration of romance and allegory, and the last of which surveyed the later nineteenth century, affording him an opportunity to consider for the first time several important Victorians who had died during the 1890s. *A History of Criticism*, in its three majestic volumes, astonished the academic world, and in several respects has not yet been superseded. A three-volume *History of English Prosody from the Twelfth Century to the Present Day* (1906–10) is a compendium of refined 'tasting', and has been brutally condemned by those who hear poetical lines differently from Saintsbury; but, as one literary historian noted, 'The people who are truly enthusiastic over these topics could be gathered in quite a small dinner party.'[55] Saintsbury's vivid prose, despite its vague definitions and its scandalous ignoring or rejection of practically all earlier investigators of the field (Sidney Lanier, William Thomson, Paul Verrier and Edwin Guest, among others), has gusto and readability. *A History of English Prose Rhythm* (1912) is a significant pioneering study. Saintsbury contributed twenty chapters to *The Cambridge History of English Literature* (1907–16), wrote a study of Matthew Arnold, edited a three-volume anthology of *Minor Poets of the Caroline Period* (1905–21), and completed full-scale works on the

English lyric, the English novel, the Augustan Age, the French novel to the close of the nineteenth century, several scrapbooks of essays, a 'consideration' of Thackeray, as well as introductions to a large number of English and French authors whose works, he felt, deserved wider attention. All this, of course, in addition to his regular teachings duties, which did not end until his resignation in June 1915. He moved from Edinburgh to Bath, to the Royal Crescent. His final years were spent quietly within book-lined rooms. At the age of eighty-seven he died (28 January 1933), and was buried in the Old Cemetery, Southampton.

Like Lang, he did not want a biography written to commemorate his achievements (though he was really following the precedent set by his hero Thackeray), and those who knew him well expected some such decision. His essays, though they used biographical information freely, avoided petty gossip, and the thousands who have enjoyed his scrap books of the 1920s never encountered scandal there. Saintsbury was sensitive to criticism, but refused to respond publicly to Churton Collins's review of his deficiencies, and never attacked by name a critic with whose views he disagreed. Matthew Arnold, for example, may have been formally polite in his censure of living writers; but the application of his opinions proved much too personal for Saintsbury. In a memorable footnote to his treatment of Arnold's style, Saintsbury wrote, in volume III of *A History of Criticism,*

> He has been largely imitated in this, and I cannot help thinking that it is a pity. If a man is definitely and ostensibly 'reviewing' another man's work, he has a perfect right, subject to the laws of good manners, to discuss him *quoad hoc*. But illustrations of general discourses by dragging in living persons seem to be forbidden by those laws as they apply in the literary province.[6]

For this reason, he refused to consider living authors at the time of his writing of the *History of Nineteenth Century Literature*, and even those who had passed away too recently (Robert Buchanan, William Ernest Henley and Sir Leslie Stephen, among others) at the time he was completing *A History of Criticism*. In one sense, all books and all authors were his contemporaries, and E. M. Forster's vision of every writer who had ever lived working simultaneously in the Reading Room of the British Museum would have struck Saintsbury as an amiable conceit.

Dorothy Margaret Stuart, in a brief recollection of her relationship to Saintsbury that began in 1926, speaks of his 'passionately
(and, alas, archaically) chivalrous attitude towards women'. She
remembers his comment to her: 'All but the very *worst* of you are so
much too good for all but the very *best* of *us*.' Her mother's portrait
pleased him, and he 'ceremoniously removed his skull-cap. "You
must tell her", he said, "that I could not stand covered before
her." '7 Toward the end he had his share of problems: the nursing of
an ill wife, the dispersal of his 15,000-book library as a preliminary to
removal from Edinburgh, the selling of his cellar accompanied by
medical advice against drinking his beloved wines, and a race
between blindness and death. But even if his funeral party consisted
only of six persons – David Nicol Smith, as a representative of
Merton, had to request permission to attend – he had finally come
home to Southampton, to the city where he had been born.

He was not a writer of long, wittily phrased letters, though his
habit of answering all communications by return post was remarkable enough in one whose duties were both multiple and pressing;
and, indeed, his injunction against the publication of posthumous
bits and pieces related to his own life specifically included all letters.
There was always the danger that his concern with modern manners
and codes of behaviour might be misunderstood as a failure to
understand the ceaselessly shifting standards of morality in both the
nineteenth and twentieth centuries; the charge that he levied against
Sterne's 'considerable indulgence, not in coarseness of the
Smollettian kind, but in indecent hint and innuendo'8 was consistent
with his attitude that much of Zola, and practically all of naturalistic
fiction, had transgressed against civilisation itself. He praised
Baudelaire as a music-maker, and did a great deal to make his
success in England possible; but he did so by ignoring what Arthur
Symons, in protest, called a 'sub-stratum of vice', and just about
everything that made Baudelaire important to the Decadents and,
for that matter, to T. S. Eliot early in the new century. In the
classroom, as one admirer pointed out, 'He excluded politics, and
religion, and more matters of controversy than might have been
expected.'9 The instant one reflects on the implications of the
classroom omission of these major areas of concern to most of the
great English writers, the more difficult it is to recall extended
treatment of these same matters in the literally tens of thousands of
pages turned out by Saintsbury: pages that are always a pleasure to
read, that are always saying something worth paying attention to

despite the likelihood that Saintsbury may be treating for the twentieth time the same author or the same literary work, that are the obvious product of a well-stocked mind and an original personality.

Helen Waddell believed that Saintsbury's repeated failure to win his Fellowship 'cost him something more than the initial sharpness of humiliation – Leisure for an absolute exactness of scholarship, even though it was more than made up for by his depth and range'.[10] John Gross is saying substantially the same thing, though perhaps with more astringency, when he writes, 'For all his weight of learning Saintsbury was not, in the modern sense, a fully paid-up professional scholar.'[11] Saintsbury recorded dates inaccurately, occasionally misremembered quotations, got small facts a little off; and aggravated those who offered mild corrections by dismissing the problem with an unconcerned shrug, a light and pleasant rejoinder. Even those who admire Saintsbury's occasional swelling rhetoric and masterful formulation cannot endorse with unqualified enthusiasm the Saintsburian style, with its qualifications, asides, parentheses, and exfoliating images. For 'knowingness', Saintsbury may be compared to Kipling, the author who brought to him, for scholarly vetting, that extraordinary tale about Shakespeare, 'Proofs of Holy Writ', and to whom ('the best poet and taleteller of his generation') Saintsbury dedicated *Notes on a Cellar-Book*; but knowingness is usually regarded as being inferior to knowledge.

Yet, astonishingly, the charge of writing too much and of being too copious in his literary productions can be levied only by those who have not sampled a true cross-section of Saintsbury's wares. It is impossible to read any essay or book-chapter by Saintsbury that does not contain some characteristic, well-turned observation. In his essay 'Oxford Sights and Scenes' he recorded Southey's remark that he never dreamt of Oxford, and added, within parentheses, 'It was the only bad thing that he ever said of himself or that is ever said of him on good authority.'[12] The editors and publishers to whom Jeffrey sought to introduce himself in 1798 – and who rebuffed his efforts to become a professional man of letters – 'were either inaccessible or repulsive'.[13] Saintsbury admired Donne's satires, for their brilliant employment of intellect:

> It is a constant fault of modern satirists that in their just admiration for Horace and Juvenal they merely paraphrase them, and, instead of going to the fountainhead and taking their

matter from human nature, merely give us fresh studies of *Ibam forte via sacra* or the Tenth of Juvenal, adjusted to the meridians of Paris or London.[14]

A comparison of Voltaire and Rabelais turns out very much to the former's disadvantage: Voltaire 'believes in nothing, wishes for nothing very much, can excite himself about nothing. With Rabelais, on the contrary, the steam is not only always up, as modern slang says, but up with a full head, and escaping through every safety valve.'[15] There has never been a more vigorous defence of Malory's principles of editing his materials than that which Saintsbury records in *The English Novel*:

It is what the artist does with his materials, not where he gets them, that is the question. And Malory has done, with *his* materials, a very great thing indeed. He is working no doubt to a certain extent blindly; working much better than he knows, and sometimes as he would not work if he knew better; though whether he would work as well if he knew better is quite a different point. Sometimes he may not take the best available version of a story; but we must ask ourselves whether he knew it. . . . A very remarkable compiler! It is a pity that they did not take him and cut him up in little stars for a light to all his brethren in compiling thereafter.[16]

Saintsbury admired Macaulay, and appreciated particularly the author's habit of checking impressions by visiting the actual sites where history had taken place; but Macaulay, who never told a falsehood, 'not seldom contrives to convey one', a judgement that many readers of Macaulay's historical essays have uneasily shared.[17] In speaking of the notorious unequalness of Hazlitt's writings, Saintsbury argues that the inequality is

due less to an intellectual than to a moral defect. The clear sunshine of Hazlitt's admirably acute intellect is always there; but it is constantly obscured by driving clouds of furious prejudice. Even as the clouds pass, the light may still be seen on distant and scattered parts of the landscape; but wherever their influence extends, there is nothing but thick darkness, gusty wind and drenching rain.[18]

Saintsbury did not care for *Gorboduc*, which (with the exception of the choruses) 'is couched in correct but ineffably dreary decasyllables, in which the sense usually lapses with the line, and the whole stumps on with a maddening, or rather stupefying, monotony'.[19] Reviewing Prévost's life as a hack writer in an effort to understand whence came the moment's falsh of genius that produced *Manon Lescaut*, he pointed out that Prévost undoubtedly imitated not only his own countrymen Marivaux and Crébillon, but two English writers as well, Defoe and Richardson, the latter of whom he actually translated; and then, with irresistible puckishness, Saintsbury felt compelled to add, within parentheses, 'Fancy translating Richardson!'[20] He admired Dickens, but shuddered at the excesses of idolators of Dickens; he cited as one example the statement made 'in a most respectable book of reference', that 'Agnes is perhaps the most charming character in the whole range of fiction'. He exploded, '*Agnes!* No decent violence of expletive, no reasonable artifice of typography, could express the depths of my feelings at such a suggestion.'[21] And in his Inaugural Address at the University of Edinburgh, when he sketched in masterly fashion his ambitions as a professor of English literature for the coming years, he said what most lovers of literature have doubtless felt, and seldom expressed as cogently:

> It has been complained of modern geography and travel by the fanciful, that the nice blank spaces, so comfortable to imagi-nation, are being too fast filled up. There is no danger of that in literature, even in a single one. There are plenty of things that you can never find out at all – plenty of them that in the conditions of time and space there is no chance of finding out. But you can always be finding out something, and always, as you find it, the old things that you knew have fresh light shed on them – the old enjoyment that you felt acquires a fresh keenness.[22]

If the true test is a reader's ability to enjoy a novel, poem or play – a test that Saintsbury, in the same address, admitted was 'rebel-liously simple' – the professional study of literature had to beware lest it take guidance from the pernicious example of German universities, and encourage the cataloguing of syllabic lengths in lines of poetry or the analysing of sex in animals in Shakespeare. Saintsbury's exuberant self-confidence, his relating of specific insights to a more generalised sense of the value of his own responses to literature, could not convert all readers; the scoffing at the possibility of absolute standards whereby a genre or a literary school might be judged led inevitably to the counter-reaction of new styles in literary analysis.

It is not unexpected, therefore, that Saintsbury should have enjoyed his own century (the nineteenth much more than the twentieth) fully as much as any previous one. True that he could not remember clearly details about the publication of Dickens's novels of the 1850s, and true that much of what he wrote about the first six decades of the century was based on what he had read in the study rather than on what had come to him in the reviewer's way. One would give much to have Saintsbury's comments on some of the greatest Victorians, written not after their death, but while they still lived and their works were most controversial. The reasons for his reluctance to discuss living authors – which, at a later time, included his reluctance to seem to be making judgements *ex cathedra* from his Chair at Edinburgh – have already been mentioned, and do him credit; but Saintsbury's relationship to his century was, in some respects, affected by both this chronological remoteness from the events of the first half of the century, and – in the final decades – by an understandable unwillingness to interpose himself between a reader and a living writer whose work could not yet be judged in relation to what Dryden had called the 'firm perspective of the past'.[23]

Nevertheless, Saintsbury's observations about nineteenth-century English writers are expressed with an idiosyncratic pungency. He regarded Matthew Arnold – whose career he had followed with interest – as the best critic of his century, and admired him as one who knew what he meant, and who meant something not anticipated by any earlier critic. But Arnold's faults, as enumerated by Saintsbury, are quite serious. Arnold was given to formulas, and to repetition of phrases such as 'criticism of life', 'lucidity' and 'grand style' ('misleading and snip-snap phrases', Saintsbury wrote with some exasperation). Arnold's arrogance in believing that what he did not like no person of taste could like either, originated in a narrow, crotchety personality. Moreover, Arnold frequently violated his own canons: 'At least,' said Saintsbury, 'I am myself quite unable to reconcile that doctrine of confining ourselves to "the best", which it seems rules out the *Chanson de Roland* and makes Shelley more remarkable as a letter-writer than as a poet, with the attention paid to Sénancour and the Guérins.' Arnold contributed greatly to the awakening of the Victorian sense that appreciation might justifiably precede codification (the doctrine was novel in his time), but his criticism suffered because he admired classical literature so highly that to be un-Greek was to follow inferior gods. 'Now I will yield to no man in my respect for the classic,' said Saintsbury; 'and I do not think that, at least as far as the Greeks are concerned, anyone will ever do better the things that they did. But it is absurd to suppose or maintain that the canon of literary perfections was closed when the Muses left Philemon's house.'[24]

Arnold suffered from an unhistorical attitude toward Celtic literature, and worked with a limited number of translations and undated works as if they justified very large generalisations about 'melancholy', 'natural magic' and so forth. Saintsbury disdained 'theory divorced from history'. Arnold's later work, with notable exceptions, was inferior because much of the ebullience had 'frothed and bubbled itself away'; because his critical views had matured, but not altered. Moreover, Arnold's dedication to the Poetic *Subject* rather than to the Poetic *Moment* was sometimes inconsistent with his admiration of such lines as '*In la sua volontade è nostra pace*', quoted to demonstrate Dante's greatness, and to serve 'as an infallible touchstone for detecting the presence or absence of high poetic quality in other poetry'.

Arnold at the top; the others, lamentably farther down the mountain's side. Froude's criticism was damaged by political and philosophical prejudices; it had been tainted by Froude's admiration of Carlyle. Ruskin talked poetically, but was given to paroxysms of unreason: 'You may admire the budding of a flower, but not a display of fireworks.'[25] George Henry Lewes may have been important as George Eliot's mentor and companion, and he wrote some decent dramatic criticism; but to perpetrate upon the public a work entitled *The Principles of Success in Literature* was to confess the existence of an ingrained vulgarity. 'Fame may be the last infirmity of noble minds; Success is but the first and last morbid appetite of the vulgar.'[26] Everywhere, even in his best essay, 'The Inner Life of Art', 'the stamp of the Exhibition of 1851 is upon him also'[27] Bagehot, praised for sanity, sense, and good humour, spread himself wide and thin, though his 'odd moments were far from unprofitable'.[28] Richard Holt Hutton, on the other hand, hated criticism as criticism, and always allayed or sweetened its bitter cup 'by sentimental, or political, or religious, or philosophical, or anthropological, or pantopragmatic adulteration'.[29] Saintsbury harbours a rather curious disapproval of Hutton's approach to Carlyle (Hutton persists in thinking of Carlyle as a man, teacher, philosopher, moralist, not as a writer); after all, Carlyle entertained a savagely low opinion of most writers, and did not wish to be regarded primarily as a writer, since he dealt with Truths; and Hutton's treatment was in line with Carlyle's own wishes. Pater could not be considered less than a second-rank Coleridge or Arnold, and might have been treated as their equal if he had not been trite in his championing of the pleasure-giving quality of literature, and if it were not that his style had been a little precious and his facility had interfered with the reader's appreciation of the importance of his subject-matter. Saintsbury gives full marks to Pater's emphasis on the definition of feeling, however, and adds, after quoting Pater's remarks on Amiel, 'Indeed, I really do not know that "to define feeling" is not as good – it is certainly as short – a definition of at least a great part of the business of the critic as you can get.'[30]

Saintsbury's attitude toward English critics of the second half of the nineteenth century is distinctly unsatisfactory, since he deals with broken lights. Pater, who comes closer to being an ideal appreciator of moments of pleasure than a fussy, patronising Arnold could, is not Arnold's equal in comprehensiveness of interests, and his disciples, though fierce in adoration, were fewer in number, and more narrowly selective in the kinds of literature that they would willingly endorse. It may be that Saintsbury was justified in his refusal to group *kinds* of critics, since they had stubbornly refused to form schools, as in the eighteenth century, or for that matter as in the first half of the nineteenth; but the net impression after reading Saintsbury's brusque treatment of dozens of late Victorian critics is that he saw their occupation as harried, and the essays that they churned out, on demand, in the crowded periodical world to which he himself had belonged was – on the whole – an uninspiring business.

With the Victorian novel Saintsbury was more at ease, and his appreciation of that particularly productive period from 1845 to 1855 was very enthusiastic. Thackeray then wrote his best, and *David Copperfield* came out in 1850; Lever, Kingsley and Trollope were all publishing major works; there was 'a stirring of the waters, a rattling among the bones, such as is not common in literature'.[31] Saintsbury did not want to attribute this flowering to the simple fact that good novelists were mature, and enjoying their camaraderie, in the same decade. The examples set by the works of Scott and Jane Austen had been studied, and assimilated. England had triumphed in the Napoleonic Wars; travels of both the aristocracy and the middle class were becoming more extensive; people were better educated; the change in manners and society by mid century affected all branches of creative endeavour, and the novel especially. The domestic novel, artistically treated, became the new favourite of both writers and readers. Scattered throughout *The English Novel* are brief analyses (less than 500 words) of specific examples of the craft that, for good sense and straightforward communication of one reader's 'pleasure', can hardly be bettered. In his chapter 'The Mid-Victorian Novel' (a subject that he kept treating in a surprisingly large number of essays and other books), he offers a concise statement of the reason why Mrs Gaskell so often disappoints midway through a narrative such as *North and South*:

> Mrs Gaskell seems to me one of the chief illustrations of the extreme difficulty of the domestic novel – of the necessity of exactly proportioning the means at command to the end to be achieved. Her means were, perhaps, greater that those of most of her brother-and-sister novelists, but she set them to loose ends, to ends too high for her, to ends not worth achieving. . . . She 'means' well in Herbert's sense of the word: but what is meant is not quite done.[32]

Of a minor writer as Elizabeth Sewell, Sainstsbury could say, in a judgement that remains final,

> Though she wrote good English, [she] possessed no special grace of style, and little faculty of illustration or ornament from history, literature, her own fancy, current fashions, even of the most harmless kind, and so forth. Thre result is that her books have a certain dead-aliveness – that her characters, though actually alive, are neither interestingly alive nor, as Miss Austen had made hers, interesting in their very uninterestingness.[33]

Happily, the need to set individual novels within a frame of generalisations does not prevent Saintsbury from remarking on several important aspects of literary history: the way in which 'a sort of cheap machine-made' grand manner spread through the entire novel instead of being reserved for grand occasions; the temptation to make the second volume of a three-decker a convenient location for mere padding; the significant role played by circulating libraries in setting standards of content and morality for the kinds of novels they were willing to purchase from publishers; the importance of magazines in the evolution of the late Victorian novel (piecemeal production of a long work of fiction, Saintsbury maintained, was a mixed blessing for both the reading public and the novelist); and the growing perception among readers and critics that the novels of 1845–70 were, taken as a whole, as extraordinary a literary phenomenon as the drama of 1585–1625 and the poems of 1789–1825. Saintsbury believed that the note of perversity in the novels of the two most important late Victorians – George Meredith and Thomas Hardy – came from a determination to be 'peculiar' in thought, style, choice of subject, handling of subject; yet he admired their refusal to change sail in order 'to catch the popular breeze'.[34] Meredith, from one angle of vision, belonged with Cervantes, Shakespeare, Molière, Swift, Fielding and Thackeray (and 'well above Dickens'), because he 'undoubtedly enlarge[d] humanity's conscious knowledge of itself in the way of fictitious exemplification'. No book by Meredith, however, was a masterpiece, and most of his work failed to convey the sense of inevitability in the writing: 'after all, *Ich kann nicht anders* must be to some extent the mood of mind of the man who is committing a masterpiece'.[35]

There was little to be said in favour of most of Meredith's competitors. Scott wrote some four novels in one year, 'and the process helped to kill him'; but Mrs Oliphant, who equalled the feat 'over and over again', 'only killed her novels'. James Payn's novels might be readable a second time, but, as Saintsbury delicately put it, 'I have seldom come across a novelist with whom I was so little inclined to try it.' William Black began with problem novels and rapidly declined; his later work 'was not up to a very good average'. Walter Besant turned out machine-made novels, first with the collaborator James Rice, then by himself, and it made no difference one way or the other; 'the system of novel-production *à la douzaine*' encouraged the writing of tales of brick. Wilkie Collins often made the reader 'angry with him for his prudish poetical or theatrical justice, which is not poetical and hardly even just'.[36]

If Saintsbury's great love for French literature was based largely on his conviction that it was romantic, the high praise given to Robert Louis Stevenson, toward the conclusion of his chapter 'The Fiction of Yesterday', becomes more understandable as a cry from the heart: 'His style is of less importance' than the fact that he applied it almost wholly to the carrying out of a 'rejuvenescence of romance'. The novels of the second half of the century included some 'very great things', though, after Scott and Jane Austen, the ordinariness of the talents of many novel-writers was all the more vividly exposed; and the appearance of Stevenson reminded Saintsbury that the novel, as a genre, did not suffer from terminal illness.

In 1923, Saintsbury took one of his final looks at the novel, and sniffed disapprovingly of books written 'in accordance with a definite scheme', inasmuch as 'the best stories of the past have not as a rule been constructed in such a fashion'.[37] There is an endearing crustiness to the plea Saintsbury addressed to the novelist who tried to beguile him with some 'plan' or 'purpose'. 'Never mind your significance, old man! . . . Give us story! Give us character!'

Those who regard Saintsbury as hopelessly old-fashioned, however, would do well to take a look at the chapter 'The Second Poetical Period' in *A History of Nineteenth Century Literature (1780– 1895)*. Its ordering of poets was exceptionally perceptive for the time of its writing. It was based on enormously wide and intelligent reading of minor poets as well as in the total work of all the major ones (Saintsbury treated, with his usual zest, the humorists, the Spasmodics, the London Bohemian school, and a crocodile of women poets); and practically all its judgements have been accepted as the common wisdom of modern anthologies. It is true that the basis of judgement keeps shifting, and that he is sometimes particularly severe on a transgression in one poet that he has no time to annotate in the case of another; but there is little doubt at any given moment what Saintsbury is reacting to, or why. The number of illustrations that he provides of Mrs Browning's wilful and 'tastelessly unusual vocabulary', careless rhymes, and tendency to run on and on, is, to say the least, generous.[38] He has little patience with the argument that Martin Farquhar Tupper was, in private life, 'an amiable and rather accomplished person', though he writes it down as a fact worth noting; he feels constrained to add, 'But *Proverbial Philosophy* remains as one of the bright and shining examples of the absolute want of connection between literary merit and popular success.' While conceding the unsettled condition of the merits of Lord Lytton, he encapsulates a later generation's disdain: 'Though he frequently rewrote, it seemed impossible for him to retrench and concentrate.'[39]

Saintsbury never doubted that Tennyson was the best poet not merely of his generation, but of the entire second half of the century. In some respects Tennyson exceeded Keats, for he had 'a wider range of interest and capacity', 'the enormous advantage of thorough and regular literary training', and the capacity for taking infinite pains with editing of his own work. This did not mean that Tennyson's mannerisms were dismissed as trivial interferences with a reader's enjoyment. *In Memoriam* probably talked too much about the ineffable and the unprovable; what Saintsbury, in another context, called 'the *Schwatzerei*, the endless, aimless talkee-talkee about "thoughtful" things in which the nineteenth century has indulged beyond the record of any since what used to be called the Dark Ages'.[40] He conceded merit to the charge that Tennyson's dandyism (also called 'finicalness' or '*mignardise*') produced over-rhetorical passages and manifested itself in a tendency to pile up tribrachs in his blank verse. *Maud* dragged in too many casual things such as 'adulteration, popular politics, and ephemera of all kinds'; while *Idylls of the King* ran on too long, and belonged neither to the medieval nor to the modern period. But Tennyson was important not merely because of the breathtaking variety of his poems, or because he had come before the public with a great volume of such work, but because he had dominated his contemporaries longer than any other poet of the century: 'The influences of Pope and Dryden were weak in force and merely external in effect, the influence of Byron was short-lived, that of Wordsworth was partial and limited, in comparison with the influence of Tennyson.'[41]

Next to Tennyson, Browning's work, for all its virtues, shone palely. Saintsbury, while not dismissing the charge of obscurity, termed the problem one of 'breathlessness', or the expression 'of a man who either did not stop at all to pick his words, or was only careful to pick them out of the first choice that presented itself to him of something not commonplace'.[42] Browning's masterpieces were 'Christmas Eve and Easter Day' (1850) and *Men and Women* (1855), though *Bells and Pomegranates* and *Dramatis Personae* (1864) contained some fine poems, too. His dramas were involuted and uneven, his Greek translations indulged 'a sort of hybrid and pedantic spelling of proper names', and his later works, from *The Ring and the Book* onwards, were riddled by 'an eccentric and almost burlesque phraseology'. What Lang had disliked in Dickens's admirers, Saintsbury found particularly repellent in the Browning Society, to which, he said sternly, the poet had allowed 'a kind of countenance which would certainly not have been extended to it by most English men of letters'. Handbooks and the *Browning Dictionary* provided 'for his disciples something to make up for the ordinary classical and other dictionaries with which, it seemed to be presumed, their previous education would have made them little conversant'.[43]

It may reasonably be concluded, therefore, that Saintsbury rated the Victorian novel more highly than the Victorian poem. But he sought diligently for shards of talent or promise in the disappointing poetry that duty compelled him to review. He believed that Arnold's genius – like that of most poets in the last two-thirds of the century – expressed itself best in shorter pieces; Rossetti's *The House of Life* was not (despite contemporary reactions) an indecent sonnet sequence; O'Shaughnessy lacked originality and human interest, and suffered from morbidity, but he had the *unum necessarium*, 'the individual note of song'; Thomson suffered from 'a monotonous, narrow, and irrational misery', but his stately verse contained splendid passages; Clough's work suffered from that brand of scepticism which had 'neither the strength to believe nor the courage to disbelieve "and have done with it"'. The end of the century was notable, among other things, for a flagging of energy among the poets, and Saintsbury gloomily contemplated the growth in popularity of free verse: 'It is quite clear that this kind of freedom is certain to indulge itself in mere anarchy at first. As to what some people seem still to think and do more than seem to say – that metre and rhyme will be superseded – one may be rash enough to pronounce this impossible . . . .'[44]

Saintsbury's sympathy with literary effort of almost all varieties was, somewhat curiously, limited in so far as drama was concerned. He did not attend the theatre, preferring his study; and there are some indications that, given choices of how to pass his reading time, he preferred almost anything to a play. He certainly never speaks of the printing or the production of a new drama with the same enthusiasm that led him to bring home, along with a first-edition copy of Swinburne's *Poems and Ballads* (1866), 'divers maroons' for accompaniment.[45] Verse dramas had proved disastrous. Talfourd's *Ion* enjoyed what little success it had because of Macready's popularity and skill. Browning's plays continually raised the question, 'Why are all these people behaving in this way?' As for Knowles, he was 'content to dwell in decencies forever',[46] a damning encomium. Perhaps the drama suffered because those who wrote the most ambitious plays for the nineteenth-century theatre were, in one sense, play-acting; their primary artistic interests did not lie in the writing of dramas so much as in acting, producing, the law, poetry or the novel. Saintsbury's final judgement is completely negative: 'In this period the dramatic work of those who have been really men and women of letters is generally far inferior to their other work, and . . . with the rarest exceptions, the dramatic work of those who have not excelled in other kinds of literature is not literature at all.'[47]

It is not necessary to consider, in this context, Saintsbury's views on nineteenth-century historians, journalists, theologians and philosophers, beyond marvelling again at how much of the printed product turned out by men and women of fundamentally non-belletristic bias Saintsbury had taken some effort to master. But Saintsbury's feeling about the nineteenth century was intensely positive. *Bliss was it in that dawn to be alive*: for Saintsbury is really saying that after the giants – after the Romantics, who benefited from the renewal of interest in medieval and foreign literature, the excitement of the French Revolution and its aftermath, and the growing conviction that theirs would be an age of 'Progress' – came a sequel scarcely less interesting than the original renaissance between 1798 and 1824. A brief period of imitation ('school work'), and an undeniable falling-off; but Hood, Praed, Macaulay, Taylor, Darley, Beddoes, Hartley Coleridge and Horne had 'singular excellence', and an eccentric and spasmodic orginality; and after them, of course, Tennyson, Browning, Arnold, and all the others who made poetry so watchable a profession fully half a century. 'For total amount, total merit, total claims of freshness and distinctness, no period of poetical literature can much, if at all, exceed the ninety years of English verse from *The Ancient Mariner* to *Crossing the Bar*.'[48]

Thus, unlike Lang, whose strictures against almost anything new became more severe as the century ended, Saintsbury looked back on what he considered to be an extraordinary period of talents, enthusiasm and achievement, and his 'Huzzah!' could be heard everywhere. It may be argued that Saintsbury, who outlasted Lang by a full two decades, simply took longer to agree with Lang that English literature had exhausted itself, and was enduring a period of transition while a new yeast prepared to work itself out in the later years of the twentieth century. Saintsbury was well aware that the end of the Victorian Age was also the end of a number of literary movements. Saintsbury underestimated the merits of Yeats, Eliot, Pound, Joyce and a number of other modernists; he entertained more nostalgia than was necessary for the three-decker novel, an art form that had collapsed by the early 1890s; and he entertained dark suspicions that the kinds of periodicals for which he had laboured so valiantly over a twenty-year period had vulgarised everyone's reading-tastes.

Novels had become the only books for many men and women, who assumed that it was legitimate to adopt the standards found therein as the standards of both nature and life. The authors of these novels, in turn, had frequently imitated what they had found in earlier novels. There was, in brief, a second-hand look to ideas that Saintsbury found disconcerting, even distressing; and literary craftsmanship, or over-abundance of information about the 'past and present of literature', did not compensate for the public's strong demand for quantity rather than quality, and for its willingness to pay handsomely for reading-pleasure of an inferior variety.

But Saintsbury believed in change, not only in its certainty, but also in its desirability, and he was willing to entertain the proposition that a new *Lyrical Ballads* might appear at any moment; that after Stevenson a new master of the romance might begin to publish; and that public taste might improve if genuine artists came forward to treat nature again at first-hand. The nineteenth century, which had ended on a note of diminuendo, might well be followed by stronger and newer chords played by a master musician, and, though Saintsbury saw few or none on the immediate horizon when he came to the end of his lengthy and productive life, he never forgot that English literature – if only the record could be trusted – continually renewed itself. The point, of course, is that he did trust the record, and in his own way had done a great deal to make journalistic and academic criticism respectable elements of that record.

At least one master-work deserves a closer look before we conclude this discussion of Saintsbury's work: *A History of Criticism*, which appeared in three volumes (1901, 1902 and 1904). It is both magisterial and surprisingly diffident. As Saintsbury indicated in his Preface to volume I, such a review had not been undertaken by anyone else on quite the scale that Saintsbury believed essential for a judicious consideration of the subject-matter. Dr Johnson had intended to write a *History of Criticism, as it related to Judging of Authours*, but never proceeded to do more than collect notes. B. Mazzarella's *Della Critica* (1866) 'seems to be merely a torso' (though Saintsbury had not seen it personally); Théry's *Histoire des Opinions Littéraires* (c. 1830) dismissed too many important subjects too swiftly, in a page or a paragraph, and knew nothing about

English criticism after Campbell and Blair. Forced to identify the major critics of European tradition and to trace their doctrines for himself, Saintsbury decided to put together the atlas that he himself had needed. 'He may have put elephants for towns, he may have neglected important rivers and mountains, like a general from the point of view of a newspaper correspondent, or a newspaper correspondent from the point of view of a general; but he has done what he could.'[49]

Saintsbury did not disguise his disdain of attempts of critics to smash literary works which did not live up to theoretical laws that they had themselves devised; such critics hammer home the dubious propositions that this poem will not do because it fails to resemble the ideal epic, or that that poem, a romance, is too loose to be accounted an epic, and hence is barred altogether. Not too long ago one form of tragedy became the only permissible form; lyric 'became a mere appendage to Tragedy', and history was relegated to 'a sort of baggage-waggon to oratorical Rhetoric'. The critics of antiquity – Aristotle followed by Dionysius of Halicarnassus and Longinus – began this notion of hierarchies of genres. Saintsbury did not much like the direction in which the rhetoric of classical times was moving, and he spoke often in terms such as 'the bread-winning chicanery of forensic' and 'the desert and chaos of wasted industry' that stretched in an 'endless procession of some fifty generations'. Aristotle, Plato, Plutarch, all had their eyes 'mainly off the object', which means, essentially, that reading and examining a text in an untiring quest after 'the secret of its charms' were seldom, if ever, regarded as worth the trouble until Longinus.

Latin literature, Saintsbury claimed, benefited from being able to refer its standards to the language and literature of the Greeks. The Greeks had had to evolve their own standards, and their diagnosis of the qualities that made a literary work distinctive suffered accordingly; but comparative techniques afforded the Roman critics an opportunity to see both the degree of orginality and the acceptable variations in form of a given creative work. They were men of letters 'almost always by accident, and on the way to being something else'. Moreover, they kept fastening down upon themselves hard and fast rules.

If Saintsbury detested the false claims for the virtues of oratory made by the Greeks, he was driven to distraction by the even more exaggerated claims made by Romans for orators whose speeches survive only in fragments, or not at all. Rhetoricians who insisted on classifying the speeches of Virgil demeaned the greatness of their best poet; the emphasis on figures (antiphrasis, hyperbole, and so on) was 'topsy-turvy' and, muttered Saintsbury ominously, could 'come to no good end'. Latin grammarians knew a great deal about metre, metrical quantity, and metrical quality; but they stopped short before coming to a consideration of the 'higher criticism of literary form and charm', as if they feared being forced to render judgement on 'the *poetical* quality of the Ennian, the Lucretian, and the Virgilian hexameter'. A summing-up attempts to be generous, but succeeds primarily in reminding us how strenuously Saintsbury fought clear of restrictive rules and models meant to inspire awe rather than love: 'A literature like classical Latin, which is from first to last *in statu pupillari*, which, with whatever strength, deftness, elegance, even originality at times, follows in the footsteps of another literature, must for the very life of it have a critical creed of order, discipline, moderation.'[50] Latin literature got the criticism it deserved. Served in good stead by these carefully defined rulings of grammar and rhetoric, worked out over a period of centuries, that literature led ultimately to the development of the Trivium and the Quadrivium, legacies of the classics. Anything more, and the Middle Ages would have been unable to accomplish its own work; critical appreciation of literary texts was not part of its self-assigned business.

Saintsbury was unimpressed by the literary criticism of the medieval period; but in *De Vulgari Eloquio*, presumably by Dante (though there has been considerable debate over the question), he found 'such a diploma-piece as has been scarcely half-a-dozen times elsewhere seen in the history of the world'. Not merely because Dante's authorship provides evidence of the links between the creative and critical faculties, but because Dante wrote without indebtedness to Aristotle or to Longinus, and without being tainted by overdependence on the figures and other kinds of rhetorical jargon; with due respect to questions of 'form', with knowledge and appreciation of various prose fictions, a subtle and sophisticated awareness of the merits of literatures in other tongues, and anticipations of modern attitudes toward style. (Chaucer's efforts at literary criticism, Saintsbury maintains, are moral, and scarcely deserve the name. Only in Chaucer's discussion of Sir Thopas is there a 'crystallised' opinion as to the difference between genuine and meretricious literature.)

Saintsbury admired the originality of much medieval literature, because authors then observed only 'formal restrictions of the minor kind' which came naturally, and were of their own devising; but medieval authors, in general, rejected restrictions of literary theory. The Muse of an author of the Middle Ages 'will wear no stays, though she does not disdain ornaments'. Thus, the invention of story, the development of romance as a genre, the new understanding of the love motive, the cultivation of the short tale, and the originality of the medieval drama, made possible for later generations of critics the hammering-out of an entirely new calculus of critical variations. The signal contribution of the Middle Ages to the Renaissance grew out of two facts: 'the immense provision of new kinds of literature by the Middle Age, side by side with its almost total abstinence from criticism', which, Saintsbury concludes, 'was the best thing that could have happened'.[51]

Renaissance criticism, understandably, becomes a class of literary endeavour. Besides its ancient books, of the law (the Greek and Latin authorities are generally recognised to have survived because of their intrinsic quality), this body of criticism now has 'quite a library of modern prophets, commentators, scribes'. The sixteenth century brought together in recognisable form 'the dogmas of the Neo-Classic creed, its appeal to the ancients and its appeal to Reason or Nature or Sense, its strict view of Kinds, its conception of Licence and Rule, its Unities', and the business of the seventeenth century was to 'codify precedent case-law' rather than do anything new. Saintsbury notes that Renaissance criticism limits itself, rather surprisingly, to poetry, and more than compensates for those earlier times when oratory took precedence; but it also slights the prose romance, the essay, and other departments that now justify careful consideration. In addition, Ronsard, Du Bellay, Tasso, Sidney and Ben Jonson are not the great critics that earlier or later ages produced, so that the whole critical system came into existence 'by a process of haphazard accretion'.

As Saintsbury reviews 'the crystallising of the Neo-Classic creed', his disapproval of pedantry, absurdities, literary history reshaped to fit a critic's preconceptions, and overdogmatic assumptions affect what he wants to say about Malherbe, Chapelain, Malebranche, La Bruyère, Fénelon and Boileau; Spanish writers never 'kept creation and criticism separate' and had no critic of 'real authority' to keep them honest; the Germans did not know enough about other cultures to develop 'the comparative stimulus'; and intellects such as Milton, Cowley, Davenant and Hobbes served primarily to prepare the way for one greater than themselves in the field of English criticism.

Dryden (there is an almost audible sigh of relief) was never afraid to ask 'Why?' He asked 'not whether he ought to like such and such a thing, but whether he does like it, and why he likes it, and whether he does like it, and why he likes it, and whether there is any real reason why he should not like it'. Dryden, of course, was not perfect, but he was a genuine and catholic critic, and his interest in discovering for himself the reasons why he enjoyed a particular literary work was the very interest that Saintsbury declared every critic should cultivate. A critic (so Saintsbury concluded in his final chapter, 'The Present State of Criticism')

> must read, and, as far as possible, read everything – that is the first and great commandment. If he omits one period of a literature, even one author of some real, if ever so little, importance in a period, he runs the risk of putting his view of the rest out of focus; if he fails to take at least some account of other literatures as well, his state will be nearly as perilous. Secondly, he must constantly compare books, authors, literatures indeed, to see in what each differs from each, but never in order to dislike one because it is not the other. Thirdly, he must, as far as he possibly can, divest himself of any idea of what a book *ought to be*, until he has seen what it is.[52]

On these grounds the critics of the Neo-Classic period, however meritorious their individual insights might be, failed to satisfy Saintsbury. They were too ready to accept unquestioningly the authority of an ancient, of Aristotle or Horace; they believed too slavishly in the need of a drama to observe the 'Unities' and in the indisputable greatness of the 'Heroic Poem'. Nor did Saintsbury accept the conventional view of the unbridgeable chasm between the Ancients and the Moderns, despite their notorious quarrel:

> The Moderns were, as a rule, just as 'classical' in their ideas as the Ancients. They were as incapable of catholic judgment; they were even more ignorant of literature as a whole; they were at least as apt to introduce non-literary criteria; they were as much under the obsession of the Kind, the Rule (cast-iron, not leaden), the sweeping generalisation.

Hence, it was not surprising that the eighteenth century, with its hardening orthodoxy, neither deserved nor received the praise that Saintsbury felt more properly due to the succeeding century. But English criticism, at least, was saved from the worst excesses of the school of 'correctness' by the fact that Dryden had championed Shakespeare and Milton, and Englishmen who took an intelligent interest in poetry had already agreed that Chaucer and Spenser were great practitioners of the craft. Pope was succeeded by Dr Johnson, and both were humane and liberal enough to admit the difficulties that prevented them from issuing categorical imperatives. Saintsbury noted that Dr Johnson had refused to 'judge genius merely by the event', and had said, in reference to Shakespeare, that, 'if genius succeeds by means which are wrong according to rule, we may think higher of the genius but less highly of the work'. To which Saintsbury replied that, if Shakespeare showed genius in neglecting the Rules, the inexorable voice of Logic was bound to point out that the Rules were evidently not necessary.

A History of Criticism reviewed, with enormous authority, the critical judgements of eight cultures and more than two thousand years. But Saintsbury's criteria for judging the worth of a critic, no matter where or in which century he lived, are no more complicated than has already been indicated. He opposed schematic criticism. The more rigorously a writer insisted on ignoring any possible exceptions to a morphology and a set of precedents that he had adopted, the less reliable would he be whenever he came to treat a fellow author whose work transcended predefined categories. Saintsbury maintained consistently that a critic must never neglect the artistic criterion, even if it suggests the existence of more things in heaven and earth than are dreamed of in his philosophy; even if it unnerves his self-confidence. Thus, while repudiating much of Dr Johnson's argument about the relative worth of English poets, Saintsbury conceded that Dr Johnson had 'kept in constant touch with life', and that he easily passed the test of a great critic. With generosity, he speaks of the fact that Johnson's critical opinions were formed quite early in life: it is not necessarily true that regarding everything as an open question, or being willing to change any opinion 'at a moment's notice', is worthy of praise. 'As a matter of fact, we have record of not many men who have proceeded in this way; and it may be doubted whether among them is a single person of first-rate genius, or even talent.' This is sensible stuff; the fact that Saintsbury, personally more rabidly Tory than Dr Johnson ever was, appreciated the conservative politics of Dr Johnson does not take away from the well-turned piquancy of the observation.

Criticism, as Saintsbury outlines its history, is not as ancient or as honourable a profession as its practitioners sometimes pretend. There have not been many good critics over the centuries; fortunate the nation that can boast, as Italy does, of a poet who also had original and useful things to say about the nature of his art.

> No Muse, or handmaid of the Muses (let it be freely confessed) has been less often justified of her children: none has had so many good-for-nothings for sons . . . . The purblind theorist who mistakes the passport for the person, and who will not admit without passport the veriest angel; the acrid pedant who will allow no one whom he dislikes to write well, and no one at all to write on any subject that he himself has written on, or would like to write on, who dwells on dates and commas, who garbles out and foists in, whose learning may be easily exaggerated but whose taste and judgment cannot be, because they do not exist; – these are too often justified patterns of the critic to many minds. The whole record of critical result, which we have so laboriously arranged and developed, is a record of mistake and of misdoing, of half-truths and nearly whole errors.

So stern a summing-up would be depressing save that, again, Saintsbury admits the delights inherent in the quest; and what has been known once and appreciated for what it is in all its splendour can never be less than what it was then seen to be. If Saintsbury expands Arnold's notion of the goal of criticism from an endeavour to know and recommend 'not only the best, but all the good, that has been known and thought and written in the world', the enthusiasm is not unbecoming to a critic who has obviously read more and written more than practically all his contemporaries; and it is a truism throughout this enormous study that the best critic is one who first satisfies himself as to why he likes a work before he attempts to expand its reading audience.

To be a modern critic, one must disregard the precedents established by either the ancients or our contemporaries who assume, with some dogmatism, to speak for the ancients. Saintsbury's position is that 'the most modern of works is to be judged, not by adjustment to anything else, but on its own merits'. A critic, we are told, 'must always behave as if the book he takes from its wrapper might be a new *Hamlet* or a new *Waverley*, – or something as good as either, but more absolutely novel in kind than even *Waverley*, – however shrewdly he may suspect that it is very unlikely to be any such thing'. To some extent this argues with another proposition that one should know as much about the literary past as possible, and thus be able to judge on the basis of an awareness of the heritage of any new literary work. We can hardly evaluate intelligently the new *Hamlet* unless we know the old *Hamlet*. Saintsbury never satisfactorily reconciled these two positions, and his neglected law of criticism, that 'B is not bad because it is not A, however good A may be', would be more widely accepted if one remembered Saintsbury's corollary law, that B and A must be compared and contrasted before the singularity of B may be established.

Perhaps Saintsbury stressed, more than most twentieth-century critics, the importance of the critic's response. His own appetite being omnivorous, he could read swiftly through enormous quantities of material (reading was not work, he once said, but writing criticism was), and decide which works were worth thinking about, and which could be safely discarded. An analogy with tasting grew naturally from consideration of such an image. The classic formulation by Bacon as to how books are to be digested must have been what Saintsbury had in mind when, in his book for all enthusiasts of drink, *Notes on a Cellar-Book* (1920), he repeatedly linked his love of spiritous liquors with his love of literature. One learns to trust the critic when his appetite has been proved sound, and his ability to discriminate between tastes has been demonstrated.

No Victorian critic exposed himself more often or willingly to the kind of scrutiny that precedes trust than Saintsbury did. *A History of Criticism*, despite its 1800 pages, fulfils its author's claim that here, for the first time, the major critical texts have been reviewed to discover what, in fact, their authors had to say. Saintsbury has little patience with the notion that one must review what critics of the critics have had to say before one can estimate fairly what poems, plays, and novels are driving at; there is no fussing with Victorian views of what Dr Johnson meant when he wrote about Milton's opinions on the epic. Saintsbury's footnotes record aperçus and afterthoughts rather than citations to the secondary and tertiary literatures that have grown up around, and sometimes over, the critical texts. Saintsbury is not a technical critic in the modern sense. Yet René Wellek's *A History of Modern Criticism 1750–1950* is highly respectful of

Saintsbury's 'atlas of the actual facts', even as Wellek measures its limitations. Like Croce and Spingarn, Wellek disliked Saintsbury's neglect of theory and aesthetics, his occasional errors in dates and titles, his treatment of poetry as more sound than sense, his dismaying tendency to discuss form independently of the subject, his vagueness whenever he uses the term 'grand style', his subjective readings, 'the poverty and haziness of his concepts and criteria of genres, devices, style, composition', and his near-total impressionism. But Wellek concedes that Saintsbury, for all his faults, was a map-maker in the *History of Criticism*; his influence on academics has been not only 'enormous' but also, we gather, helpful in the encouragement Saintsbury gave to those interested in comparative literary studies, including Wellek himself; and he was, throughout, a 'lively commentator'.[53]

7 Edmund Gosse

A review of Gosse's life and work must confront the difficulties that recent generations of scholars have had with the evidence. There is, to begin with, the remarkable memoir *Father and Son, A Study of Two Temperaments*, which appeared anonymously in 1907, and which was greeted with high praise by those who believed that at last the mask of Victorian piety had been ripped away, revealing humbug and hypocrisy; the hubbub created by its reception more than matched the sensationalism of its content. In *Father and Son* Gosse portrayed himself as the sensitive, much-oppressed son of a famous biologist, and the unwilling participant in the religious activities of the glum Plymouth Brotherhood of St Marychurch, South Devon. Restricted to a narrow range of church literature, Gosse knew little or nothing of most creative writing, of any literature, until his adolescent years. Evan Charteris, his discreet biographer, fixes on Gosse's seventeenth year as the true beginning of his appreciation of English literature.

But *Father and Son* is a self-serving document; it would be astonishing if the memoir were not; and questions about the accuracy of Gosse's depiction of his father's character, the Plymouth Brotherhood, and the glacially paced development of his own reading-tastes have been raised by more than one analyst. James Hepburn, in a scholarly edition of the text published in 1974, asks the pointed question, 'Why should he who was inaccurate about Sir Philip Sidney, Donne, Gray, and Swinburne be taken at face value about himself and his father unless it were that he charmed his modern readers with their own prejudices?'[1] John Churton Collins had a right to expect from the new appointee to the Clark Lectureship in English Literature at Trinity College, Cambridge, more respect for factual accuracy than Gosse had been willing to show in the late 1880s,[2] but Hepburn's question might easily be extended to the remainder of Gosse's life – a full four decades – and to most of his critical books.

This second bothersome aspect of Gosse's career provokes an

argument that the graces of a lucid and straightforward style, enlivened by anecdote and by personal reminiscence, must always be judged in relation to our suspicion that Gosse is not a completely reliable witness to what he knows or what he has read. A similar feeling of unease overwhelms more than one literary historian looking into the numerous Thomas J. Wise forgeries; how much Gosse knew, and when he knew it (to paraphrase Senator Baker's questions about an American President on the eve of impeachment proceedings), are still obscure issues, though Gosse must have known the pernicious consequences of becoming even more deeply involved with Wise than he was.

Moreover, Gosse's trimming of opinions to suit those above him, and his occasional brutality of manner to those below, cannot help but be disconcerting. Gosse was a snob of the worst kind. Perhaps no post offered him more of an opportunity to perfect his equivocal – and occasionally exasperating – manners than that of librarian to the House of Lords (1904–14). The printing of more of his letters (they continue to turn up) has shown how skilfully he sought to win the favour of writers with talent, and how he frequently changed his own opinions of an author or a literary work to complement another's view that he had carefully solicited in advance. A strong smarminess is present in the edited texts printed in *The Life and Letters of Sir Edmund Gosse*, by Evan Charteris (1931); but it is even stronger than one had suspected it might be in the volumes that print the correspondence between André Gide and Gosse,[3] and between various American writers and Gosse.[4]

It is certain that Gosse benefited in his studies of the literature of Scandinavia – particularly Denmark and Norway, though he also wrote at some length on the career of Johan Ludvig Runeberg, the great Swedish poet – from the facts that he came early upon the scene, knew personally some of the writers whose plays and poems he was introducing to England, and exploited the Victorian appetite for new techniques and new subject-matter. His work in this field suffered from the same lacunae in needed informaton that plagued his numerous studies of French literature, though it is not surprising that Gosse should have regarded his own pioneering with some complacency, even after he had returned his major attention to English literature. We may generalise: Gosse never knew enough to be accounted a professional, but he earned, relatively soon after Collins's attack, a wide, respectful, and at times affectionate readership. (In the United States, Collins's well-documented charges against Gosse's brand of scholarship were disregarded, or greatly minimised.) Tennyson's oft-quoted characterisation of Collins as 'a Louse on the Locks of Literature' more than compensated Gosse for the cruel gibe, repeated most often at Oxford, that a don who got his facts wrong had 'made a Gosse of himself'.

The issue of trustworthiness is related not so much to Gosse's personality, which can be (and has been) described as oleaginous, as to the fact that Gosse represented, almost without suspecting it, the dying tradition of the English man of letters. Collins, for all his faults – his betrayal of his friendship with Gosse, his jealousy over Gosse's friendship with Swinburne, his disappointment over failure to win the Merton Professorship of English at Oxford (which gave rise to sombre thoughts at the sight of Gosse's academic successes in both the United States and England), and his delight in overkill – was a portent of the future that would soon end the kind of sovereignty exercised by critics like Gosse. Collins was the technical man, the professional scholar, who preferred accuracy to graciousness of style, and solid research to impressionistic maundering on literary topics. Hardy implied more than he knew when he exclaimed – on receipt of Gosse's biography of Raleigh – 'How indefatigable your pen is!'[5] Even Charteris, who forgave almost everything, was writing, within a few years of Gosse's death, a damning critique of this lifelong habit of hasty writing:

> He had the impatience of the imaginative man. He possessed the dangerous boon of a powerful but not always accurate memory, and he trusted it with the eager alacrity of a poet . . . . He never had the discipline of examinations and 'schools', no don had drilled his mind, he was pitchforked into the world . . . . His knowledge was wide and stimulating but it was not minute. His mind was vividly alert but not meticulous. He had 'emulation', but with him it was not 'the scholar's melancholy'.[6]

In the growth of a new cultural climate, as new critics with their armed vision turned to the closer examination of texts and applied hitherto-unused (and only recently developed) disciplinary tools to those texts, Gosse's reputation was bound to go into a long decline.

Yet, for all its deficiencies, Gosse's approach to literature was remarkably consistent over a half-century, and made such good sense in its own time that the bases for its favourable reception must be better understood before Gosse's long bibliography is written down as irrelevant to the modern world. To begin with, Gosse was not alone in his conviction that a writer's life was relevant to a consideration of a writer's art. It is true that this emphasis upon 'personal character' was, to an important degree, affected by contemporary moral standards; he judged writers, perhaps not unexpectedly, in terms of decorum and the presence or absence of common sense. Though he avoided scandal in the anecdotes he chose to recount, he claimed that he sought to tell the truth about the writer behind the work. Character traits might be peculiar, but, if they threw light on the writer's intellect and imagination, he intended to record them faithfully. Gosse believed that it was far more difficult to relate a life to the verses that a writer produced than it would have been for a critic such as he to concentrate wholly upon the verses. In his Preface to *Portraits and Sketches* he wrote, 'To analyse the honey is one thing, and to dissect the bee another; but I find a special pleasure in watching him, myself unobserved, in the act of building up and filling the cells.'[7] In *Critical Kit-Kats* he argued that the biographical element in the mixed sketch that he had begun to perfect as his own distinct contribution to late Victorian reviewing eliminated the temptation to be polemical:

> We cease to be savage and caustic when we are acquainted with the inner existence of a man, for the relentlessness of satire is only possible to those who neither sympathise nor comprehend. What is here essayed is of the analytical, comparative, and descriptive order; it hopes to add something to historical knowledge and something to aesthetic appreciation.[8]

He took pride in the personal element in his criticism, and justified it in much the same ways as Saintsbury. He had a broad-ranging curiosity about many kinds of literature, about their themes, and about the men and women who had transferred to paper the product of their imaginations. How else could he impose order and unity upon his treatment, unless he emphasised the subjectivity of his response? And the fact that it was a personal response? 'It would be disconcerting to believe', he wrote in *Books on the Table*, 'that a man of fair intelligence can be the incessant and insatiable reader of good books for fifty years without discovering some pathway through the maze. That pathway must be his personal response . . . .'[9] The corollary of this view is that a judgement delivered *ex cathedra*, a dictum recorded as if the authority that lay behind it were absolute, imposes a critic's version of the truth in too tyrannical a fashion. What Gosse most wanted, as a writer expressing personal opinions for the benefit of those who might be interested in receiving them, was to pass on to others the pleasure which he had experienced. 'If the poet is allowed to create his sonnet out of the emotions awakened by a sunset or a statue, of which he is not bound to supply scientific description, may I not dare a swallow-flight in prose without being called upon to give an architectural plan of the roof from which I start?'[10]

Gosse's judgements were not backed by rigorously defined aesthetic principles. When he looked into Arthur J. Balfour's *Foundations of Belief* (1900), he was disconcerted by the negative response Balfour had given to his own question, 'Is there any fixed and permanent element in beauty?' He rejected Balfour's 'brilliant and paralysing logic', which claimed, perhaps too stridently, that 'there is no such thing as a principle of taste, but only a variation of fashion'. He conceded the difficulty of producing a yard stick whereby all works of imagination might be measured.

But when we observe, as we must allow, that art is no better at one age than at another, but only different; that it is subject to modification, but certainly not to development; may we not safely accept this stationary quality as a proof that there does exist, out of sight, unattained and unattainable, a positive norm of poetic beauty? We cannot define it, but in each generation all excellence must be the result of a relation to it. It is the moon, heavily wrapt up in clouds, and impossible always to locate, yet revealed by the light it throws on distant portions of the sky.[11]

Beauty in brief, has a fixed existence, though perceptions of beauty may vary from age to age; but the beauty of a literary work may not be brutally seized; the tangential, oblique approach will work better.

Gosse was eager to discover in a writer of any age the merits which were distinctive to that writer's art, whether or not he resembled Jane Austen or Pope or Keats. Dismissing a writer because – here we adapt Saintsbury's formulation – A was not like B, without caring to examine the reasons why A was distinctively and pleasurably A, was to fall into schismatic error. 'All my life long I have been wandering in the gardens of Armida', Gosse wrote as he introduced still another selection of his essays, prepared for the Travellers' Library, 'never rejecting the rose because it was not a jasmine, and never denying the beauty of orchids because they were not daisies'.[12]

These tenets of faith have fallen into disfavour, perhaps not least because of the unwillingness of English men of letters to believe, late in the nineteenth century, that small matters of fact created large suspicions about their interest in being truthful. Basically, Gosse was saying that his approach to literary works emphasised the importance of biographical data, and relating the life to the literary achievement was much more difficult than most people realised; that a critic was entitled to be personal and digressive, if only because he sought to transmit his enthusiasm, and could do so more effectively if he spoke of himself rather than remained anonymous; and that an interest in literary excellence, pursued over a half-century of diligent reading in several languages, entitled him to believe that good writing might be found almost anywhere, and *was* found unexpectedly so often that one should not be dismayed by fluctuations of taste from one culture to another, or from one generation to the next.

How well were these precepts carried through in particular studies? We may begin with a closer look at two volumes, written for the English Men of Letters series, that were well regarded in their time, though they have been superseded by more detailed and informative works of scholarship: *Gray* (1882, revised in 1889) and *Sir Thomas Browne* (1905). Thomas Hardy admired *Gray*, perhaps as much because the eighteenth-century poet's melancholy appealed to him as much because Gosse and he got along so well. Gosse's eye in this book is more on the life than the poetry. In discussing 'Ode on a Distant Prospect of Eton College' Gosse notes the actual appearance of the land near 'Stoke-Pogis'; expresses confidence in the poet's sincerity; and muses with some wistfulness (along with Gray) that the 'illusions of boyhood' cannot last through life. Yet Gosse knows that the notion of youthful innocence in Gray's 'Ode' is circumscribed by the 'elementary' notion of ethics that accompanies the poem. Gosse refrains from carping, though he believes (and regrets) that the poem has been overpraised; famous lines have not only been honoured by millions of readers, they have been degraded (the phrase Gosse uses is 'vulgar traffic', and this note, struck fairly often, suggests an occasional – and surprising – reluctance to share with just anyone the pleasures of his reading).

'Hymn to Adversity', written in Gray's mature style, maintains the severe elevation of a Milton and a Shelley, but it represents a 'pure and cold' manner that Gosse does not warm to. He finds, for instance, that Gray does not do enough to differentiate the 'shadowy personages of allegory', and he objects, even while paying homage to Gray's art, to the problems a careful reader might have in remembering the terrors or allurements of Adversity when that abstraction operates on so high a level of generalisation. Gosse likes best the last stanza, which wriggles free from allegorical personages; and enjoys speculating about the possibility that Gray, in veiled fashion, is referring to his quarrel with Walpole.

The biographical connection is stressed even more in Gosse's consideration of the 'Elegy Wrote in a Country Church-yard'. Gosse scrupulously notes the difficulties inherent in reviewing the stages of composition, its original form, the retention of lines and thoughts from the earliest drafts; but he connects its composition with the death of Gray's uncle, Jonathan Rogers, which completely altered Gray's prospects at the age of twenty-five. Only enough money was left to support Mrs Rogers and her two sisters, Mrs Gray and Miss Antrobus. Their lives progressed in genteel poverty until their respective deaths; Gray, unwilling to impose on his aunts, returned to Cambridge, becoming a middle-aged man. 'From this time forward we find that his ailments, his melancholy, his reserve, and his habit of drowning consciousness in perpetual study, have taken firm hold upon him, and he begins to plunge into an excess of reading, treating the acquisition of knowledge as a narcotic.'[13] Gosse goes on to say that the death of his aunt Mary Antrobus, in 1749, led Gray to resume the writing of the 'Elegy' at Cambridge, though the poet finished it at Stoke Poges in 1750.

The test of Gosse's discernment lies here, in his consideration of the most famous poem written betwen Milton and Wordsworth. There are the usual acknowledgements of the poem's universal appeal, its countless translations into other languages, its role as a model for poets everywhere. Gosse notes that Swinburne, the only writer who has depreciated Gray's poetry since Dr Johnson's time, was forced to concede the poem's perfection. But he has something fresh to say about Gray's use of the heroic quatrain, based upon his investigation of the manuscripts at Pembroke College, Cambridge. Notes taken by Gray on the *Nosce Teipsum* of Sir John Davies (1599), and Gray's almost certain knowledge of Davenant's *Gondibert*, Dryden's *Annus Mirabilis*, and James Hammond's *Love Elegies*,

contributed – in Gosse's view – to the brilliance of the newly imagined form.

> The measure itself, from first to last, is an attempt to render in
> English the solemn alternation of passion and reserve, the
> interchange of imploring and desponding tones, that is found in
> the Latin elegiac, and Gray gave his poem, when he first
> published it, an outward resemblance to the text of Tibullus by
> printing it without any stanzaic pauses.[14]

Gosse reviews a number of incidents illustrating the sudden, and
in some respects unwelcome, fame that overtook Gray as a
consequence of Walpole's circulation of the 'Elegy' in manuscript
form. He adds, in his final chapter, 'Posthumous', a succinct analysis
of Gray's fate at the hand of various biographer–critics, particularly
in William Mason's *Life and Letters of Gray* (1774) and Dr Johnson's
Lives of the Poets, the fourth volume of which, containing the famous
essay on Gray, was published in 1779. Gosse's dislike of Mason's
work is based partly on the fact that Mason's literary tastes were
inferior to those of Gray, and that Gray had reproved him a number
of times for writing 'nonsense', as in the case of *The English Garden*, a
poem that Mason wrote in 1767 but dared not publish until Gray
had died. Mason preferred 'artificial cascades and myrtle grots to all
the mountains in Christendom', and Gray, who preferred the
mountains, chided both manner and matter in ways that Mason
could only regard as nettling; so much so, indeed, that he attempted
to have the last word in a third book, added in 1772 (the year after
Gray's death), to *The English Garden*, which creates a dialogue
between Gray and Mason over the merits of Mason's poem. But
Gosse also laments the pitifully small use that Mason made of all the
primary materials in his possession; the tamperings with the
correspondence, including transposing parts of the letters, interpo-
lations and erasures of passages, concealment of proper names,
mutilations of original manuscripts, and alterations of dates and
opinions. One might therefore expect that Gosse would have a
completely negative view of Mason's attempt to present only the
attractive side of Gray; but, rather unexpectedly, Gosse finds that
some aspects of Mason's 'meagre and slipshod narrative' are worth
commendation. It is, for one thing, a sketch from the life, and it
shows literary ability; and Mason's intimacy with Gray, cultivated
over a long period of years, means that it is, in some ways, an
unrivalled source of information.

Gosse is unable to dismiss Dr Johnson's essay in quite so summary a fashion, though he finds little there of biographical value. Perhaps, as Gosse maintains, Johnson was tired of the whole task, 'and longing to be at rest again'.[15] A graver charge has to do with Johnson's misuse (or inadequate use) of anecdotes and sayings collected from Gray's Cambridge friends, material that was dispersed and lost after Johnson had finished drafting his biographical sketch.

Johnson did not care much for Gray's kind of poetry. Without the commendations of critics he respected (Warburton and Hurd) and friends he could not easily dismiss (Boswell and Garrick), Johnson might not have found anything to praise in Gray's performance. But even his tempered praise for the 'Elegy Written in a Country Churchyard' and the 'Ode on Adversity' would not have persuaded many to read Gray for the first time, because, as Gosse puts it, 'Where he approves . . . no praise could be fainter; where he objects he is even more trenchant and contemptuous than usual.'[16] Against Johnson's commendation of the picturesque grace contained in Gray's descriptions of the country, Gosse sets Johnson's whimsically inconsistent failure to object to the allegorical machinery of the 'Ode on Adversity', and his strictures against specific points in the 'Prospect of Eton College', such as the ability of every beholder to think and feel exactly the same thoughts as Gray. ('This, so far from being a fault,' Gosse writes with asperity, 'is the touch of nature which makes the poem universally interesting.') Johnson deplored Gray's asking Father Thames to say 'who drives the hoop or tosses the ball', inasmuch as 'Father Thames has no better means of knowing than himself'. But Gosse points out that Johnson called on Father Nile 'for information exactly analogous' in the pages of *Rasselas*. And Johnson's attack on Gray's use of the term 'redolent' (Gray, Johnson urges, had misunderstood a phrase used by Dryden) might have been less severe had he known, or remembered, that sixteenth-century Scottish poets used the term. 'The phrases above quoted', Gosse concludes, 'constitute Johnson's entire criticism of the "Eton Ode", and it is of a kind which, however vigorously expressed, would not nowadays be considered competent before the least accredited of tribunals.' Johnson – Gosse has, of course, constituted himself as a tribunal of sorts – is 'absolutely deaf' to experiments in metre and to the verbal and quantitative felicities of the two Pindaric odes; he misses the fidelity of Gray to his Pindaric source in the first stanza of 'The Progress of Poetry'; and he accuses

Gray of having invented the term 'velvet-green', without remembering that Pope and Young (poets whom Johnson admired) had first devised and employed the term.

This detailed analysis of another critic's commentary is relatively rare in Gosse, as his emphasis upon broad surveys and biographical data militates against close consideration of what any critic, even such a major one as Dr Johnson, has to say about the works under examination. Then, too, the format of the English Men of Letters series did not allow much space for a review of the secondary literature. But it is surely noteworthy that Gosse's dislike of Johnson's style leads him to single out as capricious a number of particular points of attack. He fails to relate Johnson's guarded commentary to a shift in critical taste of respectably large proportions, one which inevitably altered readers' perceptions of what Gray had actually accomplished, a shift that took place during the last quarter of the eighteenth century. Arnold may not have been so far from Johnson's position when he proclaimed that Gray was 'the scantiest and frailest of classics in our poetry', but a classic nevertheless; yet Gosse's hectoring of Johnson's views allows no room for the possibility that Johnson spoke not only for himself, but for a growing number of readers who had come to believe that the time had come for something less Greek, less classical, in English poetry.

Gosse's enthusiasm for 'The Bard' provides an even more illuminating passage of extended criticism. Gosse may overemphasise the impact on Gray's sensibility of attendance at a number of concerts at Cambridge, given by John Parry, the famous blind harper, in 1757, though Gray himself admitted that Parry had put his ode 'in motion again' and had 'brought it at last to a conclusion'. A poet has as much difficulty as any critic in disentangling cultural and literary influences from personal impressions and the excitement of specific events, and 'The Bard' must be set against a larger background of developing interest in myths and folklore of the mid eighteenth century than Gosse is interested in sketching.

Nevertheless, several points made by Gosse remain as true today as when his biography was published. Gosse was reacting against the claims of 'extremely refined critics' that Collins's 'Ode to Liberty' and Blake's 'Book of Thel' were superior to Gray's 'Bard'. He does not deny that these works possessed merit, and beauty of a high order. 'But we must beware of the paradox which denies beauty in a work of art because beauty has always been discovered there.'[17]

'The Bard', Gosse maintains, has a greater 'human sympathy, historical imagination, and sustained dithyrambic dignity' than two poems to which it has been compared; it uses its machinery with greater effect; and it represents a welcome advance in technique and concept of subject-matter over what had been done in Gray's Pindaric odes. Gray was writing on an historical theme, but he 'was diverted from his purely abstract consideration of history into a concrete observation of its most picturesque forms', as in his treatment of Edward II undergoing torture at Berkeley Castle, or in his description of the massacre of the Bards at the battle of Camlan. Gosse was willing to put up with 'some use of allegorical abstraction', because it was 'necessary to the very structure of poetry', but Mason and other imitators of Gray use such abstraction excessively, tediously; a mythology cannot be forced out of the emotions of the human mind, a new Olympus cannot be fitted out with brand-new gods of a moralist's making, without the running of risks and the possible disenchantment of even the most sympathetic reader. 'The Bard', like the 'Elegy Written in a Country Church-yard', is restrained in its use of abstraction, and these, concludes Gosse, are Gray's two greatest works.

Sir Thomas Browne, also written for the English Men of Letters series, includes a chapter, entitled 'Language and Literature', that usefully summarises Gosse's views on the isolation of a major intelligence. For Browne lived in Norwich, not Cambridge or Oxford, and he was remote from London and his father, despite frequent exchanges of correspondence. He had disciples, letter-writers, friends; but their stimuli waned as his years advanced. Perhaps thinking of his own tortured upbringing, which fully deserved the epithet 'provincial', Gosse identified some consolations in Browne's remoteness from urban centres. Browne was in between the sixteenth century (book-learning for its own sake') and the new age (which went 'straight to nature, determined to make new, stiff, half-mathematical treatises that should be mere records of experiment, repertories of hard fact'). Hence, he handled facts, but not because he deemed them of supreme importance. He has no claim to our gratitude for having discovered or classified information on biology, medicine, ethics, horticulture or any other science. 'Wherever we lean on the substance of Browne's treatises, it cracks and gives way, it is worm-eaten and hollow.'[18] Gosse's admiration of Browne's achievement is, to some extent, a statement of his own case. Browne aimed at the 'translation of temperament by style'. He paid relatively little attention to the current literature, to the modern vernaculars. It was the supreme paradox of his life that he should write for the divine pleasure of writing; he did not find writing easy, nor did his audience find reading what he had written an easy assignment. Browne's style is a 'language of a wanton ingenuity', marked by themes, illustrations and digressions introduced 'for their own sakes'.[19] Browne is 'less a man of science, an all-round naturalist, than a dreamer of philosophic dreams, satisfied with brief and partial experiences'.[20]

Gosse admires the 'deep stoic tone' with which Browne describes death, so unlike 'the slightly hysteric manner' of the descriptions recorded by his contemporaries[21]. He has little interest in defining the precise nature of Browne's religious beliefs (indeed, several pages of the monograph confess to an ignorance of Browne's intention and meaning when the language produces effects in excess of the author's needs); but he vibrates sympathetically to Browne's invocation to avoid dogmatism, to his 'serenity' in both personal demeanour and writings, and to his very careful cultivation of a large number of friendships. Gosse quotes with admiring approval a passage from a letter written by Browne in 1635: 'I hope I do not break the Fifth Commandment, if I conceive I may love my friend before the nearest of my blood, even those to whom I owe the principles of life. I never yet cast a true affection on a woman; but I have loved my friend as I do virtue, my soul, my God.'[22] Of all the characteristics of Browne on which he might have ended his study, the one chosen – Browne's plainness, carried 'almost to affectation', in manner and speech – is affectingly personal: 'He was excellent company when he was not distracted by his professional responsibilities. Those who knew him only by his books were sometimes disappointed to find the man so quiet and sedate; nor did he ever wake up in society to a high note of eloquence.'[23]

In several important respects Browne is not a congenial figure for Gosse's kind of literary analysis. Gosse does not much care for Browne's subject-matter, or consider it sufficiently important (taken by itself) to 'preserve' Browne 'among the foremost literary oddities of his time'. As a consequence, he all too easily separates form from substance, and admires Browne for style, for writing in the 'service of beauty', and for using language of 'a wanton ingenuity'. Throughout the text, and particularly in the final chapter, 'Language and Influence', Gosse praises Browne as an 'architect of phrases', a builder skilled in the 'mere verbal development' of 'cloud-castles'. He does not choose to grapple with his subject's philosophy because it is easy enough, and sufficiently dismissive, to speak of Browne's intellect as marked by 'something abnormal'. Picturesqueness and artificiality have moved Browne's meaning beyond the pale:

> He was conscious of no controlling taste around him, holding him in, subduing the most daring elements in his vocabulary. In consequence, he built up the music of his sonorous balanced periods as he pleased, without any criticism to restrain him, and the consequence is the irregular splendour that we see in the *Urn-Burial* and *A Letter to a Friend*.[24]

The unexamined assumptions behind Gosse's evaluation of Browne's contribution to English letters are, in this case, troubling. Gosse evidently believes in something he calls 'the integrity of the English language', which has been violated by Browne's Latinisms. He may admire Browne the man, and Browne the stylist in so far as exuberant conceits convey music to the reader's ear; but Browne's vocabulary is occasionally 'so servilely Latin as to be ugly', and its adherence to classical forms is, in Gosse's view, deplorable. 'We owe no thanks to persons like Browne, who have tried to make us call man an equicrural animal when all we mean is that his legs are of a bigness',[25] writes Gosse, ignoring the possibility that many readers would prefer to have men called 'an equicrural animal' rather than a creature whose legs 'are of a bigness'. If Gosse is to complain about Browne's habit of 'wrapping the trite in the coronation-robes of fine language', he is obligated, as part of his inspection of Browne's contribution to English letters, to explain how or why Browne's thought was so popular during the seventeenth century. And it will not do, save in an over-reductive fashion, to imply that Browne's lucidity benefits from the use of 'the shortest and plainest of words'. 'Verbal sonority' and what Pater called Browne's 'learned sweetness of cadence' are not that separable from what Browne is saying. Browne's subject-matter, after all, is frequently the elaborateness of the strategies devised to cope with the unnerving fact of death.

Gosse admires Browne's emotion, and measures a reader's enjoyment of a given passage by the amount of emotion present.

> When Browne is extremely moved by his imagination he can hardly be too grandiloquent; we accept his most audacious

'Brownisms' with delight. He leads us, at his will, through his labyrinths of language, and with every turn of the path displays some new sombre beauty, brings forward to our ears some new strain of melancholy faery music.[26]

If deep truly calls to deep (for language such as this tells us little or nothing about what Browne is *saying*), then Gosse most enjoys not the message of Browne's meditations on death, meditations which he describes as Browne's finest achievement, but the fervour which moves behind them:

> He is the laureate of the forgotten dead. . . . In the presence of a haunting sense of the fragility of time, of the faint mark we all make on life, something less durable than the shadow of a leaf or a breath upon a mirror, Sir Thomas Browne decides that 'restless unquiet for the diuturnity of our memories seems a vanity almost out of date, and a superannuated piece of folly'.[27]

Thus, for two writers whom he genuinely admires, Gosse chooses to relate biographical detail to the works whenever possible, treating in fuller richness those literary productions for which the circumstances of genesis, composition and publication have been recorded, and moves rapidly past those productions for which such data are unavailable. It is almost as if he distrusts his own abilities to assess a poem or essay that does not carry its own dossier of minute particulars. Gosse enjoys using the first person; his puzzlement over Browne's meaning makes its employment more imperative than in the case of the Gray study, but a reader is seldom allowed to forget for long the fact that a reader like himself, properly humble in the presence of genius but never struck dumb if due cautions have to be sounded, is guiding him from start to finish of a distinguished writer's career. And he speaks of quality in works so diverse in ambition, scope and achievement that his catholicity of taste may seem to be increasingly impressive, and his occasional demurrals at failed art all the more trustworthy. But his failings as a critic are closely related to some idiosyncratic views on the possibility of judging the beauty of a literary style in isolation from the meaning of the thing communicated, and on the overstressing of emotion as an aid to the achieving of literary greatness.

It is clear that for more than half a century Gosse felt compelled to make amends, furiously, and with considerable self-consciousness,

for a youth that he persisted in regarding as ruined or – at the very
least – stunted in growth. At the age of twenty-four he wrote to
Philip Henry Gosse, 'I think you are the most difficult Father to
satisfy in all the wide world',[28] but he was objecting at the time to
the necessity for defining still again his attitude toward religion. The
edginess in his remarkable characterisation of family relationships
in *Father and Son* – a document written more than three decades after
this letter – indicates that he neither forgot nor forgave. Two
anecdotes recounted in that work may be seen (depending on the
perspective of a modern reader) as either charming or horrendous in
their indication of how 'the interests of daily life were mingled' in
the Gosses' 'strange household, with the practice of religion'.

> We had all three been much excited by a report that a certain
> dark geometer-moth, generated in underground stables, had
> been met with in Islington. Its name, I think, is *Boletobia
> fuliginaria*, and I believe that it is excessively rare in England. We
> were sitting at family prayers, on a summer morning, I think in
> 1855, when through the open window a brown moth came
> sailing. My Mother immediately interrupted the reading of the
> Bible by saying to my Father, 'O! Henry, do you think that can be
> *Boletobia*?' My Father rose up from the sacred book, examined
> the insect, which had now perched, and replied: 'No! it is only the
> common Vapourer, *Orgygia antiqua*!', resuming his seat, and the
> exposition of the Word, without any apology or embarrass-
> ment.[29]

The second anecdote begins with Gosse's father asking his son
whether he would like to have a new mamma. 'I was never a
sentimentalist,' writes Gosse, 'and I therefore answered, cannily,
that that would depend on who she was.' On being informed as to
her identity, the eleven-year-old, recalling that it is his duty to
testify 'in season and out of season', asks, 'with much earnestness',
'But Papa, is she one of the Lord's children?' His father replies in the
affirmative.

> 'Has she taken up her cross in baptism?' I went on, for this was
> my own strong point as a believer. My Father looked a little
> shame-faced, and replied: 'Well, she has not as yet seen the
> necessity of that, but we must pray that the Lord may make her
> way clear before her. You see, she has been brought up, hitherto,
> in the so-called Church of England.'

Our positions were now curiously changed. It seemed as if it were I who was the jealous monitor, and my Father the deprecating penitent. I sat up in the coverlid, and I shook a finger at him. 'Papa,' I said, 'don't tell me that she's a pedobaptist?'[30]

It is not my intention to review the history of Gosse's troubled family relationships. More important in terms of his professional vocation is the record of his reasons for responding, one by one, to reading-discoveries. There is the moment when his father recites Virgil's verses from memory, and the delighted Edmund asks for an explanation of the 'adorable verses'. But he really didn't pay much attention to the meaning; what, after all, was beautiful Amaryllis to him? 'She and her love-sick Tityrus awakened no image whatever in my mind', Gosse writes. 'But a miracle had been revealed to me, the incalculable, the amazing beauty which could exist in the sound of verses.'[31] He reads *Tom Cringle's Log* (1829), by Michael Scott, that 'wild masterpiece', as if he has been on a milk diet and somebody has given him a glass of brandy neat. 'The scenes at night in the streets of Spanish Town surpassed not merely my experience, but, thank goodness, my imagination.'[32] That work, more than any other, fortifies Edmund's individuality, and gives him the strength to resist his father's pressure to conform to a narrow, religiously constricted way of life. He responds to Scott's *Lady of the Lake* with mounting waves of excitement ('I almost gasped'), and a shudder floats down his backbone. His 'unresisting humorous appreciation' of *The Pickwick Papers* is similarly emotional: 'My shouts of laughing at the richer passages were almost scandalous, and led to me being reproved for disturbing my father while engaged, in an upper room, in the study of God's Word.'[33] He succumbs willingly to the graveyard poems of Dr Young, Blair, Bishop Beilby Porteus and Samuel Boyse: 'Who shall explain the rapture with which I followed their austere morality?' He pores over Bailey's *Etymological Dictionary*, 'delighting in the savour of the rich, old-fashioned country phrases', and when he comes to Shakespeare he revels in the glossary, and the lovely, obvious and inevitable language that clothes the sentiments.[34] He even uses the word 'exquisite' to characterise almost the entire contents of *The Golden Treasury*.[35]

These scattered allusions to the pleasures of reading do not count for much in *Father and Son*, a memoir aimed at settling old scores. It is curious, however, that the great majority of these brief references amount to commentaries on the sensory excitement that Gosse derived from sound patterns, and that a reference is often extended only because it serves a dual function – that is, it remarks on Gosse's entry into 'a heaven of passion and music' as a consequence of reading a particular work, and it serves as illustration of the deafness to verbal music of either his stepmother or his father, or both. If Edmund enjoyed the poetry of Ben Jonson and Christopher Marlowe, such enjoyment was bound to lead to the displeasure of his guardians:

> I can but admit that my Father, who was little accustomed to seventeenth-century literature, must have come across some startling exposures in Ben Jonson, and probably never reached 'Hero and Leander' at all. The artistic effect of such poetry on an innocently pagan mind did not come within the circle of his experience.[36]

A classic anecdote is the one recounting his horror at the damnation of Shakespeare during an 'enormous Evangelical conference' in London. 'I remember', Gosse writes,

> my short-sighted sense of the terrible vastness of the crowd, with rings on rings of dim white faces fading in the fog. . . . An elderly man, fat and greasy, with a voice like a bassoon, and an imperturbable assurance, was denouncing the spread of infidelity, and the luke-warmness of professing Christians, who refrained from battling the wickedness at their doors. . . . 'At this very moment,' he went on, 'there is proceeding, unreproved, a blasphemous celebration of the birth of Shakespeare, a lost soul now suffering for his sins in hell!'[37]

Gosse's depressed spirits fall 'to their nadir' because nobody comes to Shakespeare's defence, and cheer up only after his father – later, in their hotel – reminds him that we really do not know enough of the poet's history to render such a judgement. 'The light of salvation was widely disseminated in the land during the reign of Queen Elizabeth, and we cannot know that Shakespeare did not accept the atonement of Christ in simple faith before he came to die.' Philip Gosse provides thus a 'meagre' comfort to his son.

Edmund Gosse's bequest to modern criticism is thus more problematical than that of most major Victorian critics. Gosse left behind five kinds of legacies. His first legacy, more than a dozen collections of essays on miscellaneous subjects, however readable, are chatty, digressive, excessively arch, not consistently or clearly focused on particular ways of seeing the world despite Gosse's oft-expressed reverence for a given author's vision, and surprisingly bland and uninformative. Gosse recognises the distinction between major and minor talents, but the requirements of periodical length seem to reduce every writer to the same height, width and breadth; the occasional expansive essay turns out to be more a matter of a congenial home for an essay on James than a matter of conviction that James counts for more than, say, Leconte de Lisle, whose centenary is being commemorated. *Aspects and Impressions* devotes seven of its fifteen essays to French authors, but has no unifying theme or attitude; Gosse is as interested in bringing up to date his life of Congreve, published decades before, as he is in defining Rousseau's influence on England in the nineteenth century; and observations on Spenser's *The Faerie Queene* (such as the eccentric but quite seriously argued proposition that Spenser's major poem is not 'about' anything, and that 'There is nothing of serious import to be deduced from its line of argument'[38]) melt gently into a paean of praise for Albert Mockel's *Chantefable* of 1891 ('Here, once more, we enter a world as audaciously designed as Ariosto's, as intricately splendid as Spenser's'[39]). In *Silhouettes*, published toward the very end of his life, Gosse moves easily from early French poets to Lafcadio Hearn, from Claudian to Bernard Mandeville to Vauban and American folksong. Nothing in print is alien to him; but nothing he touches is shaped to withstand the handling of later generations of critics, and the end result, an essay ranging from three to ten thousand words, almost invariably suggests rather than defines an approach to subject-matter. There may not have been often enough in Gosse's responses to literary endeavours spread over five centuries and a dozen cultures a sufficient quantity of exasperation, anger, puzzlement or humility. It is all too even, too serene, and ultimately too unresponsive to what is being said.

A second bequest is a series of textbook-type studies. These are profoundly indebted to conventional concepts of dividing-lines between ages, or periods, of literary history, even though Gosse protests that 'It would not be wise, doubtless, to make a general habit of regarding literary history through artificial barriers of this kind'.[40] John Churton Collins's scorn for slipshod dating in *From Shakespeare to Pope* (1885) had a salutary effect for decades afterwards on Gosse's treatment of a writer's career, but there may be too many constraints on Gosse's view of what a textbook survey ought to contain for the genre ever to become interesting for more than a few sentences at a time. Here is an unfortunately all-too-common example:

> Late in 1605 Ben Jonson added a cubit to his literary stature by producing his noble comedy of *Volpone or the Fox*. All these years he was not merely a frequenter of the wits' meeting at the Mermaid Tavern in Friday Street, but the very centre and main attraction of the club. In 1609 his comedy of *Epicene, or the Silent Woman*, was brought out, and in 1610 *The Alchymist*. This was Ben Jonson's blossoming-time, and everything he now did was admirable . . . .[41]

Gosse praises, a dangerous number of times, the writer who 'can write about Nothing like a gentleman' (in this case Sir William Temple, who is cited as one of the progenitors of modern English prose).[42] He never masters Saintsbury's knack of returning, with undiminished enthusiasm, to the same literary figures in new histories. One can anticipate Gosse's judgements; they are, after all, the conventional wisdom of a century ago. What we yearn for when we approach the poetry of the third quarter of the eighteenth century is a sense of delight or discovery, based on boldly independent reading, instead of the view, already trite in Wordsworth's time, that it was 'singularly dull, mechanical, and dusty'.[43]

In *A Short History of Modern English Literature* (1898) Gosse's critical dicta suffer keenly by comparison with those of Andrew Lang and George Saintsbury, who undertook similar works. Gosse professes to keep always before him 'as the central interest' expression, form and technique, rather than biography, or sociology, or more unrelated criticism. This volume, which begins with 'the Age of Chaucer', omits from consideration all literature written in England in languages other than English, i.e. Latin and French, and stresses the art of poetry: 'For it is in verse that style can most definitely and to greatest advantage be studied, especially in a literature like ours, where prose has mainly been written without any other aim than the naive transference of ideas or statement of facts . . . .'[44] This facile distinction between prose and poetry makes any writer – as one illustration, Sir Thomas Browne – more interesting when his prose exercises approach the condition of poetry; and it is another way of formulating the opinion, recorded in the Preface to one of Gosse's final volumes, *Leaves and Fruit* (1927), that 'by dint of gazing interminably over the vast expanse of literature' he had learned, 'gradually and unconsciously', to regard 'with equal interest all forms of passionate expression, whether grave or gay, profound or superficial'. He asks of books 'only that they should be amusing, that is to say, competently enough executed to arrest an intelligent observer'. Holding such a view, the critic makes judgements that inevitably become 'so many pieces of broken looking-glass held up to catch the figures and gestures of life as they pass by',[45] not, as Matthew Arnold had argued, a criticism of life, or a charged interaction with the best that has been thought and said in the history of culture.

Gosse understands well enough that literature changed its definition in the eighteenth century, and became increasingly belletristic as a reaction against the tyranny of fact and the multiplying subdivisions of science. Nevertheless, his reaction against utilitarian prose leads him onto thin and cracking ice; leads him to declare that a literary historian should restrict himself 'to what remains in some degree linked with the art of poetry, to what aims at giving delight by its form, to what appeals to the sentiments and the pleasure-receiving instincts'[46] – and this interpretation of his function minimises intellectual content. If to the scrappy one- or two-page treatments of individual writers are added vague dithyrambs whenever Gosse encouters an 'easy style', a sense of the precise nature of the contributions made by these writers will have difficulty in communicating itself to even the most sympathetic reader of Gosse's pages. Gosse is most at ease when, in these literary histories, he can relate a writer to a well-defined school; but to some extent this desire to work with ready-made tags (one example: the 'three equal parts' into which the 120 years following the Restoration might be divided) works against Gosse's equally strong interest in personality – either that of the writer or his own. All things considered, Gosse, who writes frequently on the eighteenth century, take a rather chilly stance toward some of its more notable literary achievements ('the strong leaden sceptre of Dryden'[47] is how Gosse marks the passage of four decades). Even 'the Age of Johnson' is described as hard to enjoy: 'Here, to secure more strength, needless weight was superadded to language; elasticity was lost in a harmony too mechanically studied.'[48]

Yet there are fields of study that Gosse enjoyed more, and his third legacy, groupings of essays hung loosely round literary movements that he does not feel constrained to define too narrowly, is worth taking more seriously. More specifically, Gosse is at his best in treating the seventeenth century, the literature of northern Europe (he uses the phrase as the title of his most important single book of literary criticism) and the literature of France. In these essays – for Gosse has difficulty in sustaining a critical thesis for the length of an entire volume – he is able to communicate his personal excitement in more than a generalised and tired language.

Seventeenth Century Studies: A Contribution to the History of English Poetry (1883), for example, has a reasonably scaled objective, the writing of a series of 'exhaustive' critical biographies in miniature of 'less monumental figures', and a sensible awareness of the difficulties inherent in achieving that objective. One problem has to do with the vagueness of the biographical information available for such a figure as Thomas Randolph; another, the vastness of the materials available for any consideration of John Donne. To write fully of Donne's work 'would be to write the history of the decline of English poetry, to account for the Augustan renascence, to trace the history of the national mind for a period of at least a century'. Gosse confesses that he feels Donne to be as far beyond the scope of his work as Ben Jonson would have been. Moreover, Gosse is becomingly aware of the problems created by unreliable texts; only three of the writers under consideration at the time he began his book had been edited and 'only one in the exact modern method'. He may exaggerate the newness of some of his topics in a work devoted to this period: 'the influence of contemporary politics, the relation to foreign literatures, the relative aspect of divergent schools'. The limitations of some of the authorities he had consulted in this field were more severe than he imagined, and he assumed, too confidently, that printing his studies 'in a provisional form' might compensate for the lack of unity in his work. But no reader can read Gosse on Thomas Lodge, John Webster, Samuel Rowlands, 'Captain Dover's Cotswold Games', Robert Herrick, Richard Crashaw, Abraham Cowley, 'The Matchless Orinda', Sir George Etherege, and Thomas Otway without learning a surprising amount about the flavour of the age as well as the lives of the writers involved.

A fourth type of bequest is contained in the services that Gosse rendered to Scandinavian, French and American literatures, as well as a number of other literatures (such as Russian) in which he maintains intermittent but genuinely sincere interests. He is not as unique a conduit for the popularisation of these cultures as he assumes, and sometimes claims; his critical essays seldom probe deeply; his work is rapidly superseded by younger scholars and critics who have more than dilettantish interests. Yet he has a right to feel proud about his prominence in the movement that led to the opening-up of Victorian publishing-houses, to the multiplication of translations and literary histories, and to the growing awareness among English intelligentsia that the exhausted springs of creative literature could be, and must be, replenished by waters flowing in from across the North Sea, the English Channel and the Atlantic Ocean. The full dimensions of the story of England's relationships to European and American cultural traditions during the crucial period of transition, 1880 to 1920, have not yet been traced by literary historians, nor has an authoritative study of the subject been written, although the need for it has long been recognised by such organisations as the Modern Language Association. Whenever it is undertaken, however, the name of Edmund Gosse, and the value of his efforts at propagandising on behalf of writers whose reputations in England were still insecure, must count for a great deal.

The final legacy is that of the comfort and appreciation Gosse provided creative writers whose talents exceeded those he himself possessed. This matter is also not easy to assess, inasmuch as the written record provides ample evidence that Gosse is not only obtuse about much of what he is praising, but also singularly incurious as to what is intended. Gosse, after all, is the first English critic to introduce the name of Ibsen to his fellow countrymen, in a *Spectator* review of 1870; yet, in his revised edition of *Studies in the Literature of Northern Europe*, published under the title *Northern Studies* (1890), he is fully capable of writing about *The Wild Duck* – a relatively straightforward and often-produced drama of domestic relationships – that it may be a medicine, but that he does not understand how the dose is expected to act; that it is 'by far the most difficult of Ibsen's dramas for a reader to comprehend'; and that he has been 'told' that it is 'effective enough' on the stage.[49] He is an early champion of Tolstoy, but reacts angrily when Tolstoy refuses to continue writing the kind of fiction that he feels comfortable with; in 1907 he writes to Bliss Perry that Tolstoy is 'a nodule of pure imaginative genius floating about in a quite barbarous cocoon of folly, preposterous idealism and even (not a little) insecurity'.[50] Moreover, Gosse's ability to adapt himself to a given audience may explain, but does not always excuse, his two-faced comments on writers whose personal friendships he assiduously cultivates. The case of Thomas Hardy is an intriguing illustration of the problem. Gosse is the author of that devastating sentence in *Cosmopolis* (January 1896), 'What has Providence done to Mr Hardy that he should rise up in the arable land of Wessex and shake his fist at his Creator?' which so upset Hardy because Gosse seemed to be calling public attention to the religious differences between himself and Emma, his wife, and because Gosse well knew the answer to his own question. Only a few years before, on the occasion of a hostile review about *Tess* that appeared in the *Saturday Review*, Gosse had written to Hardy (1 January 1892) that such critics were 'vultures', waiting to swoop down and tear one's liver, and that their reviews manifested 'bad faith' and were '*of no importance whatever*'.[51] Gosse, nine years younger than Hardy, calls Hardy his 'dear Child' in letter after letter; the astonishing thing is that Hardy responds with touching gratitude to Gosse's continuing expressions of faith in his poetry, particularly *The Dynasts*, when such encouragement is rarely expressed even by Hardy's oldest literary acquaintances. The final volumes of Hardy's letters, co-edited by Richard L. Purdy and Michael Millgate, have not yet been published by Oxford University Press, and these, we are told, will contain a large number of Hardy's animated, candid comments on a variety of matters, written to Gosse as a close confidant: Gosse can, and does, say some wounding things about such writers as Robert Louis Stevenson and Henry James; but he keeps their friendship, and the friendships of an astonishingly large number of first-rate talents.

The story that Charteris tells about Gosse's bold self-introduction to the retired poet Frederik Paludan-Müller in 1872 may be taken as an example of Gosse's extraordinary ability to make literary friends. The Danish poet, considered by his contemporaries as the peer of Kierkegaard and Hans Christian Andersen, was startled by Gosse's thick-brushed flattery, but much taken by it as well. 'Before the interview ended,' Charteris writes,

> Paludan-Müller declared his intention of going to London 'and visiting his young friend', and in parting announced that he would once more take up the role of poet. It was very much as if the Archbishop of Canterbury of the day had introduced into the presence of Tennyson a Danish youth of no outstanding eminence and with an imperfect knowledge of English, and as though the seer of Farringford, after the rays of adulation had adequately

penetrated his being, had declared that in spite of three years of silence he would again resume his pen.[52]

We may doubt the story, circulated by Gosse's cousin, that Arnold, Tennyson and Browning supplied the three testimonials that Gosse submitted in support of his application to become Clark Lecturer at Cambridge (1880). But Gosse was always seeking out great writers, and his relationship to Swinburne became one of the longer-lasting joys of his life; he championed Swinburne's verse in a wide variety of publications, and wrote a readable, carefully laundered biography, *The Life of Algernon Charles Swinburne* (1917). He seems to have known everyone, and, in Ezra Pound's caustic phrase, to have retreated to 'the safety of his annual pension of £666, 16 shillings, 8 pence', so that his criticisms are 'safe', and filled with 'cant and fustiness'.[53] But it may be precisely this unwillingness to offend anyone who might do him a good turn, or provide matter for his essays or pleasurable experiences for his reading-time, that endears him to so many authors. The record of his American friendships, begun in 1881 with his appointment as London agent for Richard Watson Gilder's *Century Illustrated Monthly Magazine*, and blossoming exuberantly during Gosse's visit to the United States in the winter of 1884–5, is a crowded one. If Gosse in his old age became the convenient target of those who rebel against orthodoxy, snobbery and the *ancien régime*, it should never be forgotten that for most of his life Gosse was well liked as a man, as a hard-working man of letters, as a patron of younger writers, and as a source of moral support to his intellectual superiors.

The net result of all these friendships, if measured only by the amount of literature produced that might not otherwise have come into being, is probably small in bulk, and of little consequence. No serious writer with genuine vision and talent needs the warm effusions of a Gosse, or will learn much from them, though he may welcome such voluntary contributions as well as the personal companionship of the critic who offers them. It is true that in some important respects Gosse failed to exploit the opportunities made available to him by his early awareness of genius at work in a number of foreign cultures. To most readers of this late decade of the present century he is important primarily for the scandalising, and largely non-literary, memoir *Father and Son*. His life and works after the period covered by that autobiography (which cuts off at approximately December 1866) have become emblematic of the reasons why the role of a man of letters became less important after the Great War.

Nevertheless, Gosse's presence during one of the more fertile periods of English literature is worth remembering. Over all, his influence may be characterised as bland, moderately stimulative, and benign. It is not enough to ensure immortality, but only a churlish posterity would deny the value of Gosse's multiple legacy – for all its limitations – and of Gosse's role as a man of letters before the Great War.

Notes

NOTES TO CHAPTER 1: GEORGE HENRY LEWES

1. *The Life of Goethe*, 2nd edn (London: The London Library, George Routledge & Sons, 1864), has a lengthy discussion in Bk VI, ch. 7, of the problems of translation from German, particularly German poetry.
2. Ibid., p. 305 (Bk V, ch. 6).
3. Ibid., p. 455 (Bk VI, ch. 7).
4. Ibid., p. 547 (Bk VII, ch. 7).
5. Ibid., p. 546 (Bk VII, ch. 7).
6. Ibid., pp. 127–60 (Bk III, chs 4 and 5).
7. Ibid., pp. 264–76 (Bk V, ch. 2).
8. Ibid., p. 420 (Bk VI, ch. 4).
9. Ibid., pp. 545–54 (Bk VII, ch. 7).
10. Ibid., pp. 108–9 (Bk III, ch. 2).
11. 'Realism and the Art of the Novel', *Fortnightly Review*, vol. XVII (1872) pp. 141–54.
12. 'Causeries', *Fortnightly Review*, vol. VI (1866) pp. 759–61.
13. 'Grote's History of Greece: The Homeric Poems', *Westminster Review*, vol. XLVI (1846) pp. 408–12.
14. 'Percy Bysshe Shelley', *Westminster Review*, vol. XXXV (1841) pp. 317–22.
15. *Leader*, 26 Nov 1853, pp. 1146–7, and 3 Dec 1853, pp. 1169–71.
16. 'Principles of Success in Literature', *Fortnightly Review*, vol. II (1865) pp. 259–64.
17. 'Another Pleasant French Book', *Blackwood's Magazine*, vol. LXXXVI (1859) pp. 672–7. Lewes was reviewing Renan's *Essais de Morale et de Critique* (Paris, 1859).
18. *The Principles of Success in Literature*, ed. Fred N. Scott, 3rd edn (Boston, Mass.: Allyn and Bacon, 1891) pp. 100–1.
19. Ibid., pp. 136–8.
20. *Dramatic Essays: John Forster and George Henry Lewes*, ed. William Archer and Robert W. Lowe (London: Walter Scott, 1896).
21. Ibid., pp. 112–18.
22. Ibid., pp. 76–8.
23. Ibid., pp. 156–61.

24. Ibid., pp. 240–2.
25. Ibid., pp. 118–22.
26. Ibid., pp. 101–4.
27. Ibid., pp. 274–5.
28. Ibid., p. xxxvi.
29. 'Principles of Success in Literature', *Fortnightly Review*, vol. II.

NOTES TO CHAPTER 2: WALTER BAGEHOT

1. *The Collected Works of Walter Bagehot*, ed. Norman St John-Stevas (Cambridge, Mass.: Harvard University Press, 1965) vol. I, p. 173.
2. Ibid.
3. Ibid., p. 174.
4. Ibid., p. 176.
5. Ibid., p. 177.
6. Ibid., p. 178.
7. Ibid., p. 181.
8. Ibid.
9. Ibid., p. 183.
10. Ibid., p. 185.
11. Ibid., p. 188.
12. Ibid.
13. Ibid., p. 192.
14. Ibid., p. 195.
15. Ibid., p. 203.
16. Ibid., p. 204.
17. Ibid., p. 209.
18. Ibid.
19. Ibid.
20. Ibid., p. 210.
21. Ibid., p. 211.
22. Ibid., p. 212.
23. Ibid.
24. Ibid.
25. Ibid.
26. Ibid.
27. Ibid., p. 213.
28. Ibid.
29. Ibid., pp. 97–8.
30. Ibid., p. 98.
31. Ibid., p. 198.
32. Ibid., p. 213.
33. Ibid., p. 175.
34. Ibid., p. 180.

35. Ibid., p. 184.
36. Ibid.
37. Ibid., p. 185.
38. Ibid., p. 187.
39. Ibid., p. 192.
40. Ibid., p. 344.
41. Ibid.
42. Ibid.
43. Ibid., p. 310.
44. Ibid.
45. Ibid., pp. 310–11.
46. Ibid., p. 311.
47. Ibid.
48. Ibid., p. 313.
49. Ibid., pp. 330–1.
50. Ibid., p. 331.
51. Ibid.
52. Ibid.
53. Ibid., pp. 332–3.
54. Ibid., p. 333.
55. Ibid., vol. II, p. 365.
56. Ibid.
57. Ibid., p. 366.
58. Ibid., vol. I, p. 166.
59. Ibid., p. 380.
60. Ibid., vol. II, p. 48.
61. Ibid.
62. Ibid.
63. Ibid., p. 52.
64. Ibid., p. 53.
65. Ibid.
66. Ibid., p. 56.
67. Ibid., p. 62.
68. Ibid., p. 68.
69. Ibid.
70. Ibid., p. 75.
71. Ibid.
72. Ibid., vol. I, p. 402.
73. William Irvine, *Walter Bagehot* (London: Longmans, Green, 1939) p. 175.
74. Bagehot, *Collected Works*, vol. II, p. 120.
75. Ibid., p. 121.
76. Ibid., p. 124.
77. Ibid., p. 135.

78. Ibid., p. 136.
79. Ibid.
80. Ibid., p. 137.
81. Ibid.
82. Ibid., p. 138.
83. Ibid., p. 142.
84. Ibid.
85. Ibid., p. 143.
86. Ibid.
87. Ibid.
88. Ibid., p. 144.
89. Ibid., p. 145.
90. Ibid.
91. Ibid., p. 147.
92. Ibid.
93. Ibid., p. 109.
94. Ibid., p. 113.
95. Ibid., p. 119.
96. Ibid., p. 127.
97. Ibid., pp. 128–9.
98. Ibid., p. 136.
99. Ibid., vol. I, p. 264.
100. Ibid.
101. Ibid., p. 292.
102. Ibid.
103. Ibid., p. 441.
104. Ibid., pp. 462–3.
105. Ibid., vol. II, p. 46.
106. Ibid., p. 71.
107. Ibid., p. 79.
108. Ibid., p. 163.
109. Ibid., p. 207.
110. Ibid.
111. Ibid., vol. I, p. 397.
112. Ibid., vol. II, p. 181.
113. Ibid.
114. Ibid., pp. 182–3.
115. Ibid., p. 332.
116. Ibid., vol. I, p. 291.
117. Ibid., vol. II, p. 352.
118. Ibid., p. 361.
119. Ibid., p. 356.
120. Ibid., p. 321.
121. Ibid., p. 322.

122. Ibid., p. 323.
123. Ibid., vol. I, p. 165.
124. Ibid.
125. Ibid., vol. II, pp. 200–1.
126. Ibid., vol. I, p. 434.
127. Ibid., p. 435.
128. Ibid., p. 437.
129. Ibid.
130. Ibid., p. 438.
131. Ibid., p. 441.
132. Ibid.
133. Ibid., p. 460.
134. Ibid., p. 462.
135. Ibid., pp. 462–3.
136. Ibid., p. 472.
137. Ibid.
138. Ibid., p. 474.
139. Ibid., p. 475.
140. Ibid., p. 476.

NOTES TO CHAPTER 3: RICHARD HOLT HUTTON

1. 'Memoir by the Editor', in Walter Bagehot, *Literary Studies*, ed. Richard Holt Hutton (London: Longmans, Green, 1884) vol. I, p. xii.
2. Ibid.
3. Ibid., p. xiii.
4. Ibid.
5. Ibid., pp. xiii–xiv.
6. Ibid., p. xv.
7. Ibid., pp. xv–xvi.
8. Ibid., p. xvi.
9. Ibid.
10. Ibid., p. lviii.
11. Ibid., p. xxxv.
12. Ibid.
13. Ibid., p. liii.
14. Ibid., pp. xlv–xlvi.
15. Ibid., pp. ix–x.
16. Ibid., p. lxiv.
17. Ibid.
18. Ibid., p. lxv.
19. *Sir Walter Scott* (New York: Harper & Brothers, 1881) pp. 46–7.
20. Ibid.

21. Ibid., p. 49.
22. Ibid.
23. Ibid.
24. Ibid., pp. 49–50.
25. Ibid., p. 50.
26. Ibid., p. 59.
27. Ibid., p. 114.
28. Ibid., pp. 116–17.
29. Ibid., pp. 42–3.
30. Ibid., p. 43.
31. Ibid., p. 54.
32. 'Nathaniel Hawthorne', in *Essays Theological and Literary* (London: Strahan, 1871) vol. II, p. 424.
33. Ibid.
34. Ibid., p. 425.
35. Ibid., p. 427.
36. Ibid.
37. Ibid., p. 429.
38. Ibid., p. 431.
39. Ibid.
40. Ibid., p. 432.
41. Ibid.
42. Ibid., p. 433.
43. Ibid.
44. Ibid.
45. Ibid., p. 436.
46. Ibid., p. 437.
47. Ibid., p. 438.
48. Ibid., pp. 440–1.
49. Ibid., p. 441.
50. Ibid., p. 449.
51. Ibid., p. 442.
52. Ibid., p. 445.
53. Ibid., p. 446.
54. Ibid.
55. Ibid., p. 447.
56. Ibid.
57. Ibid.
58. Ibid., p. 448.
59. Ibid.
60. Ibid., p. 449.
61. 'The Future of English Humour. Mr Ainger's "Charles Lamb"', in *Criticisms on Contemporary Thought and Thinkers* (London: Macmillan, 1894) vol. I, p. 104.

62. Ibid.
63. 'Emerson as Oracle', ibid., p. 54.
64. '*Democracy*: An American Novel', ibid., pp. 69–75.
65. 'Longfellow', ibid., p. 83.
66. 'Goethe and his Influence', in *Essays Theological and Literary*, vol. II, p. 7.
67. Ibid., p. 9.
68. Ibid.
69. Ibid., p. 43.
70. Ibid., pp. 46–7.
71. Ibid., p. 48.
72. Ibid., p. 49.
73. Ibid., p. 50.
74. 'Swinburne', in *Literary Essays* (London: Macmillan, 1896) p. 394.
75. Ibid., p. 393.
76. Ibid., pp. 393–4.
77. Ibid., p. 394.
78. Ibid.
79. Ibid.
80. Ibid.
81. 'The Genius of Wordsworth', ibid., pp. 90–2.
82. Ibid., pp. 99–100.
83. Ibid., p. 111.
84. Ibid., p. 112.
85. Ibid., p. 113.
86. Ibid.
87. Ibid., pp. 114–15.
88. Ibid., p. 116.
89. Ibid., p. 117.
90. Ibid.
91. Ibid., p. 118.
92. Ibid., pp. 121–2.
93. 'Shelley and his Poetry', ibid., p. 132.
94. Ibid., p. 126.
95. Ibid., p. 127.
96. Ibid., p. 130.
97. Ibid., p. 129.
98. Ibid., p. 133.
99. Ibid., p. 134.
100. Ibid., p. 142.
101. Ibid., p. 144.
102. Ibid., p. 147.
103. Ibid., p. 149.
104. Ibid.

105. Ibid.
106. Ibid., p. 152.
107. Ibid.
108. Ibid., p. 156.
109. Ibid., p. 163.
110. Ibid.
111. Ibid., p. 173.
112. This position is argued in several places, e.g. pp. 112–13.
113. Ibid., p. 177.
114. Ibid.
115. Ibid., p. 186.
116. Ibid.
117. Ibid., p. 187.
118. 'Shelley as Prophet', in *Brief Literary Criticisms Selected from the Spectator*, ed. Elizabeth M. Roscoe (London: Macmillan, 1906; repr. Port Washington, NY: Kennikat Press, 1970) p. 98.
119. Ibid., p. 102.
120. Ibid.
121. Ibid., p. 103.
122. 'Emerson as Oracle', in *Contemporary Thought and Thinkers*, vol. 1, pp. 57–8.
123. Ibid., p. 58.
124. Ibid.
125. 'Mr Leslie Stephen on Johnson', ibid., p. 168.
126. 'Ralph Waldo Emerson', ibid., pp. 46–52.
127. 'The Poetic Place of Matthew Arnold', in *Brief Literary Criticisms*, p. 272.
128. 'George Eliot', ibid., pp. 181–2.
129. 'Shelley and his Poetry', in *Literary Essays*, p. 176.
130. 'Tennyson', ibid., p. 361.
131. Ibid., p. 363.
132. Ibid., p. 364.
133. Ibid., p. 375.
134. Ibid.
135. Ibid.
136. Ibid., p. 376.
137. Ibid., p. 392.
138. Ibid.
139. Ibid.
140. Ibid.
141. Ibid., pp. 400–7.
142. Ibid., p. 405.
143. Ibid.
144. Ibid., p. 407.

145. Ibid., p. 417.
146. Ibid., p. 421.
147. 'Tennyson's Poem on "Despair"', in *Contemporary Thought and Thinkers*, vol. II, p. 198.
148. Ibid., p. 199.
149. Ibid., p. 200.
150. Ibid., p. 203.
151. '"Locksley Hall" in Youth and Age', ibid., p. 205.
152. Ibid.
153. Ibid., p. 212.
154. 'The Poetry of Matthew Arnold', in *Literary Essays*, p. 312.
155. Ibid., pp. 312–13.
156. Ibid., p. 332.
157. Ibid., p. 343.
158. Ibid., p. 350.
159. Ibid., p. 359.
160. Ibid.
161. Ibid.
162. Ibid., pp. 335–6.
163. 'Matthew Arnold as Critic', in *Contemporary Thought and Thinkers*, vol. I, p. 221.
164. Ibid., pp. 222–3.
165. Ibid., pp. 223–5.
166. Ibid., p. 225.
167. Ibid.
168. Ibid., pp. 225–6.
169. Anthony Trollope, *Autobiography* (New York: Dodd, Mead, 1905) p. 177.
170. *Essays on Some of the Modern Guides of English Thought in Matters of Faith* (London: Macmillan, 1887) p. 160.
171. Ibid., pp. 169–70.
172. Ibid., p. 233.
173. Ibid., p. 171.
174. Ibid., p. 233.
175. Ibid., p. 237.
176. Ibid., p. 185.
177. Ibid., p. 263.
178. Ibid., pp. 278–9.
179. Ibid., p. 286.

NOTES TO CHAPTER 4: LESLIE STEPHEN

1. 'The Study of English Literature', *Cornhill Magazine*, n.s., vol. VIII (May 1887) p. 486.

2. Ibid., pp. 486–7.
3. 'Walter Bagehot', in *Studies of a Biographer (Second Series)* (London: Duckworth, 1902) vol. III, p. 167.
4. 'Sterne', in *Hours in a Library*, new edn (London: Smith, Elder, 1909) vol. III, p. 130.
5. 'Autobiography', *Cornhill Magazine*, vol. XLIII (Apr 1881) p. 427.
6. 'Gibbon's Autobiography', *Studies of a Biographer*, vol. I, p. 157.
7. Ibid., p. 158.
8. Ibid., p. 159.
9. Ibid., p. 162.
10. Ibid., p. 164.
11. Ibid., p. 167.
12. Ibid., p. 168.
13. Ibid., pp. 168–9.
14. Ibid., p. 179.
15. Ibid.
16. Ibid., p. 180.
17. Ibid.
18. Ibid., p. 181.
19. Ibid., pp. 186–7.
20. Noel Gilroy Annan, *Leslie Stephen, his Thought and Character in Relation to his Time* (London: MacGibon & Kee, 1951) p. 2.
21. Ibid., p. 4.
22. Frederic William Maitland, *The Life and Letters of Leslie Stephen* (London: Duckworth, 1907) pp. 263–4.
23. Ibid., p. 277.
24. This position is argued at length in 'Thoughts on Criticism, by a Critic', *Cornhill Magazine*, vol. XXXIV (1876) pp. 556–69.
25. *National Review*, vol. XXVII (1896); repr. in *Studies of a Biographer*, vol. I, pp. 1–36.
26. Ibid., pp. 7–8.
27. Ibid., p. 8.
28. Ibid., pp. 8–9.
29. Ibid., p. 12.
30. Ibid., p. 22.
31. Ibid.
32. Ibid., p. 23.
33. Ibid., pp. 26–7.
34. Ibid., pp. 29–30.
35. 'Emerson', ibid., vol. IV, p. 146.
36. Ibid.

37. Ibid., pp. 146–7.
38. *National Review*, vol. XXXIII (1899) pp. 401–15; repr. in *Studies of a Biographer*, vol. III, pp. 1–35.
39. Ibid., p. 1.
40. Ibid., p. 2.
41. Ibid., p. 30.
42. Ibid., vol. III, p. 40.
43. 'New Lights on Milton', ibid., vol. IV, p. 93.
44. 'Autobiography', *Cornhill Magazine*, vol. XLIII (Mar 1881) p. 410.
45. Ibid., p. 411.
46. Ibid.
47. Ibid., p. 412.
48. Ibid., p. 422.
49. Ibid., p. 423.
50. Ibid.
51. *Studies of a Biographer*, vol. IV, p. 232.
52. Ibid., pp. 270–2.
53. Ibid., vol. II, p. 88.
54. Ibid., p. 92.
55. Ibid., vol. III, p. 111.
56. 'Gray and his School', *Hours in a Library*, vol. III, p. 124.
57. Ibid.
58. 'John Ruskin', *Studies of a Biographer*, vol. III, p. 93.
59. Ibid., vol. I, pp. 105–46.
60. *Hours in a Library*, vol. III, p. 89.
61. Ibid.
62. Ibid.
63. Ibid.
64. Ibid. pp. 89–90.
65. 'Carlyle's Ethics', ibid., p. 264.
66. Ibid., p. 263.
67. Ibid., p. 264.
68. 'Matthew Arnold', *Studies of a Biographer*, vol. II, p. 77.
69. 'Life of Tennyson', ibid., p. 198.
70. Ibid., p. 199.
71. Ibid., p. 201.
72. Ibid., vol. III, p. 255.
73. Oliver Elton, *A Survey of English Literature, 1800–1880* (London: Edward Arnold, 1920) vol. I, p. 295.
74. Stephen's attitude toward the moral doctrine implicit in George Eliot's fictions affords a fascinating contrast to views held by Hutton.

For example, Stephen was suspicious of any claim that novels exerted much ethical influence; he held *Adam Bede* to be less of a masterpiece than Hutton did (Mrs Poyser was for Stephen a far more interesting character than either Dinah Morris or Adam); his judgement of George Eliot's ability to draw masculine characters (e.g. Stephen Guest in *The Mill* on *the Floss*) was considerably harsher than Hutton's; and, in general, he disliked the way in which George Eliot attempted to make a novel illustrate a philosophical tendency, or to symbolise a general formula. He insisted on reading her work as 'implicit autobiography'. Hutton demanded more from George Eliot; the psychological analysis of women that satisfied Stephen was less interesting to Hutton than the ethical truths contained in her novels. A close study of the differences between Hutton and Stephen on this complex issue might well define two distinct generations of critical taste.

75. *English Literature and Society in the Eighteenth Century, Ford Lectures, 1903* (London: Duckworth, 1904) p. 22.
76. Ibid., p. 25.
77. Ibid.
78. Ibid., p. 4.
79. Ibid., pp. 9–10.
80. Ibid., p. 14.
81. Ibid.
82. Ibid., pp. 15–17.
83. IbId., p. 20.
84. Ibid., p. 22.
85. Ibid., p. 24.
86. Ibid., p. 29.
87. Ibid., pp. 30–1.
88. Ibid., p. 159.
89. Ibid., p. 161.
90. Ibid., p. 162.
91. Ibid., pp. 165–6.
92. Ibid., p. 167.
93. Ibid.
94. Ibid. p. 168.
95. Ibid., p. 169.
96. *George Eliot* (1902; repr. London: Macmillan, 1926) pp. 200–1.
97. 'Robert Louis Stevenson', *Studies of Biographer*, vol. IV, p. 233.
98. Ibid., p. 240.
99. Ibid., p. 233.

100. 'The Story of Scott's Ruin', *Cornhill Magazine*, n.s., vol. II (Apr 1897) pp. 448–65; repr. in vol. IV, pp. 1–37.
101. Ibid., p. 32.
102. Ibid.
103. Ibid., p. 33.
104. Ibid., p. 34.
105. *Cornhill Magazine*, vol. XXVII (Mar 1873) pp. 345–54.
106. Ibid., p. 346.
107. Ibid., p. 347.
108. Ibid., p. 348.
109. Ibid., p. 349.
110. Ibid.
111. Ibid., p. 350.
112. Ibid.
113. 'Anthony Trollope', *Studies of a Biographer*, vol. IV, p. 168.
114. Ibid., p. 188.
115. Ibid., p. 198.
116. Ibid., p. 201.
117. Ibid., p. 203.
118. *George Eliot*, p. 63.
119. 'William Godwin's Novels', *Hours in a Library*, vol. III, p. 152.
120. 'Charles Kingsley', ibid., p. 48.
121. 'Charlotte Brontë', ibid., p. 6.

NOTES TO CHAPTER 5: ANDREW LANG

1. Roger Lancelyn Green, *Andrew Lang, A Critical Biography* (Leicester: Edmund Ward, 1946) p. x.
2. A. Blyth Webster, in *Concerning Andrew Lang* (Oxford: Clarendon Press, 1949) p. ix. Each essay in this anthology is individually paged.
3. Green, *Lang, A Critical Biography*, pp. 241–59.
4. Alexander Shewan, 'Andrew Lang's Work for Homer', p. 21, in *Concerning Andrew Lang*.
5. Ibid., p. 23.
6. Ibid., p. 27.
7. R. R. Marett, 'The Raw Material of Religion', p. 20, ibid.
8. Quoted ibid., p. 22.
9. Ibid.
10. Green, *Lang, A Critical Biography*, pp. 145–6.
11. Ibid., p. 146.

12. Robert S. Rait, 'Andrew Lang as Historian', p. 17, in *Concerning Andrew Lang*.
13. J. D. Mackie, 'Andrew Lang and the House of Stuart', pp. 20–2, ibid.
14. Ibid., p. 22.
15. Ibid., p. 26.
16. Louis Cazamian, 'Andrew Lang and the Maid of France', p. 15, ibid.
17. Ibid., p. 16.
18. Bernard Darwin, 'Andrew Lang and the Literature of Sport', p. 10, ibid.
19. H. J. C. Grierson, 'Lang, Lockhart and Biography', pp. 3–38, ibid.
20. John Buchan, 'Andrew Lang and the Border', p. 12, ibid.
21. *Shakespeare, Bacon, and the Great Unknown* (London: Longmans, Green, 1912) p. xiv.
22. Ibid., p. xvi.
23. Ibid.
24. Ibid., p. xvii.
25. Ibid.
26. Ibid., p. xix.
27. Ibid., p. xx.
28. Ibid., p. xxviii.
29. Ibid., p. 281.
30. Ibid., p. 290.
31. Green, *Lang, A Critical Biography*, p. ix; but compare Green's own statement in a later monograph: ' "My mind is gay, but my soul is melancholy", Lang once said, and to read his poetry and his prose fiction is to catch here and there a haunting glimpse of the melancholy soul, the soul of the true poet, behind the brilliant façade of the gay mind' – *Andrew Lang* (London: The Bodley Head, 1962) p. 67.
32. Green, *Lang, A Critical Biography*, p. 164.
33. *Letters to Dead Authors* (New York: Charles Scribner's Sons, 1895) p. 206.
34. Ibid., p. 213.
35. Ibid., p. 214.
36. Ibid., p. 140.
37. Ibid., p. 146.
38. Ibid., p. 141.
39. Ibid.
40. Ibid., p. 2.
41. Ibid., pp. 2–3.

42. Ibid., p. 11.
43. Ibid., p. 12.
44. Ibid., p. 15.
45. Ibid., p. 6.
46. Ibid., p. 19.
47. Ibid., p. 176.
48. Ibid.
49. *History of English Literature from 'Beowulf' to Swinburne* (London: Longmans, Green, 1914) p. v.
50. Ibid., p. 573.
51. Ibid., p. 570.
52. Ibid., p. 571.
53. Ibid.
54. Ibid., p. 575.
55. Ibid., p. 576.
56. Ibid., p. 575.
57. Ibid., p. 587.
58. Ibid.
59. Ibid., p. 588.
60. Ibid., p. 589.
61. Ibid.
62. Ibid.
63. Ibid., p. 590.
64. Ibid.
65. Ibid., p. 588.
66. Ibid., pp. 592–3.
67. Ibid., pp. 594–5.
68. Ibid., p. 596.
69. Ibid., p. 597.
70. Ibid., p. 598.
71. Ibid., p. 599.
72. Ibid., p. 601.
73. Ibid., p. 604.
74. Ibid., p. 616.
75. Ibid., p. 620.
76. Ibid., p. 619.
77. Ibid., p. 624.
78. Ibid., p. 636.
79. Ibid., p. 633.
80. Ibid., p. 638.
81. Ibid., p. 640.

82. Ibid., p. 641.
83. Green, *Lang, A Critical Biography*, p. 206.
84. *Adventures among Books* (London: Longmans, Green, 1905) p. 43.
85. Ibid., p. 48.
86. Ibid., p. 46.
87. Ibid., p. 54.
88. Ibid., p. 55.
89. Ibid., p. 54.
90. Green, *Lang, A Critical Biography*, pp. 169–70.
91. Ibid., pp. 51–2, 56.
92. *Essays in Little* (New York: Charles Scribner's Sons, 1894) p. 24.
93. Ibid., pp. 29–30.
94. Ibid., p. 30.
95. Ibid., p. 33.
96. Ibid., pp. 34–5.
97. Peter Keating, 'The Fortunes of RLS', *TLS*, 26 June 1981, pp. 715–16.
98. *Adventures among Books*, p. 53.

NOTES TO CHAPTER 6: GEORGE SAINTSBURY

1. A. Blyth Webster, 'A Biographic Memoir', in *A Saintsbury Miscellany: Selections from his Essays and Scrapbooks* (New York: Oxford University Press, 1947) p. 29.
2. *Notes on a Cellar-book* (1920; repr. London: Macmillan, 1963) p. 203.
3. Oliver Elton, 'George Saintsbury', in *A Saintsbury Miscellany*, p. 9.
4. Sir Herbert Grierson, 'Some Personal Memories', ibid., p. 12.
5. Elton, ibid., p. 8.
6. *A History of Criticism and Literary Taste in Europe from the Earliest Texts to the Present Day* (1900–4; repr. Edinburgh and London: William Blackwood & Sons, 1919) vol. III, p. 529.
7. Dorothy Margaret Stuart, 'The Last Years', in *A Last Vintage: Essays and Papers by George Saintsbury*, ed. John W. Oliver, Arthur Melville Clark and Augustus Muir (London: Methuen 1950) p. 21.
8. *A Short History of English Literature* (1898; repr. London: Macmillan 1948) p. 608.
9. Webster, in *A Saintsbury Miscellany*, p. 65.
10. Helen Waddell, 'The Man of Books', in *A Last Vintage*, p. 27.
11. John Gross, *The Rise and Fall of the Man of Letters: Aspects of English Literary Life since 1800* (London: Weidenfeld & Nicolson, 1969) p. 142.
12. *A Saintsbury Miscellany*, p. 152.
13. *Essays in English Literature 1780–1860, First Series* (1890; repr. London: Percival, 1891) p. 105.

14. *A History of Elizabethan Literature* (1887; repr. London: Macmillan, 1928) p. 150.
15. *The Earlier Renaissance*, vol. v of *Periods of European Literature* (New York: Charles Scribner's Sons, 1901) p. 202.
16. *The English Novel* in *the Channels of English Literature* series (London: J. M. Dent & Sons, 1913) pp. 25, 27.
17. *A History of Nineteenth Century Literature (1780–1895)* (New York: Macmillan, 1896) p. 231.
18. *The Collected Essays and Papers of George Saintsbury 1875–1920* (London and Toronto: J. M. Dent and Sons, 1923) vol. i, p. 107.
19. *A Short History of English Literature*, p. 230.
20. *A Last Vintage*, p. 159.
21. *Corrected Impressions: Essays on Victorian Writers* (New York: Dodd, Mead, 1895) p. 124.
22. *George Saintsbury, The Memorial Volume* (London: Methuen, 1945) p. 182.
23. Ibid., p. 203. The quotation, a favourite of Saintsbury, turns up in several contexts.
24. *Corrected Impressions*, p. 270.
25. *A History of Criticism*, vol. iii, p. 539.
26. Ibid., pp. 540–1.
27. Ibid., p. 542.
28. Ibid., p. 543.
29. Ibid.
30. Ibid., p. 550.
31. *The English Novel*, p. 237.
32. Ibid., p. 255.
33. Ibid., pp. 260–1.
34. Ibid., p. 276.
35. Ibid., p. 286.
36. Ibid., p. 291.
37. *A Last Vintage*, p. 35.
38. *A History of Nineteenth Century Literature*, pp. 276–81.
39. Ibid., p. 311.
40. Ibid., p. 267.
41. Ibid., p. 266.
42. Ibid., p. 269.
43. Ibid., p. 273.
44. *A Last Vintage*, p. 33.
45. *Corrected Impressions*, p. 61.
46. *A History of Nineteenth Century Literature*, p. 422.
47. Ibid., p. 424.
48. Ibid., p. 440.
49. *A History of Criticism*, vol. i, p. vi.

50. Ibid., p. 366.
51. Ibid., pp. 469–80.
52. Ibid., vol. III, p. 609.
53. René Wellek, *A History of Modern Criticism 1750–1950* (New Haven, Conn.: Yale University Press, 1965) vol. IV, pp. 416–28.

NOTES TO CHAPTER 7: EDMUND GOSSE

1. James Hepburn, Introduction to his edn of *Father and Son, A Study of Two Temperaments* (London: Oxford University Press, 1974) p. xiii.
2. *Transatlantic Dialogue, American Correspondence of Edmund Gosse*, ed. Paul F. Mattheisen and Michael Millgate (Austin: University of Texas Press, 1965) pp. 20–1.
3. *The Correspondence of André Gide and Edmund Gosse 1904–1928*, ed. Linette F. Brugmans (New York: New York University Press, 1959).
4. *Transatlantic Dialogue*, pp. 20–1.
5. *The Collected Letters of Thomas Hardy, 1840–1892*, vol. I, ed. Richard Little Purdy and Michael Millgate (London: Oxford University Press, 1978) p. 150.
6. Evan Charteris, *The Life and Letters of Sir Edmund Gosse* (New York: Harper & Brothers, 1931) pp. 196–7.
7. *Portraits and Sketches* (London: William Heinemann, 1913) p. viii.
8. *Critical Kit-Kats* (New York: Dodd, Mead, 1896) p. 8.
9. *Books on the Table* (London: William Heinemann, 1921) p. vii.
10. *More Books on the Table* (London: William Heinemann, 1923) p. viii.
11. *Some Diversions of a Man of Letters* (New York: Charles Scribner's Sons, 1919) p. 11.
12. *Selected Essays (First Series)* (London: William Heinemann, 1928) p. 5.
13. *Gray* (New York: Harper & Brothers, 1885) p. 66.
14. Ibid., p. 99.
15. Ibid., p. 215.
16. Ibid., p. 216.
17. Ibid., p. 130.
18. *Sir Thomas Browne* (London: Macmillan, 1905) p. 190.
19. Ibid., p. 192.
20. Ibid., p. 83.
21. Ibid., p. 172.
22. Ibid., p. 185.
23. Ibid., p. 187.
24. Ibid., p. 194.
25. Ibid., p. 197.
26. Ibid., p. 201.
27. Ibid., p. 205.

28. Charteris, *Life and Letters of Sir Edmund Gosse*, p. 52.
29. *Father and Son*, p. 21.
30. Ibid., p. 121.
31. Ibid., pp. 92–3.
32. Ibid., p. 114.
33. Ibid., p. 129.
34. Ibid., p. 155.
35. Ibid., p. 161.
36. Ibid., p. 160.
37. Ibid., p. 155.
38. *Aspects and Impressions* (London: Cassell, 1922) p. 264.
39. Ibid., p. 269.
40. *The Jacobean Poets* (New York: Charles Scribner's Sons, 1894) p. v.
41. Ibid., p. 24.
42. *A History of Eighteenth Century Literature (1660–1780)* (New York: Macmillan, 1929) p. 88.
43. Ibid., p. 310.
44. *A Short History of Modern English Literature* (New York: D. Appleton and Company, 1898) p. vi.
45. *Leaves and Fruit* (London: William Heinemann, 1927) p. vii.
46. *A History of Eighteenth Century Literature*, p. 377.
47. Ibid., p. 380.
48. Ibid., p. 381.
49. *Northern Studies* (London: Walter Scott, 1890) p. 98.
50. Charteris, *Life and Letters of Sir Edmund Gosse*, p. 300.
51. Ibid., p. 223.
52. Ibid., p. 41.
53. *Transatlantic Dialogue*, p. 24.

Bibliographies

GENERAL HISTORIES AND BIBLIOGRAPHIES

The field which this book surveys is rich, but underappreciated by literary historians. Although intelligent analyses of Matthew Arnold's ideas may be found in numerous books, a comprehensive and thorough history focusing on Victorian literary criticism has yet to be written. George Saintsbury's *A History of Criticism and Literary Taste in Europe from the Earliest Texts to the Present Day* (Edinburgh and London: William Blackwood & Sons, 1900–4) has little room for its author's Victorian contemporaries, but is still worth consulting. René Wellek's *A History of Modern Criticism 1750–1950*, vol. IV (New Haven, Conn.: Yale University Press, 1965), is, in general, impatient with English critics of the second half of the century, with the exception of Arnold. Geoffrey Tillotson's *Criticism and the Nineteenth Century* (London: University of London, Athlone Press, 1951) is intelligent, readable, but disappointingly selective in what it treats. John Gross's *The Rise and Fall of the Man of Letters* (London: Weidenfeld & Nicolson, 1969), on the other hand, paints broad-brush, includes a great deal more, and is witty in its coverage of publishers, editors, men of letters and workaday critics; its one drawback is that not much space is devoted to any single figure.

Not a history but a most useful set of summary sketches of primary and secondary materials may be found in Wendell V. Harris's 'The Critics', in *Victorian Prose, A Guide to Research*, ed. David J. De Laura (New York: Modern Language Association of America, 1973) pp. 433–67. Here one may review bibliographies for Walter Bagehot, Eneas Sweetland Dallas, Edmund Gosse, Richard Holt Hutton, 'Vernon Lee' (Violet Paget), George Henry Lewes, George Moore, George Saintsbury, Algernon Swinburne, John Addington Symonds, Arthur Symons and Oscar Wilde. Harris expresses regret at the omission of William Rossetti, Leslie Stephen, Andrew Lang, David Masson, Augustine Birrell, Walter Raleigh, John Morley, Frederic Harrison, R. L. Stevenson and (because he lived so long into this century) William Butler Yeats.

The best place to begin any investigation of the pertinent bibliographies of all these figures is, of course, *The New Cambridge Bibliography of English Literature*, vol. III, ed. George Watson, and vol. IV, ed. I. R. Willison (Cambridge: Cambridge University Press, 1969 and 1972). The limitations of this work are clearly set forth in the Editor's Preface, but, taken as a whole, the project has heroic dimensions.

More specialised studies include several essays in *The Art of Victorian Prose*, ed. George Lewis Levine and William Madden (New York: Oxford University Press, 1968); Enid Starkie's *From Gautier to Eliot: The Influence of France on English Literature, 1851–1939* (London: Hutchinson, 1960); Richard Stang's *The Theory of the Novel in England, 1850–1870* (London: Routledge & Kegan Paul, 1959); Stephen Potter's *The Muse in Chains* (London: Jonathan Cape, 1937); George Kenneth Graham's *English Criticism of the Novel, 1865–1900* (Oxford: Clarendon Press, 1966); Alba H. Warren's *English Poetic Theory, 1825–1865* (Princeton NJ: Princeton University Press, 1950); and Ruth Z. Temple's *The Critic's Alchemy: A Study of the Introduction of French Symbolism into England* (New York: Twayne, 1953), a more specialised study than that of Enid Starkie.

Useful bibliographies are published frequently in *English Literature in Transition: 1880–1920*, a periodical edited at the University of Arizona, Tempe; and annual bibliographies of (relatively infrequent) scholarly and critical works on each of the seven Victorian literary critics treated in this study may be found in *PMLA* (*Publications of the Modern Language Association*) and *The Year's Work in English Studies*.

GEORGE HENRY LEWES

A large number of Lewes's manuscripts are at Yale University, in the Beinecke Rare Book and Manuscript Library; a smaller number may be consulted at the Berg Collection, New York Public Library.

A brief but useful Bibliographical Essay is appended to Hock Guan Tjoa's *George Henry Lewes: A Victorian Mind* (Cambridge, Mass.: Harvard University Press, 1977) pp. 149–51. There is to this day no full-length biography, and Anna Theresa Kitchel's *George Lewes and George Eliot: A Review of Records* (New York: John Day, 1933) concentrates on two issues only: Lewes's early career (1840–60), and his relationship with George Eliot. It is surprising, in light of the fact that Lewes was so widely published and read, that there has never been a collection of his diverse writings, illustrating their full range. A lengthy, but still incomplete, bibliography of Lewes's works is contained in Alice R. Kaminsky's *George Henry Lewes as Literary Critic* (Syracuse, NY: Syracuse University Press, 1968) pp. 195–206; this should be supplemented by the *Wellesley Index*. In addition to the works on Lewes's literary criticism, cited in the notes to this chapter, the reader will find that the collection of excerpts from longer essays edited by Alice R. Kaminsky, *Literary Criticism of George Henry Lewes* (Lincoln, Neb.: University of Nebraska Press, 1964), suggests the wide range of Lewes's concerns about *belles lettres*. It is not that Lewes is unknown to students of

Victorian literature, but rather that those who have not read his writings still tend to think of him as the intelligent but overshadowed consort of George Eliot. A few dissertations, and a scattering of first-rate articles, barely do justice to Lewes's contributions to the higher criticism of the Victorian Age.

A notable investigation was conducted by Robert Bernard Doremus in a two-volume dissertation (still unpublished), accepted by Harvard University in 1940: 'George Henry Lewes: A Descriptive Biography, with Especial Attention to his Interest in the Theatre'.

The following are worth looking up: Franklin Gary's 'Charlotte Brontë and George Henry Lewes', *PMLA*, vol. LI (1936) pp. 518–42; Morris Greenhut's 'George Henry Lewes and the Classical Tradition in English Criticism', *Review of English Studies* , vol. XXIV (1948) pp. 126–37, 'George Henry Lewes as a Critic of the Novel', *Studies in Philology*, vol. XLV (1948) pp. 491–511, and 'G. H. Lewes's Criticism of the Drama', *PMLA*, vol. LXIV (1949) pp. 350–68; and M. Glen Wilson Jr's 'George Henry Lewes as Critic of Charles Kean's Acting', *Education Theatre Journal*, vol. XVI (1964) pp. 360–7. A workmanlike survey, but overcompressed because of space limitations, may be found in Edgar W. Hirshberg's *George Henry Lewes* (New York: Twayne, 1970). The standard biography, Gordon S. Haight's *George Eliot* (Oxford: Clarendon Press, 1968), contains important insights about the Lewes–Eliot relationship. Other scholarly and critical items of some importance include nineteenth-century statements by Frederic Harrison, 'G. H. Lewes', *Academy*, vol. XIV (1878) pp. 543–4; James Sully, 'George Henry Lewes', *New Quarterly Magazine*, vol. II (1879) pp. 356–76; and Anthony Trollope, 'George Henry Lewes', *Fortnightly Review*, vol. XXXI (1879) pp. 15–24. Fred N. Scott contributed an introduction and notes to *The Principles of Success in Literature* (Boston, Mass.: Allyn and Bacon, 1892). William Archer's essay 'George Henry Lewes and the Stage' was published in the *Fortnightly Review*, vol. LXV (1896) pp. 216–30. In this century Havelock Ellis wrote an introduction to Lewes's biography of Goethe, as reprinted in the Everyman edition (London: Dent: 1908), which is now – regrettably – out of print. See, also, Leslie Stephen's sketch in the *DNB*, vol. II (1937–8) p. 1044. General surveys of Lewes's literary interests include R. L. Brett's 'George Henry Lewes: Dramatist, Novelist and Critic', *Essays and Studies*, vol. XI (1958) pp. 101–20; Alice R. Kaminsky's 'George Eliot, George Henry Lewes, and the Novel', *PMLA*, vol. LXX (1955) pp. 907–1013; and Allen R. Brick's unpublished dissertation '*The Leader*: Organ of Radicalism' (Yale University, 1957). More specialised articles have been written by Kenneth W. Davis, 'George Henry Lewes's Introduction to the Blackwood Circle', *English Language Notes*, vol. I (1963) pp. 113–14; Franklin Gary, 'Charlotte Brontë and George Henry Lewes', *PMLA*, vol. LI (1936) pp. 518–42; Gordon S. Haight, 'Dickens and Lewes', *PMLA*, vol. LXXI (1956) pp. 166–79; Edgar Hirshberg, 'George Eliot and her Husband', *English Journal*, vol. LVI (1967) pp. 809–17; and Mathilde

Parlett, 'The Influence of Contemporary Criticism on George Eliot', *Studies in Philology*, vol. xxx (1933) pp. 103–32.

In addition to Alice R. Kaminsky's collection, *Literary Criticism of George Henry Lewes* (a tantalising sampler), the following works are in print: *The Life of Goethe*, a reprint of the 1864 edition (Norwood, Penn.: Norwood Editions); *On Actors and the Art of Acting* (Westport, Conn.: Greenwood Press); *Principles of Success in Literature*, with an introduction by Geoffrey Tillotson (Farnborough, Hants: Gregg International); and *The Spanish Drama: Lope de Vega and Calderon* (Staten Island, NY: Gordon Press).

WALTER BAGEHOT

The previous editions of Walter Bagehot's works – those prepared by Bagehot himself under the title *Estimates of Some Englishmen and Scotchmen* (1858); Richard Hutton (a two-volume *Literary Studies* in 1879, *Economic Studies* in 1880, and a two-volume *Biographical Studies* in 1881); Forrest Morgan's five-volume edition of 1889, published (rather mysteriously) by the Travelers Insurance Company of Hartford, Conn.; and Mrs Russell Barrington (*Works and Life* in ten volumes, 1915) – have been superseded by *The Collected Works of Walter Bagehot*, ed. Norman St John-Stevas (Cambridge, Mass.: Harvard University Press, 1965–). *The Literary Essays*, complete with the addition of several hitherto-unattributed pieces, form the first two volumes. Alistair Buchan's *The Spare Chancellor: The Life of Walter Bagehot* (London: Chatto & Windus, 1959) is highly recommended as a survey of Bagehot's total accomplishment. Charles H. Sisson's *The Case of Walter Bagehot* (London: Faber & Faber, 1972) is largely hostile to Bagehot's literary criticism, but is perceptive and very well written. William Irvine's *Walter Bagehot* (New York: Longmans, Green, 1939) is a workmanlike and consistently interesting study of Bagehot's ideas, particularly those relating to literature. The most valuable biographical treatments are contained in sketches by Richard Holt Hutton (included in Mrs Barrington's edition) and in Norman St John-Stevas's *Walter Bagehot: A Study of his Life and Thought together with a Selection from his Political Writings* (Bloomington: Indiana University Press, 1959); the major part of the latter book, however, concentrates on Bagehot's political essays. Woodrow Wilson's two essays may be found in *Mere Literature, and Other Essays* (Boston, Mass.: Houghton Mifflin, 1896) and *The Atlantic Monthly*, vol. LXXXII (1898) pp. 527–40. G. M. Young's *Today and Yesterday: Collected Essays and Addresses* (London: Rupert Hart-Davis, 1948) contains a perceptive critique. Bagehot, of course, has attracted a number of first-rate minds who are primarily interested in his political and historical writings; these need not be cited here; but one more literary appreciation may be mentioned, Richard Stang's *The Theory of the Novel in England: 1850–1870* (New York: Columbia University Press, 1959).

Less useful as critiques of Bagehot's literary criticism, but still worth reading, are the following: a privately printed *Walter Bagehot, In Memoriam* (1878); Leslie Stephen's essay in *Studies of a Biographer* (New York: G. P. Putnam's Sons, 1907) vol. III, pp. 144–174; an introduction by George Sampson contributed to his edition of Walter Bagehot's *Literary Studies* (London: Latchworth, 1912); Arthur A. Baumann's 'Walter Bagehot' in the *Fortnightly Review*, n.s., vol. XCVIII (Sep 1915) pp. 568–74; Augustine Birrell's 'Walter Bagehot', in *The Collected Essays and Addresses of the Rt Hon. Augustine Birrell* (London: J. M. Dent & Sons, 1922) vol. II, pp. 213–35; and Robert Henry Murray's 'Bagehot's Seminal Mind', in *Studies of the Political and Social Thinkers of the Nineteenth Century* (Cambridge: Heffer & Sons, 1929). Kenneth Clinton Wheare's 'Walter Bagehot', a lecture on 'a Master Mind', is reprinted in the *Proceedings of the British Academy* (London: Oxford University Press, 1974) vol. LX.

The most up-to-date survey of Bagehot's total career is Harry R. Sullivan's *Walter Bagehot* (Boston, Mass.: Twayne, 1975).

Regrettably, the first two volumes of St John-Stevas's *Collected Works* are no longer in print. The 1879 edition of *Literary Studies with a Prefatory Memoir*, ed. Richard Holt Hutton, has been reprinted as a two-volume set by AMS Press, New York; a two-volume *Estimations in Criticism*, reprinting the 1908 edition, is available from Arden Library, Darby, Penn.; and three editions of *Biographical Studies*, one a reprint of the 1881 edition (AMS Press), another of the 1885 edition (Scholarly Press, Saint Clair Shores, Mich.), and still another of the 1895 edition (Richard West, Philadelphia), are available. *Estimates of Some Englishmen and Scotchmen* (the edition of 1858) has been reprinted by both Folcroft Library Editions, Folcroft, Penn., and Darby Books, Darby, Penn. The long essay *Shakespeare the Man* is available in three editions, published by AMS Press, Folcroft and Arden Library.

RICHARD HOLT HUTTON

It is rather surprising that so much of Hutton's work is in print: *Criticisms on Contemporary Thought and Thinkers* in two volumes, originally printed in 1894; *Literary Essays*, a new printing of the 1896 edition; and *Aspects of Religious and Scientific Thought*, a new edition of a collection that appeared in 1899. All three titles are published by Gregg International (Farnborough, Hants). Elizabeth M. Roscoe edited *Brief Literary Criticisms* in 1906; this has been reprinted by Kennikat Press. *Essays on Some of the Modern Guides to English Thought in Matters of Faith*, despite its title, is primarily about literature, and is available in two editions, one from Folcroft Library Editions (Folcroft, Penn.) and the other from Arno Press, New York (the 1887 edition). *Richard Hutton of the Spectator*, a reprint of the 1899 edition, has the imprint of Richard West, Philadelphia. *Sir Walter Scott* has four publishers: AMS Press (New York), Arden Library (Darby, Penn.), Folcroft, and Darby Books (Darby, Penn.).

For a comprehensive listing of Hutton's writings, see Robert H. Tener's 'The Writings of Richard Holt Hutton: A Check-list of Identifications', *Victorian Periodicals Newsletter*, vol. 17 (1972) pp. 1–179; Tener has since added items in various short notes and articles in scholarly journals, an article on Hutton in *TLS*, 24 Apr 1959, p. 241, and short articles in *Blake: An Illustrated Quarterly* (1978) and *English Language Notes* (1978); several essays on Hutton's editorial career were printed in *Victorian Periodicals Newsletter* in 1974 and 1975. Unfortunately, two dissertations on Hutton, one by Glyn M. Thomas (University of Illinois, 1950) and another by Albert K. Stevens (University of Michigan, 1950), remain unpublished. Both have substantial discussions of Hutton's literary criticism. An interesting, if somewhat specialised, essay entitled 'Richard Holt Hutton on Matthew Arnold', written by Patrick J. Creevy, appeared in *Victorian Poetry*, vol. XVI (1978) pp. 134–46. To this list should be added Sir William Beach Thomas's *The Story of the Spectator, 1828–1928* (London: Methuen, 1928); Robert A. Colby's ' "How It Strikes a Contemporary" : The *Spectator* as Critic', in *Nineteenth-Century Fiction*, vol. XI (1956) pp. 182–206; John Hogben's *Richard Holt Hutton of 'The Spectator'; A Monograph* (Edinburgh; Oliver & Boyd, 1899); and Gaylord C. LeRoy's 'Richard Holt Hutton', *PMLA*, vol. LVI (1941) pp. 809–40, which discusses Hutton's literary criticism as an important element in a larger body of work.

William Watson has a chapter on Hutton in *Excursions in Criticism, being Some Prose Recreations of a Rhymer* (London: E. Mathews & J. Lane, 1893). Frederick Samuel Boas, in 'Critics and Criticism in the Seventies', has some interesting observations; the essay is one of several contributed by fellows of the Royal Society of Literature to *The Eighteen-Seventies*, ed. Harley Granville-Barker (Cambridge: Cambridge University Press, 1929). Julia Wedgwood wrote 'Richard Holt Hutton' for the *Contemporary Review*, vol. LXXII (Oct 1897) pp. 457–69, and noted, 'Nothing that he has written is bitter or stinging, or pregnant with *innuendo*' (p. 458); a remarkable claim (she believed) because nineteenth-century reviewing depended so heavily on scorn and other 'pungent condiments'.

LESLIE STEPHEN

Leslie Stephen's writings have never been collected in a complete edition; for that matter, the majority of his periodical essays, written over a period of more than forty years, have never been reprinted. *Hours in a Library*, *Studies of a Biographer*, *English Literature and Society in the Eighteenth Century*, and the lives of Dr Johnson, Pope and Swift have been reprinted, and are currently available. *Essays on Freethinking and Plainspeaking* (1873), which contains essays on Shaftesbury's 'Characteristics', Mandeville's 'Fable of the Bees' and Warburton, has been reprinted by Gregg International (Farnborough, Hants). Eleven essays representing a wide range of Stephen's interests have been gathered by S. O. A. Ullmann under the title *Men, Books, and Mountains* (Minneapolis: University of Minnesota Press, 1956); the most complete check-list of Stephen's works is printed as an appendix. (Ullmann wrote his Harvard dissertation on Stephen: 'The Philistine Pose', 1954.) The Albert A. Berg Collection, New York Public Library, has recently acquired a large number of Stephen letters. More important still is *Sir Leslie Stephen's Mausoleum Book*, owned by the British Museum, with an introduction by Alan Bell (Oxford: Clarendon Press, 1977), which was written, in the form of a lengthy 'letter', to the children of Julia, Stephen's second wife; it contains invaluable – and otherwise unobtainable – insights into the private life of a great Victorian man of letters. Stuart Hampshire's essay 'The Heavy Victorian Father' reviews the *Mausoleum Book* in *TLS*, 10 Feb 1978, p. 159. Virginia Woolf's complex feelings about her father are recorded in the portrait of Mr Ramsay in *To the Lighthouse*, in that of Mr Hilbery in *Night and Day*, and in an essay entitled 'The Captain's Deathbed'. A substantial biography by F. W. Maitland, *Life and Letters of Leslie Stephen* (London: Duckworth, 1906), appeared shortly after Stephen's death. An intellectual biography, written with style and wit, is Noel Gilroy Annan's *Leslie Stephen, His Thought and Character in Relation to His Time* (London: MacGibon & Kee, 1951). More recent, but based primarily on the insights of others, is David D. Zink's *Leslie Stephen* (New York: Twayne, 1972). Important short essays are Desmond MacCarthy's *Leslie Stephen* (1937) and John Dover Wilson's *Leslie Stephen and Matthew Arnold as Critics of Wordsworth* (1939); both were published by Cambridge University Press. A bird's-eye view of Stephen's life and work is available in Phyllis Grosskurth's *Leslie Stephen*, published for the British Council and the National Book League by Longmans, Green (1968); its cool and sometimes disapproving tone is hardly justified by the astonishing accomplishments by Stephen listed in the text. Stephen is one of Janet Elizabeth Courtney's *Freethinkers of the Nineteenth Century* (1920; repr. Freeport, NY: Books for Libraries Press, 1967). A reader may also wish to consult René Wellek's hostile assessment in *A History of Modern Criticism, 1750–1950*, vol. IV (New Haven, Conn.: Yale University Press, 1955).

Worthwhile studies of Leslie Stephen as Victorian sage include James C. Livingston's article 'The Religious Creed and Criticism of Sir James Fitzjames Stephen', *Victorian Studies*, vol. XVII (1974) pp. 279–300; Benjamin E. Lippincott's *Victorian Critics of Democracy* (Minneapolis: University of Minnesota Press, 1938; repr. New York: Octagon Books, 1964), in which Stephen is aligned with Carlyle, Ruskin, Arnold, Maine and Lecky; Francis W. Knickerbocker's *Free Mind: John Morley and his Friends* (Cambridge, Mass.: Harvard University Press, 1943), which discusses Stephen and Frederic Harrison at some length; Gertrude Himmelfarb's 'Mr Stephen and Mr Ramsay: The Victorian as

Intellectual', *Partisan Review*, vol. XIX (1952) pp. 664–79; and John W. Bicknell's 'Leslie Stephen's *English Thought in the Eighteenth Century*: A Tract for the Times', *Victorian Studies*, vol. VI (1962) pp. 103–20. More specifically literary studies are Charles R. Sanders's 'Sir Leslie Stephen, Coleridge, and Two Coleridgeans', *PMLA*, vol. LV (1940) pp. 795–801; René Wellek's 'Leslie Stephen's Stature as a Literary Critic', *Victorian Notes*, no. 11 (1957) pp. 19–22; Brijraj Singh's 'The Changing Concepts of "Charm" in Leslie Stephen's Criticism of George Eliot', contributed to *University of Rajasthan Studies in English*, no. 4, ed. R. K. Kaul, K. N. Bakaya, and J. L. Banerji (Jaipur: University of Rajasthan Department of English, 1969); Virginia R. Hyman's 'Late Victorian and Early Modern: Continuities in the Criticism of Leslie Stephen and Virginia Woolf', *English Literature in Transition*, vol. XXIII (1980) pp. 144–54; John Halperin's 'Leslie Stephen, Thomas Hardy, and *A Pair of Blue Eyes*', *Modern Language Review*, vol. LXXV (1980) pp. 738–45; and Virginia R. Hyman's 'The Metamorphosis of Leslie Stephen', *Virginia Woolf Quarterly*, vol. II (1980) pp. 48–65. A specialised but well-conceived study, with important general implications, is Oscar Maurer's 'Leslie Stephen and the *Cornhill Magazine*, 1871–1882', *Studies in English* (University of Texas), vol. XXXII (1953) pp. 67–95. A reader may also wish to look up Augustine Birrell's 'Anti-Humbug', an essay in *More Obiter Dicta* (London: William Heinemann, 1924); Noel G. Annan's 'The Intellectual Aristocracy', a chapter in *Studies in Social History: A Tribute to G. M. Trevelyan*, ed. John Harold Plumb (London: Longmans, Green, 1955); and S. T. Williams's essay 'Leslie Stephen Twenty Years Later', *London Mercury*, vol. VIII (Oct 1923) pp. 621–34.

ANDREW LANG

Book-collectors interested in acquiring copies of Lang's works in history, anthropology, folklore and fairy tales, biography and literary criticism can find more than fifty different titles in print, in both England and the United States. A surprising number of these titles are not merely photo-offset copies of original editions, but resettings of type for new editions. Lang's works are probably better represented than those of any other late-Victorian bookman.

Lang's injunction against either a biography or a collection of his letters prevented those who knew Lang best from honouring his memory; not for thirty years did anyone dare to disobey the command. Fortunately, Roger Lancelyn Green's *Andrew Lang, A Critical Biography* (Leicester: Edmund Ward, 1946) is worthy of the man, and its short-title bibliography of Lang's works is particularly helpful. Ten lectures by authorities in various fields were collected under the title *Concerning Andrew Lang, being the Andrew Lang Lectures Delivered before the University of St Andrews 1927–1937* (Oxford: Clarendon Press, 1949). Some day, we may hope, subsequent lectures – by

J. R. R. Tolkien, 'On Fairy-Stories' (1947); Gilbert Murray, 'Andrew Lang the Poet' (1948); H. P. Macmillan, 'Law and Custom' (1949); James Bell Salmond, 'Andrew Lang and Journalism' (1950); J. B. Black, 'Lang and the Casket Letter' (1951); W. C. Dickinson, 'Lang, John Knox and Scottish Presbytarianism' (1952); etc. – will be reprinted in a companion volume. T. D. Wanliss wrote two polemical books, *Scotland and Presbytarianism Vindicated: Being a Critical Review of the Third Volume of Mr Lang's History* (Edinburgh: W. J. Hay, 1905), and *Muckrake in Scottish History: or, Mr Lang Re-criticised* (Edinburgh: W. J. Hay, 1906); these indicate how live the historical issues were to some readers despite the passage of centuries. George Saintsbury's obituary on Lang was printed in the *Oxford Magazine*, 17 Oct 1912. W. P. Ker's commemorative address, delivered as part of the Proceedings of the Academic Committee of the Royal Society of Literature in 1913, is an important essay. Brief treatments worth noting are to be found in Malcolm Elwin's *Old Gods Falling* (New York: Macmillan, 1939) and Ella Christie and Alice King Stewart's 'Some Recollections of Lang', in *A Long Look at Life by Two Victorians* (London: Seeley, Service, 1940). A more recent analysis is Joseph Weintraub's 'Andrew Lang: A Critic of Romance', *English Literature in Transition: 1880–1920*, vol. XVIII (1975) pp. 5–15.

Roger Lancelyn Green's campaign to 'revive' Lang's reputation has not succeeded, but a sympathetic reader should consult Green's 'Andrew Lang, "The Greatest Bookman of his Age" ', *Indiana University Bookman*, no. 7 (1965) pp. 10–72, and Oscar Maurer's informative study, 'Andrew Lang and *Longman's Magazine*, 1882–1905', *University of Texas Studies in English*, vol. XXXIV (1955) pp. 152–78. Other investigations include Richard M. Dorson's 'Andrew Lang's Folklore Interests as Revealed in "At the Sign of the Ship" ', *Western Folklore*, vol. XI (1952) pp. 1–19; M. Demoor's 'Andrew Lang: Crusader on Behalf of Romance', *Studia Germanica Gandensia*, vol. XX (1979) pp. 87–104; Roger Lancelyn Green's 'Andrew Lang – Real Reader of Dickens', *Dickensian*, vol. LVIII (1961) pp. 124–7; and Gardner B. Taplin's 'Andrew Lang as a Student of the Traditional Narrative Ballad', *Tulane Studies in English*. vol. XIV (1965) pp. 57–73.

GEORGE SAINTSBURY

The best bibliography, which lists all the books to which Saintsbury contributed a significant fraction of the text, or which he wrote entirely by himself, is printed as an appendix in *A Last Vintage: Essays and Papers by George Saintsbury*, ed. John W. Oliver, Arthur Melville Clark and Augustus Muir (London: Methuen, 1950). Because Saintsbury requested that a biography not be written after his death, we have had to be satisfied with Adam Blyth Webster's useful, but brief, *George Saintsbury, 1845–1933* (1934), which was reprinted in *George Saintsbury, The Memorial Volume* (London:

Methuen, 1945). Walter Leuba's *George Saintsbury* (New York: Twayne, 1967), is an appreciation, sensibly written and well worth having, but it is a short critical study, and its biographical information is based largely on Webster's essay, and on David Nichol Smith's notice in the 5th Supplement of the *DNB (1931–1940)* (London: Oxford University Press, 1949).

Saintsbury's personalised brand of literary criticism has raised objections because of its politics, scholarly inaccuracies and frequent inability to focus on the specific text. John Churton Collins's review of Saintsbury's *A Short History of English Literature*, printed first in the *Saturday Review* (1898), then reprinted in *Ephemera Critica* (London: Constable, 1901), is perhaps the most notorious and intemperate attack. (Collins made something of a career of such attacks.) Nevertheless, there have been balanced assessments every reader of Saintsbury should read, particularly since scholarly publications on Saintsbury's works are far fewer than his bibliography deserves. Among the best such reviews are those of René Wellek, in *A History of Criticism 1750–1950* (New Haven, Conn.: Yale University Press, 1965) vol. IV; two essays by Edmund Wilson, reprinted in *Classics and Commercials* (New York: Farrar, Straus, 1950); two treatments by Oliver Elton, one in *Essays and Addresses* (London: Edward Arnold, 1939), and the other in *George Edward Bateman Saintsbury: 1845–1933* (London: Humphrey Milford, 1933); and an analysis of *History of English Prose Rhythm* written by Albert C. Clark as part of his influential book, *Prose Rhythm in English* (Oxford: The Clarendon Press, 1913). More specialised studies are Dorothy Richardson's 'Saintsbury and Art for Art's Sake in England', *PMLA*, vol. LIX (1944) pp. 243–60, and Gordon F. Hostettler's 'George Saintsbury's View of Rhetoric', *Western Journal of Speech Communication*, vol. 41 (1977) pp. 210–20. It is noteworthy that James R. Sutherland considered Saintsbury to be a critic worthy of treatment with Dryden, Johnson and Hazlitt, when he delivered his Inaugural Lecture at University College, London; see *The English Critics* (London: H. K. Lewis, 1952).

Although *History of Criticism* is out of print, approximately forty of Saintsbury's books, including studies of the English and French novel and the perennially popular *Notes on a Cellar-Book*, have been reprinted, and are currently available. These represent less than a third of Saintsbury's total production, however.

EDMUND GOSSE

Edmund Gosse's works have never been assembled in a single authoritative sequence. One well-known edition is *Collected Essays*, in twelve volumes (1912–27), but of course there are the individual book-length studies, the textbooks, and the occasional publications that Gosse never decided to reprint, perhaps because the potential audience for each item had been satisfied. There is a good deal of common sense in Evan Charteris's standard biography, *The Life and Letters of Edmund Gosse* (London: William Heinemann, 1931), as well as a very useful bibliography, compiled by Norman Gullick, of most of Gosse's important books. The device of telling a life through selected letters, however, has not worn well with the passing of years. Scholars who need a trusty Baedeker through a considerable secondary literature would do well to consult James D. Woolf's 'Sir Edmund Gosse: An Annotated Bibliography of Writings about Him', in *English Literature in Transition 1880–1920*, vol. XI (1968) pp. 126–72; it is comprehensive and well annotated. Gosse's correspondence with famous literary figures is by no means completely in print, although there are substantial selections in the editions prepared by Elias Bredsdorff (*Sir Edmund Gosse's Correspondence with Scandinavian Writers*, published in Copenhagen by Gyldendal, 1960), Paul F. Matheisen and Michael Millgate (*Transatlantic Dialogue: Selected American Correspondence of Edmund Gosse*, published in Austin by the University of Texas Press, 1965) and Linette F. Brugmans (*The Correspondence of André Gide and Edmund Gosse, 1904–1928*, published in New York by New York University Press, 1959). Leslie Marchand's discussion of the Symington Collection was printed in the *Journal of the Rutgers University Library* (1948), and an interested researcher should also consult *A Catalogue of the Gosse Correspondence in the Brotherton Collection* [Leeds] (1950).

A surprising amount of hostile criticism of Gosse's work turned up while Gosse was still alive, beginning with John Churton Collins's 'English Literature at the Universities', *Quarterly Review*, vol. CLXIII (Oct 1886) pp. 289–329, and 'The *Quarterly Review* and *Mr Gosse*', *Athenaeum*, 30 Oct 1886, pp. 568–70; but Gosse, able to muster such friends as Swinburne for his defence, ignored or side stepped most of his later enemies. A sampling of some of the more notable attacks may be found in Virginia Woolf's essay 'Edmund Gosse', *Fortnightly Review*, n.s., CXXXIX (1 June 1931) pp. 766–73, and subsequently printed in *The Moment and Other Essays* (New York: Harcourt, Brace, 1942); Ruth Z. Temple's lengthly chapter on Gosse in *The Critic's Alchemy* (New York: Twayne, 1953); and Eskil Sundstrom's salutary corrective, 'The Strange Case of Swedish Literature', *London Mercury*, vol. XXXI (Feb 1935) pp. 355–62. More favourable, but less sharply focused, critiques are contained in John Freeman's 'Edmund Gosse', *London Mercury*, vol. VIII (July 1923) pp. 292–302, and Harold Nicolson's *The Development of English Biography* (London: Hogarth Press, 1947). The scholars who have assessed Gosse's role in the forgeries of Thomas J. Wise include John Carter, Wilfred Partington, Graham Pollard and W. O. Raymond. Their contributions, many being short notes, are listed in Woolf's bibliography. Also, mention must be made of Max Beerbohm's masterly imitation of the Gosse style in 'A Recollection of Edmund Gosse', *A Christmas Garland* (London: William Heinemann, 1912).

During the 1970s critical interest has focused on *Father and Son* rather than on Gosse's strengths or weaknesses as a literary critic. Two notable publications are the essay by Clement H. Wyke, 'Edmund Gosse as Biographer and Critic of Donne: His Fallible Role in the Poet's Rediscovery', *Texas Studies in Literature and Language*, vol. xvii (1976) pp. 805–19, and the perceptive but regrettably brief biography by James D. Woolf, *Sir Edmund Gosse* (New York: Twayne, 1972). Other analyses of this carefully crafted 'autobiography' include James D. Woolf's 'Tragedy in Gosse's *Father and Son*', *English Literature in Transition*, vol. ix (1966) pp. 137–44; William J. Gracie Jr's 'Truth of Form in Edmund Gosse's *Father and Son*', *Journal of Narrative Technique*, vol. iv (1974) pp. 176–87; James Hepburn's introduction to his edition of *Father and Son* (London: Oxford University Press, 1974); Roger J. Porter's 'Edmund Gosse's *Father and Son*: Between Form and Flexibility', *Journal of Narrative Technique*, vol. v (1975) pp. 174–95; James D. Woolf's ' "In the Seventh Heaven of Delight": The Aesthetic Sense in Gosse's *Father and Son*', in *Interspace and the Inward Sphere: Essays on Romantic and Victorian Self*, ed. Norman A. Anderson and Margene E. Weiss (Macomb, Ill.: Western Illinois University, 1978); Nancy Baker Traubitz's 'Heavenly Mother: The Trinity as Structural Device in Edmund Gosse's *Father and Son*', *Journal of Narrative Technique*, vol. vi (1976) pp. 147–54; R. Victoria Arana's 'Sir Edmund Gosse's *Father and Son*: Autobiography as Comedy', *Genre*, vol. x (1977) pp. 63–76; Anthony Arthur's 'Gosse's *Father and Son*: Escape from "The Prison of Puritanism" ', *Modern British Literature*, vol. iii (1978) pp. 73–7; Vivian and Robert Folkenflik's 'Words and Language in *Father and Son*', *Biography*, vol. ii (1979) pp. 157–74; Philip Dodd's 'The Nature of Edmund Gosse's *Father and Son*', *English Literature in Transition*, vol. xxii (1979) pp. 270–80; and E. Pearlman's 'Father and Mother in *Father and Son*', *Victorian Notes*, vol. lv (1979) pp. 19–23.

Articles with other foci of interest have been written by Clement H. Wyke, 'Edmund Gosse as Biographer and Critic of Donne: His Fallible Role in the Poet's Rediscovery', *Texas Studies in Language and Literature*, vol. xvii (1976) pp. 805–19; Frank M. Tierney, 'Sir Edmund Gosse and the Revival of the French Fixed Forms in the Age of Transition', *English Literature in Transition*, vol. xiv (1971) pp. 191–9; Joseph O. Baylen, 'Edmund Gosse, William Archer, and Ibsen in Late Victorian Britain', *Tennessee Studies in Literature*, vol. xx (1975) pp. 124–37; and Paul Fussell, ' "My Dear Siegfried": Gosse to Sassoon', *Journal of the Rutgers University Library*, vol. xxxviii (1976) pp. 85–97; Paul F. Mattheisen, 'Gosse's Candid "Snapshots" ', *Victorian Studies*, vol. viii (1965) pp. 329–54; and Robert L. Peters, 'Edmund Gosse's Two Whitmans', *Walt Whitman Review*, vol. xi (1965) pp. 19–21.

Currently available reprints of Gosse's books include approximately forty titles; most of these are limited press runs designed primarily to replace worn-out or missing copies in university and college libraries.

(However, *Father and Son* appears in a number of inexpensive editions.) Apparently the market for Gosse items is strong enough to justify more than one publisher taking on the reprinting of *Critical Kit-Kats, History of Eighteenth-Century Literature, Modern English Literature,* and *Northern Studies.* Gosse's lives of Gray, Donne, Browne, Ibsen and Jeremy Taylor are in print.

Index